THE HUMAN PREDICAMENT
DISSOLUTION AND WHOLENESS

THE HUMAN

DISSOLUTION

George W. Morgan

REDICAMENT

ND WHOLENESS

WN UNIVERSITY PRESS : PROVIDENCE : 1968

This book was designed by David Ford, set in Linotype Janson and printed on Warren's University Text by the Crimson Printing Company, and bound by the Stanhope Bindery.

CONTENTS

Contents

Part Three WHOLENESS

Contents

INTRODUCTION

The concern of this book is man and his ways of being in the modern world: his ways of seeking understanding and conducting his life; the ways in which he exercises his powers of thought and feeling, and expresses and communicates what he thinks and feels; his views of nature and of himself; and the ways in which he relates himself to the world. The central aim is to reach toward an understanding of what constitutes human wholeness.

Perhaps at no other time has wholeness been so difficult, so nearly out of sight, and therefore the need to address ourselves to it so crucial. Today we are engulfed in the gravest of predicaments—our lives, our selves, our ways of being, are subject to dissolution. It is tempting to deny the seriousness of our predicament, to suppose that modern life is essentially good, that its chief pursuits are devoted to making it still better, and that a negative assessment merely reflects opposition to progress and a wish to live in the past. But I speak of our contemporary dissolution, not because I wish to decry whatever is modern and call for a return to some Golden Age, but because this dissolution exists and must be acknowledged if we are to extricate ourselves from it. To live in the present to the extent of our powers requires understanding, assessment, transformation, and transmutation. In this process some of the beliefs, conditions of life, and ways of being that are most widely accepted may have to be modified or rejected.

The conditions that make for dissolution are the ones I consider to be dominant in contemporary life. I am well aware that there are persons and movements in rebellion against, or moving beyond, these conditions. (Some of these persons and movements, indeed, have been vital to my own life and work.) But many rebellious movements that seem to transcend our dissolution do not really do so and are in fact mere complements of, or fallacious reactions against, the dominant conditions; indeed, some of them unwittingly aggravate the problems they seek to solve.

In Part One the nature and extent of the contemporary dissolution is discussed. Five elements of the dissolution are examined in succession: the diminution of understanding; the destruction of language; the nullification of values; man's loss of nature, his fellow man, and learning and art; and the reduction and fragmentation of the person. These elements are closely linked and can be properly understood and dealt with only in their complex totality.

In Part Two insight into the ways in which these elements are interrelated is carried to a deeper level through the introduction of a concept that will play a central role in the succeeding discussion—the concept of the prosaic mentality. This is the orientation of mind that I believe to be at the root of the contemporary dissolution. Effects of this mentality, some of its sources, and some opposing tendencies are shown through a discussion of three areas of culture—science, history, and art. A prime role in our crisis is played by science, whose effect on all our mental life is far greater than is usually recognized. The chief purpose of the chapter on science is to bring into relief certain key features of that pursuit and to place them in a coherent and illuminating perspective. History and art are discussed because they themselves have important places in our lives and because they bring into view essential elements of man's being that are usually neglected in our time, among them especially the two elements that I call self-extension and listening. The selection for discussion of these three areas of culture does not mean that other pursuits (for example, philosophy, literary criticism, and psychoanalytic thought) are less important in human life or that attention to them would yield no significant contribution to the understanding that is sought in this book; however, every human effort must be limited, and hence selective, and science, history, and art are extremely fruitful for the purposes of this inquiry.

Part Three presents a view of man's being by which our dissolution may be overcome and wholeness grasped. The five areas discussed in Part One—understanding, language, values, man's relation to the world, and the individual person—are re-examined in the light of prosaic influences, and the extent to which these elements of humanness are diminished and mutilated by the prosaic approach is made fully apparent. These five dimensions are then shown as they appear in human life that is whole. The life of the mind is considered as it manifests itself in the multiformity and interrelations of varied modes of apprehension of the world. Ways are shown of liberating language (and the larger realm of symbols of which it is a part) from prosaic enchainment and restoring the place of values and of learning and art in life. The meanings of respect, response, and responsibility are developed, and in the process man's relations to nature and to other men emerge in their fullness and crucial importance. Wholeness is seen as the never-final, discord- and risk-embracing, living unity of different approaches to the world and of the many facets of the human being.

The three parts of this book and the chapters in each part are closely interrelated, and while each chapter—and, even more, each part—is intended to have its own coherence and integrity, the full meaning of each is inseparable from its place in the whole. The numerous and vital interconnections of the salient issues require that each issue be viewed in different contexts and from different standpoints. Since initial treatment of any one question is necessarily inadequate, unbalanced, and provisional, themes reappear to disclose new points, new emphases, or new interrelations or implications. Indeed, some of the key ideas and central themes, though touched on earlier, are brought into relief only in Part Three, to which everything in the preceding parts leads.

To write this book I have had to learn, of course, from the work of a great many men, living and dead. Some have illuminated my path; others have chiefly presented me with what I judge to be fallacies, distortions, and mutilations that must be transcended. I have referred to relatively few of these sources because it is impossible for me to identify all the works that have contributed to the views and ideas that I have tried to articulate here, and because it has seemed desirable to restrict my references for the most part to those that directly contribute to my exposition. If I had tried to refer to a considerable portion of the great number of works that bear on the questions discussed or in which arguments and positions similar to, or conflicting with, the ones presented here have previously appeared, my effort would have been paralyzed and the issues concealed in a maze of elaborations and under a mountain of footnotes. I thankfully acknowledge my debt to others, though their names are but occasionally mentioned. Also, I know, and take assurance from the knowledge, that even where I can recall indebtedness to no one, my ideas will sometimes be found close to those of men who have written before me. Newness as such has not been my aim. But neither has my primary aim been to discuss or criticize older views. Instead, making use of everything I have learned and thought and lived, I have addressed myself to issues that seem to me crucial and have sought to reach a view of human existence in which its varied and often disparate elements are embraced in living wholeness.

Part One: DISSOLUTION

Chapter 1   DIMINUTION OF MAN'S UNDERSTANDING

One of the most distinctive characteristics of modern Western civilization is the eminence of knowledge. Vast sums of knowledge exist in every imaginable domain. Perpetual addition to knowledge is pressed with unbelievable energy and at an ever-increasing pace. Modern man appears to have infinite confidence in the powers of human understanding. All key institutions and interests—industry, research, education, medicine, news media, statistics, and so on—evince this confidence, and all manifest the unquestioning belief that knowledge is supremely important.

Can there be any sense, then, in beginning an assessment of our time by speaking of a diminution of man's understanding? Should not *diminution* be replaced by *glorification?* Yet there is diminution, and it coexists with, and to a considerable extent is even due to, glorification. What is glorified is a certain kind of knowing; what is diminished is understanding as a whole, in all its variety, range, and depth. And confidence in the capacity of the individual human being to understand his own self and the world in which he lives is undermined.

The power of human understanding is often equated with man's rational faculty, and the phenomenon to which we are giving attention then appears as the diminution of *reason*. At this beginning point of our inquiry this interpretation is sufficiently good, provided we remember that the reason with which we are concerned is solely a human quality and not an entity possessing the cosmic or divine properties with which reason has sometimes been endowed. Reason, having long been considered one of the chief of man's powers, no longer commands genuine confidence as an instrument of understanding our lives. Many of us do not believe that it can truly illuminate the issues that most intimately concern us, our values, judgments, decisions, and commitments. We fear that reason is weak and stumbling, prone to delusions of sovereignty and grandeur. But while it is permissible at this point to think of the problem as a diminution of reason, we shall have to ask ourselves later whether reason is really the appropriate concept for the realm that concerns us, and we shall see that this question reverberates with several of the issues central to our whole subject.

Let us take care not to commit the fallacy of supposing that to deplore a diminution of man's understanding necessarily implies a position of ultrarationalism or an opposition to all forces in conflict with reason. To help place in relief the situation that concerns us, I am indeed tempted to discuss some of the most important of these conflicts, for example, faith versus reason, emotion versus reason, action or will versus reason, romanticism versus rationalism, empiricism versus rationalism, existentialism versus rationalism. But I think it best to resist the temptation so as to avoid the misunderstandings that are likely to arise from the brevity with which these charged issues would have to be treated here. Moreover, many elements of these issues will naturally arise in later portions of our inquiry. Let me therefore content myself for the moment with the caution that my assessment by no means assumes a purely rationalist standpoint, and thence proceed straight to what, in my judgment, are the chief characteristics of the predicament of man's understanding in our time.

RELATIVISM AND SUBJECTIVISM

Man's capacity to grasp the true nature of things has been subjected to radical doubt. The ability to bring reason to bear on an issue implies the ability to entertain ideas appropriate to the issue and to judge their relevance, adequacy, and truth. To think is to be free to discover and assess such ideas, and therefore to be free from coercions and compulsions arising from extraneous sources and imposing upon the mind attitudes and conclusions that are not warranted. Imagine yourself before a political election attempting to exercise reason in the choice of the candidate for whom you will cast your vote. You reflect upon the conditions in the national and international scene and the problems that confront your country; you consider the qualifications of the candidates as manifested in their past lives, in their efforts to be elected, in the persons with whom they are associated; and you juxtapose your assessments of the candidates with the circumstances in which they will have to act. You attempt to see the relevant issues as clearly as possible, to ground your understanding of them on the best evidence, and to check the veracity and consistency of promises and actions. On the basis of all this, you choose. Reason has provided comprehension and guided action.

But perhaps this is a delusion. Could it be that your thought is not the real foundation of your choice? May there be at work upon you pressures from various sources of which you are not aware, and that propel your mind in the direction you naïvely believe reason has indicated? Perhaps the forces that led to your choice have little if anything to do with the political issues and the candidates' respective abilities. Perhaps they are rooted in your animal nature or lodged in the psychological or social mechanisms that propel you. Far from being free, far from recognizing and discharging its proper responsibility to what it seeks to understand, your thought is the prisoner and plaything of other realities.

The presence of such irrelevant realities influencing thought is evident to anyone with even a modicum of awareness who

5

scrutinizes his own mental processes. He may discover, for example, that he is being swayed by irrelevant dislike of a candidate's national background and hence may try to liberate his political reasoning from this dislike. Reason is constantly obligated to uncover and eliminate such contaminations. But precisely here the contemporary mistrust of understanding makes itself felt, by denying that the individual is capable of discovering and transcending the most powerful forces that affect his thought. These forces stem first from the society in which he lives and second from his own peculiar psychological constitution.

As to the first, the individual is seen as molded by the beliefs, desires, feelings, and modes of thought that prevail in his environment. All his efforts at understanding are subject to the local and transient characteristics of his society—to its views, traditions, and habits—that inevitably impose parochial prejudice. Assertions and judgments are permeated by the bias of their context. Visions of truth are tossed by the shifting winds of circumstance. Knowledge is held to be only the opinion and prejudice of a particular society.

This relativism has undermined our confidence in man's ability to achieve understanding that could claim greater validity. Its impact has grown with the increasing awareness —through disciplines like philology, linguistics, sociology, anthropology, and history—of the thought of other societies living and dead and of the degree to which this thought is steeped in, and dependent upon, the entire culture: language, values, social institutions, economic structure, and so on. Moreover, not only these fields of learning, but our everyday life as well, encourage this distrust of reason. The world has shrunk; we are thrown into contact with peoples of entirely different convictions and modes of thinking; we see books and works of art that speak of utterly different spiritual worlds; we have to get along with societies or groups of our own society with whom we disagree on many matters. We are therefore driven to deny the capacity of the members of any society to reach understanding that has a right to commend itself to members of another. We feel compelled to say that all men are prejudiced.

So much for the contamination of the understanding by its social setting. Now to the still more total threat that comes from the bodily and psychic forces working upon the individual: the pressures of the moment that cloud his vision, the sensations and emotions that compel his judgment, and the desires and frustrations that wield their power over reason from their seat in the unconscious. Reason is now threatened with the loss of all validity; it becomes what is commonly called rationalization, the effort of the mind to spin a web of rationality where in fact none exists. Thinking becomes wishful thinking, pushed about like a puppet by impulsions over which we have no control, serving as a cover-up for the real forces of the biological and psychological mechanisms that motivate us. The hope that we can gain true understanding is a delusion; instead of achieving what we usually call objective knowledge of reality, we have only the manifestation of the individual's subjectivity. We cannot trust the understanding to bring us illumination or to guide our actions.

The belief that whatever men do results from the operation of all kinds of forces working within and upon them, and that reason is therefore of no importance or of only minor importance, has many sources. A chief one, of course, is psychology and its widespread effects. The emphasis on irrational mental factors in much psychoanalysis (especially of the Freudian variety) seems to imply that reason is feeble; the conditioning mechanisms of behavioral psychology (and its varied present-day offspring) leave reason no room at all. The overriding role of irrational forces is seen also in a considerable proportion of the art of the twentieth century in its rejection of reasonable order, sense, and harmony, and in its emphasis on fragmented, cacophonous, and even chaotic

7

experience. These forces confront us constantly in everyday life, where the extreme rationalization and standardization of our technological and functional world is conjoined with the most blatant irrationalities in the social, political, and moral spheres. To witness the inversion of reason in nationalistic and racial fanaticism, in the hysterical restlessness of modern society, in the insane pursuit of power and speed, is quite enough to lead one to doubt that reason has even a precarious lodging in the human soul. Added to all this, a calculated attack on everything that is reasonable has recently grown to stupendous proportions in the persuasions of mass propaganda and advertising. Not only are the views and attitudes to which propaganda is bent unreasonable in the extreme, but its methods are an assault upon the reasoning faculty, designed to put it to sleep, to crush it, and to pervert it, until even the most reasonable of men are in danger of losing the distinction between a conclusion arrived at by the free exercise of thought and one on which one has been "sold."

THE SCIENTIFIC OUTLOOK

It seems paradoxical that one of the major factors in the diminution of understanding, or of reason, should be science, for science itself is a way of understanding, and it gives a central place to rational thought. But from it an outlook has grown that curtails reason's domain. This outlook is prevalent among scientists, though surely not shared by all, often in the form of general attitude rather than of reflective doctrine, and it is common among nonscientists as well.

One of the chief elements in the making of modern science was a repudiation of pure rationalism, of the attempt to gain knowledge by thought alone. The scientist views such thought as airy speculation without proper contact with the world, and insists that thought be tied to experience, that knowledge be grounded in observation, experiment, and concrete fact. Both aspects of this spirit clearly emerge at the birth of modern science in the work of Galileo. Thus, introducing the discussion of naturally accelerated motions in the *Dialogues concerning Two New Sciences,* Galileo's spokesman, Salviati, begins:

And first of all it seems desirable to find and explain a definition best fitting natural phenomena. For any one may invent an arbitrary type of motion and discuss its properties; thus, for instance, some have imagined helices and conchoids as described by certain motions which are not met with in nature, and have very commendably established the properties which these curves possess in virtue of their definitions; but we have decided to consider the phenomena of bodies falling with an acceleration such as actually occurs in nature and to make this definition of accelerated motion exhibit the essential features of observed accelerated motions.[1]

When his interlocutors begin to speculate on the causes of acceleration, he interrupts them:

The present does not seem to be the proper time to investigate the cause of the acceleration of natural motion concerning which various opinions have been expressed by various philosophers, some explaining it by attraction to the center, others to repulsion between the very small parts of the body. . . . Now, all these fantasies, and others too, ought to be examined, but it is not really worth while.[2]

Strikingly evident here are on the one hand, disdain of "arbitrary" thought, of the "fantasies" of philosophers and on the other, the insistence on anchoring thought in what is actually observed in nature.

This view has remained intrinsic to science. A modern counterpart of Galileo's position is found, for example, in a scientifically oriented philosopher's contrast between what he considers to be the procedures of the traditional philosopher, which yield no knowledge, and those of the scientist, who "does not mind if long chains of thought are involved in the proof; he is not afraid of abstract reasoning. But [unlike the traditional philosopher] he demands that somehow the abstract thought be connected with what his eyes see and his ears hear and his fingers feel." [3]

9

Now this scientific repudiation of pure rationalism is the seed from which has grown the much more sweeping *science-centered curtailment* of human understanding. Its starkest and most explicit expression is logical positivism and similar philosophical doctrines. Their spirit prevails in many areas, though the doctrines themselves have waned, at least among philosophers. The science-centered outlook is not confined, however, to those who hold positivistic views. It is widespread and often is powerful while entirely unacknowledged and even unrecognized. At this point in our discussion it will be useful to state the science-centered view in its most special and most definite form, the positivistic. It not only rejects rationalism as ungrounded speculation, but goes on to claim that there is only one path to understanding, the path found in the natural sciences, whose prototype is physics. This kind of reason alone is said to be capable of giving knowledge of the world. The positivistic thinker recognizes that some might question this and might urge that the sciences do not tell us all there is to know, "that there is mind and consciousness, that there are emotions, values in quality, religious instincts, and so on" [4] outside their scope, and that other modes of understanding are therefore also necessary. He would reply in words similar to these: "It should be remembered that whatever transcends the sphere of the special sciences transcends it precisely because it is vague and only dimly apprehended. And where facts are so vague and poorly established as to be refractory to the scientific method, we generally find that there are so many different ways of co-ordinating them loosely that almost any opinion can be expressed with the same degree of plausibility. As a result, the opinion of the wise man is on a par with that of the ignoramus." [5]

The science-centered curtailment of reason could not be stated more drastically; for here, with one clean sweep, is wiped out philosophy, theology, history, and every other realm of thought concerning social, political, educational, or artistic issues where the opinions of the ignoramus and the wise man have not been considered on a par. As concerns philosophy, for instance—specifically its competence in matters of value—a positivistic thinker claims: "Those who ask the philosopher for guidance in life should be grateful when he sends them to the psychologist, or the social scientist; the knowledge accumulated in these empirical sciences promises much better answers than are collected in the writings of the philosophers." [6] Or, with respect to history, another writer tells us that it is "a heap of data in which one can bring to light examples to prove almost any theory one wishes." [7]

The denial of the validity of knowledge gained by an approach different from that of the empirical sciences manifests itself also in another manner. The simple rejection of traditionally nonscientific activities is replaced by an effort to make them into sciences. There are two possible approaches. One is to claim that, contrary to what has been supposed, an activity is in fact scientific, or at least quasi-scientific, when practiced properly. The other is to reconceive or alter the activity according to the model provided by the natural sciences.

The first approach can be illustrated by scientific views of history.[8] It has been contended, for example, that explanation in history depends, just as in science, on deductions from general laws having predictive value.[9] Again, history has been brought close to science by the claim that "the distinction between history and theoretical science is . . . somewhat analogous to the difference between medical diagnosis and physiology, or between geology and physics." [10] And some writers attempt to drive this closeness between history and science still further by asserting that the methods of the two are in all essentials identical.

The second way of making a field scientific, by altering its character, may be illustrated by "scientific philosophy," the results of which, it is claimed, "have been established by means of a philosophic method as precise and dependable as the method of science," [11] an accomplishment that rests on so reconceiving philosophy that anything not subject to this "precise and dependable" method is excluded from its purview. In the same spirit, a modern historian[12] deplores the continued adherence of historians (specifically, students of American history) to the traditional "narrative synthesis"—that is, to history as a "narrative of men and events"—and their failure "to think or write as social scientists." In adducing the causes for this "striking intellectual anachronism" he writes that "with its great quantities of traditional literature, and its lack of accepted conceptual tools for new theoretical analysis, history probably suffers more than any other discipline from the tyranny of persuasive rhetoric," and that "the popular dramatic frame of reference has been used whenever possible" because "historians like to have their books published and are not averse to sales." To rid history of its anachronism and make it a valid and significant study, historians are advised to build a "social science synthesis" and to approach their problems "in the spirit of scientific analysis."

Suspicion of nonscientific approaches and the attempt to provide a more solid foundation for a discipline by modifying its pursuit in line with the empirical sciences is sufficiently plain from these few examples, but the pervasive influence of this attitude will become increasingly evident as we proceed. There are attempts to make aesthetic and especially literary criticism more "reliable" by assimilating it to the methods of science; there are claims that law, politics, ethics, and even religion can and must be made subject to scientific analysis; there is no realm that has not been subjected to the attempt either to reconceive it along scientific lines or to deny it all cognitive power. And, of course, a whole range of studies of man—psychology, sociology, and anthropology, for example—insist again and again that they are sciences and that it is to this that their validity is due.

It may be helpful to interrupt our theme for a moment in order to consider briefly a discussion by the Spanish philosopher Ortega y Gasset in *Toward a Philosophy of History*. Writing about a generation ago, Ortega claimed that Europeans had lost their faith in reason and that this loss was due to reason's failure to tell them anything about that which they most urgently needed to know—man. However, the reason on which they had relied was merely, he said, a particular kind of reason, namely, "physicomathematical" [13] reason— the reason of natural science. Ortega thus perceived the same curtailment of reason to scientific reason that I have just discussed; but whereas he believed that confidence in scientific reason had collapsed in Europe by 1930, my own view of the contemporary science-centered curtailment of reason supposes that the prestige and influence of science are exceedingly great at present. This apparent contradiction raises an important objection to my interpretation, which may already have occurred to the reader, that the scientific influence is an old affair—found in the tide of mechanistic thought of the eighteenth century, in the mechanistic and biological thought of the nineteenth century, and more generally, in the various strains of positivism of that age—and that these modes of thought have already been overcome, that reason is no longer identified with science.

Now it is true that, by and large, the earlier attempts to model all understanding along that of the triumphant scientific method have been abandoned; they now appear rather crude and naïve. It is just this abandonment, I believe, that Ortega has in mind when he says that Europeans have lost confidence in the reason of natural science. The great promise of the old positivism to tell us all about man by naïve emulation of the methods of science had not been fulfilled. But the positivistic orientation of which I have been speaking is a modern phenomenon. To be sure, the impetus that animates it, the exclusive confidence in scientific method, is similar to that of earlier movements, and it is to a considerable extent their offspring; but it is differently grounded, far more subtle and more eager to be faithful to the scientific method—and it is very powerful today. Science and its prestige have grown enormously, and its methods have been adopted in a great many fields—including especially the "behavioral sciences" or "sciences of man." Far from feeling that scientific reason cannot speak about man, most people have unquestioning confidence in it. True, voices have been raised in opposition, and contrary tendencies are at work, but the scientific attitude is nevertheless widespread and, on the whole, gaining momentum.

It is not relevant here to inquire further into the difference between Ortega's and my own view of the dominance of science, but two more suggestions that may be helpful can be made in passing. The first is that Ortega wrote in a European rather than an American milieu, and that European confidence in the power of science and its offspring technology to solve all human problems and to provide for continuous progress in all affairs was badly shaken by World War I, whereas American confidence was not, or not nearly so much. The other suggestion is that World War II, with its intimate reliance in every facet of its conduct on the methods and results of science, provided an immeasurable impetus not only to the pursuit of science itself and to the development of technology, but also to men's confidence in the scientific mode of thought and to the influence of this approach on every other area. (This influence is currently greater in America, but is gaining, I think, in Europe.)

People who themselves are not deliberately trying to be scientific and who believe that the positivistic orientation is misguided often dismiss it too easily. They thereby fail to appreciate the enormous power scientific thought in fact possesses, and they completely underestimate the extensiveness of the attempt to adopt it. Moreover, they are unaware that the science-centered curtailment of understanding extends far beyond those situations in which there is deliberate adoption of the positivistic spirit. It is impossible to overemphasize this fact. Many efforts at understanding have quasi- or pseudo-scientific characteristics imposed upon them. Many others that are not meant to be scientific are nevertheless imbued with true or perverted elements of scientific method. The nature of this science-centered reduction of reason can emerge only gradually in our inquiry as other matters and their interconnections are explored. It has a far-reaching influence; for example, on our everyday thought about the conduct of our lives, on the comprehension and clarification of things that intimately concern us. It discourages all large-scale thinking with the ready accusation that one is talking "mere generalities," indulging in speculation divorced from fact. It informs the distrust and contempt—existing especially in America—for the "big questions," for thoughtful reflection on the justice and value and meaning of things—traditional questions for most thinkers and questions that every man must deal with somehow in shaping his life. Often those who glibly dismiss the power and influence of scientific thinking are completely unaware that their own effort at understanding is deeply affected by its impact.

DISTRUST OF REASON AND THE SCIENTIFIC OUTLOOK

The relativistic and subjectivistic distrust of reason due to reason's domination by social and psychological forces combines with the science-centered curtailment of reason, and their joint effect is drastic. At first sight the combination seems impossible, for the first attitude belittles rational thought while the second is imbued with it. But in fact the positions reinforce each other. Sociopsychological distrust does not invalidate reason altogether, but stops short: it exempts the rationality of science. Not only that, it seconds the science-centered outlook by assuming that only the reason of science

15

or reason modeled on that of science is capable of transcending distortions from social and psychological sources. Reciprocally, a science-centered outlook—informed by studies that are, or claim to be, scientific—often fosters social relativism and psychological subjectivism. And so, many of us have little trust in our capacity to illuminate and guide our life by reason but have, at the same time, complete confidence in the rationality of science and science-informed activities (like technology), and increasingly tend to confide to scientific rationality all the areas from which reason in a more encompassing sense has been removed. One sector of reason is exalted, while reason as a whole is maimed.

PRESSURE TO DO

An obvious but nonetheless important fact to be set down as another source of the diminution of understanding is that the opportunity for genuine and sustained reflection is generally absent today in all sectors of society. We are submerged in ceaseless activity—whether in industry, government, church, education, research, or family. The pressure of things to do and the relentless pace of our lives do not permit contemplation and thought in depth.

Moreover, not only the opportunity but also the inclination is lacking. Most of us are obsessed with a hysterical impulse to be doing. We are restless, on the move, in frantic pursuit of "progress"—which is generally understood to consist of increasing the speed of already frantic activities and the extent of already mammoth possessions, material and mental. Most of us are far more concerned to "get things done" than to think, even to think about what to do. Generally, we think only enough to keep going in established grooves, whatever they be. Our reason is exercised only within the narrow confines of our one or two chief activities. Beyond this, it is ignored and avoided: ignored because apparently unnecessary for what keeps us busy; avoided because often it stands against this busyness.

This lack of an urge for deeper and larger understanding is widespread among the general population. In America, at least, it is a form of anti-intellectualism frequently present also among the "educated."

THE FLOOD OF KNOWLEDGE

One more element of the diminution of understanding must be mentioned. This has to do with what was referred to earlier as the glorification of knowledge. It is the impact that is made on the individual who seeks understanding by the staggering amount of material clamoring for attention. The sheer weight of accumulated but uncontrolled knowledge and information, of print, views, discoveries, and interpretations, of methods and techniques, inflicts a paralyzing sense of impotence. The mind is overwhelmed by a constant fear of its ignorance. It capitulates by restricting its activity to a narrowly circumscribed field in which it can feel secure. The individual man, feeling unable to gain a valid perspective on the world and himself, is forced to regard both as consisting of innumerable isolated parts to be relinquished for knowledge and control to a legion of experts. Comprehension of his world and his self is diminished. Self-determination is undermined. The function of understanding to illumine and guide the individual's life is not fulfilled.

Chapter 2 DESTRUCTION OF
LANGUAGE

When reason is in doubt, suspicion is cast on language, for language is reason's principal instrument. Nothing, indeed, is more subject to depreciation and suspicion in our disenchanted world than the word. We are much taken with semantics. We worry that our language is trapping us and are tempted to think of it as nothing but a pernicious source of confusion. We are inclined to believe that communication, or rather, miscommunication, is the locus of all human problems, that all of us would agree with each other if only we could clear up the verbal muddles that come between us—we frequently ask people to define their terms. We are much afraid that the questions we are asking and the difficulties that confront us are not questions and difficulties at all, but only deceptions and delusions created by language. For many of us, language is "mere words."

ABUSE OF LANGUAGE

Never have there been better grounds for this distrust. Words impinge upon us incessantly—spoken and written, from radio and television, from the monstrous bulk of newspapers, from the flood of journals, digests, magazines, and books, and from advertisements. All claim to give us the truth and nothing but

18

the truth, to present us with the facts, to be unbiased and objective. They advise us on everything—how to choose our professions, how to succeed, how to catch and keep a husband, how to think, how to make friends, how to find adventure and (often at the same time) how to establish security, and of course, how to be happy. They submerge us in what they claim to be art or science, to be new, original, revolutionary, exciting, and astounding. They promise by means of the latest discoveries to initiate us into the secrets of the universe and the depths of the human soul, now suddenly and for the first time made accessible to man—and what is more, by the same glory of modern ingenuity, made easily accessible.

Moreover, not only is most of this flood of words the product of ignorance, mediocrity, presumptuousness, and irresponsibility—and the effects of all that on the integrity of the word would be disastrous enough—but with terrifying frequency language is used as a means to distort facts, cloud reason, and twist judgment. Advertising and the mentality of advertising have penetrated into every corner of our life. To persuade us to buy, to change our beliefs, to gain our political support, to win our attention, the most unscrupulous and insidious use is made of language: words are mutilated, meanings are distorted, logic is inverted, associations and connotations are contaminated, sound is abused, words relating to the deepest and highest aspects of human life—love, friendship, sympathy, truth, beauty, justice, honesty, mystery, joy—are thrown at us again and again in the most trivial contexts, the most ingratiating appeals, the most blatant lies, until their effectiveness is lost; and then, to regain it, repetition and sensationalism are pushed further still, on and on in a vicious circle, so that finally the word is nothing but noise.

MISTRUST OF LANGUAGE

We have become very much aware of how language can mislead thought—by the conscious aim to distort or destroy meanings as well as the unconscious delusions and falsifications into which language may lure us. Science and critical scholarship have disclosed innumerable ways in which language's persuasive powers have hidden the truth, its capacity to arouse emotions has displaced its capacity to convey knowledge, and its endless potential of ambiguity, imagery, metaphor, analogy, and sound has worked against clarity and validity. At the very core of the modern mind is skepticism toward the written word: our critical thought encourages distrust of written authority; science (which has its historical roots in the questioning of accepted views) is permeated by a spirit of doubt of whatever is said and written; modern historical scholarship is marked to a very great degree by the same attitude, and critically and skeptically scrutinizes the authenticity and veracity of the books, papers, and memoirs that earlier were accepted at face value; philosophy has become so overwhelmingly aware of the confusions and blunders to which language tempts the mind that their exposure has often been held to constitute the chief task of philosophical thought.

Whatever places in doubt the validity of thought throws a shadow on the language into which thought is cast. If reason cannot illuminate reality, then language does not have a power it was once thought to possess. Instead of allowing us to grasp the world, it deludes us. If reason is biased by the beliefs, values, and habits of a society, then the language that embodies them is the vehicle of prejudice. If reason is obstructed by feelings and desires, then the language reason uses is a bed of error and delusion, and must be distrusted in proportion to its power to influence the mind, hence in proportion to its rhetorical qualities, its poetic strength, its literary beauty. This distrust is implicit, for example, in the view of history we have already met: "with its great quantities of traditional literature . . . history probably suffers more than any other discipline from the tyranny of persuasive rhetoric."[1] In the same spirit it is claimed by another writer that a great historian "should not write *too* well," that "the beauty of his style should not detract the attention from what he says and cloud the judgment of the reader." [2]

This fatal view of language assumes that if history is very well written, it cannot be great; that the better the style, the more it draws attention from what is said and the more it obscures the truth. This is the epitome of our contemporaries' distrust of language: its richness and power are the enemies of knowledge and truth.

Would not anyone living in a climate where language commanded more trust assert the opposite: that good language and good thought are companions? that the vast resources of language are potent vehicles of knowledge and truth? that good writing, far from distracting, concentrates the reader's attention on what is being said, and far from clouding, illuminates his judgment? But to the modern man this seems naïve. Or, at least, his fear of being misled is so great that to avoid the risk he prefers to strip language of all its dangerous qualities.

THE DIVISION OF LANGUAGE

What is the meaning of the statement that the historian "should not write *too* well"? It means "that he should not, like the novelist or the poet are wont to do, employ all the artifices of language and style in order to make his point, or to prejudice the reader in favor of his views." [3] This statement typifies the common notion that language has two very different functions: first, it serves so-called objective knowledge, and for this purpose should be stark, sterile, and devoid of power and style; second, it serves the personal interest of the writer—to vent his feelings or to persuade and prejudice—and may use all means and artifices to this end. This division is seen as the remedy for all linguistic confusions and pitfalls: make a sharp separation between these two functions of language and you will never mislead yourself, or be misled, where reason and truth are at stake.

That the division is not without foundation is obvious; you

need only turn from an article in an encyclopedia to Shakespeare. Here is language in its barest and its richest states, most neutral and most powerful, most prosaic and most poetic. But the matter is not always so clear cut. If it were, there would be no danger, for example, of a historian's writing *"too* well." The language of history, however, cannot be sterilized and deprived of style. Similarly, philosophers use language in ways neither entirely stark nor purely poetic. And the same is true in our daily lives, where our words are rarely as sterile as the encyclopedia's and never as poetic as Shakespeare's.

Since language serves different interests and accomplishes different aims, it is natural that frequently tension exists between its various and distinct possibilities and powers. This is by no means new. But what is new is that the tension has changed to antagonism and the distinction to division. The growing recognition in every field of intellectual endeavor of the temptations and deceptions with which language endangers rational thought and the decline of confidence in all exercise of reason not modeled on scientific lines have given rise to an impulse toward total cleavage. This cleavage has been formalized in a number of kindred doctrines (with somewhat different perspectives and varying degrees of rigidity). They have wide currency, although they have met with some opposition from philosophical and literary quarters. Whatever the standing of the doctrines among those who have reflected upon them, however, the underlying notion of language from which they spring colors much of contemporary life, and the doctrines crystallize this notion and thereby help us to deal with it.[4] The first function of language is supposed to belong to the realm of reason, of knowledge, of clear, precise, logical thought—the realm whose prototype or even sole representative is science; it is called "referential" or "cognitive." The second, more amorphous function is held to have nothing to do with reason and knowledge, and to be typified by poetry; it is called "emotive" or "expressive."

(Other formulations of a similar nature have also been given.) In the cognitive function language is said to refer to certain aspects of the world and thereby to enable us to describe and know the world. In the emotive function language expresses and stimulates feelings and desires. The cognitive mode is associated with objectivity, since it refers to things and makes possible objective knowledge; the emotive mode has to do only with subjectivity. The former has the privilege of conveying truth and is therefore judged according to whether its statements are true or false; the latter expresses and arouses emotions and has nothing to do with belief about the world, objective content, and questions of truth.

This division, of course, perfectly complements the science-centered curtailment of reason and the mistrust of language. For according to this division language that is not referential, not like the language of science, cannot serve reason and knowledge; hence, knowledge is accessible only to scientific or quasi-scientific reason. Reason and knowledge must avoid emotive language, for the artifices of the poet are embellishments at best, irrelevant to the content and unnecessary and even repugnant to the serious and honest thinker. Thought must be protected by stripping the word of artifice that may prejudice, of power that may persuade, or beauty that may ensnare.

What happens to literary art and especially to poetry? For people who value a clear mind and truth, such art often becomes a dubious or meaningless arrangement of words, worthless in a scientific age. Others, feeling forced to accept the cleavage of language, have striven to save poetry from such obsolescence by claiming that its impotence in the realm of knowledge and truth is in fact its strength. Its true task, they assert, is not to "say" anything but to express and arouse emotions, and it accomplishes this task by the use of emotive language. This supposed salvation has found much acclaim, but it is in fact (as we shall see in Part Two) a mutilation, and this has been increasingly recognized by poets and critics in recent times.

Poetry is not the only realm to suffer from the division of language. History, for example, is another. It is true that history has been falsified and distorted, unwittingly and deliberately, through the impact of emotional and poetic language; but it is killed if one tries to write it like physics. Division also destroys the language of our daily life, the language with which we orient ourselves and shape our actions, recall our past and plan our future, the language we need to embody innumerable meanings inherent in our existence. The division paralyzes the exercise of reason in the guidance of conduct, for it limits the language reason may use to one fragment of language; it denies that reason may speak a language that neither is, nor imitates, the language of science; it denies cognitive power to every activity whose use of language diverges from the referential.

Language is a cornerstone of our humanness. But we often treat it with total disrespect. We heedlessly abuse and corrupt it, voiding its meanings and eroding its power. And fearful that it deludes (as, alas, it often does), we mistrust it, and therefore strip and limit its meanings, reject its power, divide and reduce its resources, until language in all its dimensions —excepting only the stark and sterile concepts of science and the bare statements of everyday practicality—is reduced to impotence.

Chapter 3 NULLIFICATION OF VALUES

Values are in dissolution. Many of us have no profound convictions concerning what is good, just, beautiful, or worthy —nor their opposites. Life-fulfilling ideals are rare. Many people do not really believe that there are things that merit respect, struggle, and sacrifice. Few men are filled with a vital sense of the genuine as opposed to the spurious.

The realm of values, of course, can never be wholly without difficulties. Even in the most homogeneous communities, where most values are widely shared, there are individuals and groups who reject the common values and uphold others. Much human conflict has been engendered by commitment to disparate ideals. The modern difficulty, however, is more radical, indeed, totally radical; it lies at the very base of the whole realm of values. In the past there was disagreement over whether something was worthy or unworthy, desirable or not desirable. Sometimes there was disagreement over the way in which desirability was to be established—over the source of norms, or the human experience by which value was to be discerned. Today's predicament is that such disagreement has dissolved—not because the millennium has arrived in which all men are in harmony, but because the subject of the disagreement, value as such, has been dissolving.

In the past, one did not doubt that some things were better than others; the problem was, which things? One did not doubt that there was *some* justification for values; the problem was, what kind? Today the very existence of values is in question; the very possibility of justification is suspect. Many of us are unsure that some things are good and others bad. We are not convinced that one thing is worthy of admiration and another deserving of condemnation.

This doubt attacks the core of human life. Without values there is emptiness, boredom, and desperation. Without values individuals and society disintegrate. Or terror arises, and men frantically erect new things to function as values; they seize upon anything—idols, isms, slogans, or lies—to give purpose to their lives; and they pursue these pseudo values with fanatic and often bloody single-mindedness.

EROSION OF RELIGION AND REJECTION OF THE PAST

Religious conviction, long the foundation of basic values, is scant. Though the number of churchgoers is large, the religious spirit is not the center and ground of human existence for the overwhelming majority. Religion is a Sunday-morning interest for these people, incapable of providing inspiration and support for a vital structure of values. To the educated, religion usually seems backward and childish. They view it with indifference or hostility. To many it is the embodiment of superstition, obscurantism, and authoritarianism—an encumbrance from the past.[1]

Not only religion, but most things coming to us from the past carry little conviction. Odd remnants are cherished, historic places are visited on Sundays, traditions are invoked on public occasions; but modern man rarely sees vital meaning in the past. Usually he views it in contrast with progress, and progress he places ahead of everything else: the new, the modern, and the different exert irresistible attraction.

The past, of course, is not identical with the good. If it

has given us worthy things, it has also given unworthy ones, and much opposition to it stems from disillusionment. Old ideals have been found threadbare and hollow. There is, therefore, in this rejection of the past a spirit of cleansing and renewal without which man becomes stagnant and decays. But our rejection goes far beyond that.

It is supported by our most powerful social forces: science and technology. Science is forever forging ahead—discovering new things and voiding old views. Permeated by the spirit of science, we are disinclined to look to the precipitates of the past as sources of values. Who, apart from some classical scholars, believes that the world of ancient Greece has precious things to give to the atomic age? Who, with the exception of a few historians, is convinced that the lives of dead men have something to say to the space age? Who, apart from exceptional teachers of the arts, is certain that the creations of the past are storehouses of value for the present? The "sophisticated" consider books written before the last war outdated. Thinkers live in an atmosphere impregnated with the assumption that little of worth has been accomplished in the realm of knowledge until the most recent times. Everywhere we are told that more progress has been made in all the important departments of life during the last generation than in the previous two thousand years.

Technology is transforming our outlook and way of life with such hurricane speed that everything inherited is swept away. Without the most exhausting effort, without a constant struggle to withstand the rupturing tension between modern demands and older values, we cannot keep these values alive. Today's conditions no longer provide the ground for them. How, to use the single most glaring example in the moral realm, can a person develop and sustain an unshakable conviction in the worth and inviolability of human life when the means of destruction that have been developed and that are taken for granted are of a scale whose magnitude defies

27

description and when destruction does not bring the destroyer face to face with the men he destroys—when suffering and horror are not experienced, when extermination is talked about and may at any moment be carried out in a cool and calculating manner? Even aside from the horror of war, people's concern for human life is constantly being eroded, for example, by the fact that in the course of what we call peaceful, normal existence tens of thousands are killed yearly by automobiles—and hundreds of thousands are injured. Society generally takes this for granted as if it were an unalterable law of nature and is complacent when the yearly statistics show a decline of 1 per cent.

Technology has not only so altered the conditions of life that values from the past have been submerged, but coupled with the spirit of science it has brought about an atmosphere of unquestioned belief that everything can be changed and improved, that there is nothing that may not be tampered with—not to speak of its being sacred or holy, that nothing that is simply given to us has worth and deserves respect.

RELATIVITY OF VALUES

We are acutely aware that men's value patterns are many and that they exhibit enormous differences and disparities. Increased interaction with other nations in economic, political, and military matters confronts us with different views and ways of being that have to be acknowledged. Travel to foreign lands has expanded continuously. Information about all parts of the globe pours into our daily lives, presenting us with bewildering variety. Much mingling of groups and classes, moreover, occurs also within individual societies. This is especially true in North America, where people of different religions, nationalities, and economic, social, and educational classes are thrown into constant contact.

Awareness of different values and the obligation to live with people whose views differ from ours can have a wholesome effect. The confines of parochialism may be shaken, and horizons may be enlarged. We may be led to appreciate and respect things to which we would otherwise be blind. Under prevailing circumstances, however, another effect predominates: the spread of indifference. All values, we are led to think, are equally justified; there is no question of better or worse. Different people believe different things; some like one thing, some another—let each be happy in his own way. This appealing doctrine smoothes the pursuit of daily affairs. It removes the impulse for conflict. It furthers mutual adjustment with minimum friction.

It also empties values of all meaning. If we can never believe that one thing is better than another, if contradictory values must be accepted on equal terms, if no action, object, or ideal is preferable to another, if a conflict in values is never to be resolved by the question of merit but only by compromise, social pressure, bargaining, and expediency, then no value can continue to command respect, none can deserve commitment. All values become void. What most people call tolerance is in fact indifference. It is not caring about anything. It is not feeling strongly enough to take a stand. It is life reduced to motion with minimum pain.

Awareness of the multiplicity of human values comes not only from the actual circumstances of life, but also from a number of intellectual pursuits that have pervasively influenced the more educated classes and, through them, the less educated. History has brought to our attention the particularity of the values held by different societies at different times in the past. Anthropology has stressed again and again that the values adhered to by different peoples are enormously diverse and that there is no warrant for a judgment of merit among them. Sociology has pointed to the variability of values with social conditions and with the groups and classes of society.

All this has contributed to the emancipation of the Western world from a rigidly conceived code of values that had erroneously been regarded as universally valid. Along with this beneficial result, however, and in the long run much more influential, has come an erosion of values. Faced with diversity and contrariety, feeling the pressure to accommodate all views, persuaded of the invalidity of judgment—especially by the anthropological doctrine of cultural relativism, that values are relative to each society, and their justification is simply the fact of their being held by a people—we feel compelled to believe that the meaning of good and bad is no more than that somebody views something as good or bad. "Just" is whatever a society says is just, nothing more. No judgment transcending such affirmations is possible. Thereby all values, and value as such, dissolve. If genocide, to take the extreme example, must be considered justified for the nation that practices it and if other nations' opposition can have no grounds other than that they themselves do not want to be its victims, then moral values vanish.

SUBJECTIVITY OF VALUES

The identification of value with whatever is in fact felt to be valuable by any one group of people has the effect of eliminating the role of what is being valued and placing emphasis only on the disposition of the evaluator. The event that is admired and the act that is condemned are not essentially involved; only what people feel about them matters. This subjectivization of values receives powerful support from other quarters.

If I say, "The sunset is beautiful," I take it for granted that I am saying something about the sunset. I am making a judgment about an event in the world. In this respect I seem to be doing something quite analogous to saying, "There is a book on the table," or "This is an apple tree." My valuation refers to something other than myself, to something often called objective. This objective content, we are frequently told, is illusory. When I say, "The sunset is beautiful," I am

30

allegedly talking about myself, my feelings. I am doing something utterly different from saying, "There is a book on the table." In the latter statement, I am really referring to the world; in the former, it is claimed, I am really expressing a subjective state and falsely crediting the sunset with a quality it does not possess. I am projecting onto it something of my own. The fact that our language indicates the contrary, says the modern view, must not mislead us. Language, we dare never for a moment forget, often deludes us.

This belief about values comes to us in the first place from the prevalent view of the nature of the world. In its original form, this view is the philosophical doctrine of scientific materialism or some variation of it. The world is thought to consist of a configuration of material bodies (large and small; stars, stones, molecules, atoms) moving in space and time according to certain universal principles, the laws of physics. All that can be said about these bodies concerns their dynamic properties, the characteristics of their motions—mass, position, velocity, and so on. That is all there is to them. What about their color or their odor? They have none. The sunset is not red, the rose has no fragrance. Color and odor have to do not with bodies but with minds. In addition to the colorless, soundless, odorless bodies, there are supposed to be minds that apprehend the bodies and the laws of their motion (unless one holds to radical, monistic materialism, in which case the minds are also eventually resolved into bodies). Each mind in the process of perceiving bodies has the peculiar experience of also perceiving colors, sounds, smells, and tastes as associated with bodies. But these qualities do not in fact belong to the bodies; they are falsely projected onto them by the mind, which—except in the philosophical doctrine—does not distinguish that which comes to it from the world from that which it supplies on its own.

Just as the world has no colors and odors, so, or even more so, according to the doctrine, it has no values like goodness or beauty. It is nonsense to ask if the rose smells good or if the sunset is beautiful. Both consist of moving particles and no more. Particles simply move; they have neither fragrance nor beauty. My judgment that the sunset is beautiful is purely a disclosure of my mental state, of my subjective feeling. My judgment is not grounded in, let alone warranted by, what it purports to judge.

But the materialist doctrine of reality, based on seventeenth-century science, has lost its chief support. Modern physics is not consistent with it. Furthermore, the dominant contemporary philosophical interpretation of the nature of science holds it to be inadmissible to say anything at all about a reality allegedly disclosed by physics. The idea that physics discloses something we call reality is of a metaphysical character—beyond the compass of empirical science—and much modern philosophy denies the meaningfulness of such ideas.

Nevertheless, the materialist doctrine is very much with us, though often held unreflectively and inconsistently. We regard the world as if it consisted simply of material objects to be counted, measured, and timed. The outlook is present in numerous disciplines—very clearly, for example, in behavioral psychology and other behavioral sciences—and it pervades all of technology, concerned as it is with material things to be produced, moved, sold, and consumed. The same view is more or less consciously held by very many people, though they may never have heard of Galileo, Newton, Descartes, or Locke and the theories of primary and secondary qualities.

Even if we do not hold the materialist doctrine, however, the predicament of values is still with us, albeit in a somewhat different form. The world we accept, the world in which we have confidence, the world as we believe it to be, is the world seen through scientific eyes—and in this world there are no values. The new physics has no more need or room for them than the old. Physics considers how things are "in fact," but not whether they are good or bad; and the same is true of all natural sciences. Science, taking an "objective," or impersonal, view of the world, is, as the matter is usually expressed, value-neutral. Values, we then believe, are "subjective": they stem from a person's emotions, not from the way things are.

The objective approach of science has spread to other areas: reason has become scientific reason. We turn to the scheme of science to gain knowledge not only about nature but also about human life. Not only does our view of nature then become value-neutral, but our view of all other things as well—including those human situations and activities that are permeated by values. This value-neutral approach is the one anthropologists generally try to take to understand the ways in which different human societies live—their traditions, customs, ceremonies, social organizations, languages, thought patterns, and artifacts. Moreover, anthropologists seek objectivity not only about these things, in which values are everywhere implied, but also about the values people overtly hold and affirm, as in moral injunctions or religions. Anthropologists believe they can know what things the people they study regard as valuable, but they strive to do this while being value-neutral themselves. This, of course, is essential to their doctrine of cultural relativism: there is no question for them of something really being valuable, of its meriting the way it is regarded; there is only the neutral fact that certain people like or dislike it—they feel it is valuable and desire it; or they feel it is bad and avoid it.

The same outlook prevails in sociology, economics, many kinds of psychology, and some attempts to study politics. Valuations are eschewed. History, also, frequently tries the same approach—to give a value-neutral view of the human past, to avoid seeing human doings as good or bad. It moves from the realm of the humanities, traditionally value-soaked, to the social studies, supposedly more objective, factual, unemotional, and value-neutral, and even to the social sciences, allegedly scientific in all ways.

Even fields still counted as humanities frequently strive to follow the same path. Much modern philosophy, for example, manifests a desire to ban normative elements. Ethics is given relatively little attention, and sometimes it has been written out of the realm of philosophy. Or it has been made into a purely logico-linguistic study of propositions in the normative sphere without judgment of their ethical merit. Similarly, criticism of the arts—of music, painting, and literature—has sought to view the work of art without evaluation. Again, the study of language has been said approvingly to be no longer normative but factual, the question of how one ought to speak being resolved into how men in fact do speak.

Thus all things in human life tend to be viewed as devoid of either worth or worthlessness. They are as neutral as nature is in science. The judgments we make of human acts and the worth attributed to such acts are apparently not warranted by them. To believe that something is valuable now merely means that one likes it. The "values" of things are illusory qualities, projected onto things by ourselves according to the way we feel about them.

The same view of values emerges when the issue is approached from another direction. A fundamental difficulty with respect to values is that different people hold different values. Now if values had some basis beyond our personal likes or dislikes, there would surely have to be some way, or ways, by which these differences could be resolved. But how can we establish whether something is desirable? How can we justify the values we hold? How can we convince someone who disagrees with us that our values are the proper ones?

If we had political, military, or social power, we might be able to coerce him into agreeing with us. But however efficacious this method might be, the agreement would certainly not demonstrate the justness of our values. Beating someone into submission does not prove him wrong. Disagreement must be settled, not silenced.

There is one method that would certainly satisfy us—the method of science. Here disagreement in beliefs is settled by logical argument and observation: we show, we prove, we demonstrate. Such a process of convincing someone establishes the validity of what we are concerned with. His assent to our view is grounded in its objective basis. He is neither coerced nor merely persuaded, but is convinced on valid grounds. This method, however, cannot establish values. It is value-neutral.

Is there another way by which values can be established? Many will answer that the only valid way to discern the character of things is by science, and since science discerns no values, values cannot be known. They are not part of the cognitive realm. It is fallacious and misleading to say that we *know* right from wrong, or that we *know* the beauty of the sunset.

We should say, according to this view, that we *feel* them. Values have to do only with our emotions and desires, and these are not answerable to the character of things. They are neither appropriate nor inappropriate. Some of us have certain feelings upon smelling a rose or seeing a sunset; others have other feelings: feelings have no objective validity. Stealing is not bad. If we say it is, we really mean—or rather should really mean—that we don't like to steal or that we don't like others to steal. Expressions of value are expressions of taste, and taste, the modern view holds, is entirely subjective. "*King Lear* is a great play" is analogous to "Oysters are good." There are people who don't like oysters and people who don't like *Lear*. There is nothing further to be said about tastes, desires, and emotions.

Disagreement on values, in the contemporary view, is not a disagreement at all but merely a difference in personal reactions. There is nothing to disagree about. If I say, "The television gives me a headache," and you say, "It does not give me a headache," we have no disagreement, we have merely a difference in personal feelings. The same is true for values. Instead of saying, "The sunset is beautiful," or "*King Lear* is great," or "Genocide is evil," we should say that we like, or don't like, these things. Others may feel differently.

Disagreement and justification, it is said, belong to the sphere of the intellect, which is objective and impersonal, and apprehends the character of things. Values have to do with emotions, and emotions are purely personal, purely subjective. "Disagreements" in values, therefore, are removed by swaying people's emotions. There are many means of doing this, among them preaching, rhetoric, art, propaganda, and brainwashing. Some means are more efficacious than others; some may appeal to us less than others (there can be no question, of course, of their being right or just or desirable); but all are fundamentally the same in that they have nothing to do with validity or justification, but only with altering people's feelings.

The two reasons for the subjectivization of values—the value-neutral view of all things and the apparent impossibility of justifying our values—reinforce and substantiate each other. The neutrality of things leads us to expect that what we call values will not be justifiable; and conversely, the inability to justify values makes plausible the view that there is nothing to be justified, that the world is value-neutral.

VALUES AND THE PREDICAMENTS OF UNDERSTANDING
AND LANGUAGE

It has been evident throughout our discussion that the dissolution of values is intimately connected with the diminution of man's understanding and the suspicion of language. Values, it is thought, cannot be illuminated by the understanding: reason cannot help us in the choice of ideals; it is impotent to assess aims and purposes; it cannot judge and guide conduct and action. If reason is scientific reason and scientific reason is value-neutral, then values are not reasonable. Moreover, we now see that the activities of reason that are distrusted (that is, the activities that are not modeled on science) are generally those in which values play, or at least have played, an important role. Thus, history, philosophy, criticism, and reflection on the ends of our actions and the meaning of our commitments are—or have been—to a large extent inseparable from valuations. But if we think that values are merely expressions of personal emotions, or of the habitual feelings, tastes, and desires of a group of people, then we must think that they contaminate reason.

The issue is analogous in language. The language we distrust, which supposedly deludes and misleads us, which has poetic power, is language impregnated with values. Words that are charged with values are suspect as ejaculations of feelings, swayers of emotions—devoid of truth and objective content.

Intellect and feelings are separated in this doctrine. Intellect, reason (that is, scientific reason), objectivity, referential language, fact, knowledge, and truth belong together. Utterly different and wholly divorced from them is another cluster: feelings, subjectivity, emotive and poetic language, taste, and value.

AVOIDANCE AND CORRUPTION OF VALUES

If one is not permeated by a conviction of the meaningfulness of values, one does not trouble oneself about them, or one even deliberately avoids them. This can be seen in every area of modern activity. One area that shows the radical nature of the predicament is education, a major aim of which—it used to be thought—was to cultivate the student's capacity to discriminate values. Today, the avoidance of value judgments has become a widespread principle of teaching. Teachers, believing it their duty to be objective, often anxious to emulate the reliable method of science, suspicious of the emotional character of values, and distrustful of the very meaning of questions of worth, adopt the stance of neutrality. We must question whether they succeed in being neutral or only delude themselves and their students; for their success would have the dubious implication that psychology, anthropology, sociology—and even more dubiously, history, philosophy, literature, and all criticism of the arts—can be pursued without valuation. In any case, the profession of neutrality manifests and promotes the belief that values have no foundation.

In our value-deprived atmosphere, men's minds are easily dominated by the cluster of attributes that characterize technology and the machine—size, quantity, speed, uniformity, and efficiency. These can all be assessed objectively, by impersonal means: they are expressible in numbers. And number, that fundamental and marvellous instrument of the mind in the realm of science and technology, has become the surrogate of value: the worth of things is gauged by the number of people desiring them (note the dominant role of opinion polls) and by their price.

Without value consciousness, everything is debased. Whatever is not respected is easily trivialized. Trivialization springs from an absence of values and, in turn, seals their destruction. It surrounds us everywhere. Not an hour can be spent with radio or television, not a page of the magazines, papers, and books constituting the principal reading matter of our contemporaries can be turned, without our meeting invocations of the once most respected values in the most unfitting and trivial contexts.

This corruption complements the corruption of language. Our confidence in the word and in the value of what is meant by the word are simultaneously destroyed when the word is misused. When you are in the habit of using the salutation "Dear Friend" in thousands of identical letters to people you have never seen but want to persuade—to buy, spend, or vote—you can retain no respect for the word friend and no notion of what it truly refers to. And in the minds of the readers of these intimate communications friendship is threatened with a similar fate. When you "love" chewing gum, wash your dishes with "Joy," and see "wonder" and "miracle" in every new contrivance, only superhuman strength can maintain a sense of values.

Trivialization is incessantly dulling our minds to the perception of worth and furthering our doubt of its very existence. Even the pursuit of serious discussion concerning fundamental things in man's life is often impossible. Raise a question involving values and see how frequently people are thrown into thorough discomfort. They laugh, joke, and sidestep the issue. They say that these things must not be taken too seriously. They ridicule convictions, calling them "personal prejudice." They evade profound questions and shun significant words, because profundity and significance are suspect. Seriousness as such is avoided because of the gnawing doubt that anything worthy of seriousness exists.

Trivialization and subjectivization reinforce each other. Subjectivity of values is more readily acceptable if everything has been trivialized and if one has no conviction that there are things of real worth. Conversely, trivialization and corruption are practiced without opposition, and even with sanction, if values are purely subjective. For the doctrine of subjectivity renders invalid the judgment that something is trivial or that something valuable is being trivialized. The doctrine only allows us to say that what one person calls trivial the other deems valuable. Thus trivialization and abuse cannot be condemned, and there is even no meaning in asserting that they are being practiced—for *trivial* and *valuable* are merely expressions of personal feelings and bias. To put it bluntly lest the enormity of the issue escape: according to the doctrine of subjectivity there is no question of superiority between soap opera and Shakespeare; there is no question of

39

trivialization if your bankbook is called the second most important book you possess, or if your feeling for chewing gum is love.

In the dissolution of value, man as man disappears. Ideals and commitments are reduced to nothing when the difference between good and bad, mediocrity and greatness, triviality and worth is merely a matter of private preference. Man loses his birthright when he waives the difference between the moral and the usual, or between goodness and price.

Chapter 4 LOSS OF THE WORLD

Modern man is losing the world in which he has his being. It has receded from him—or, rather, he has become removed from it. He is feverishly busy acting upon all that surrounds him—nature, men, and men's products—but he does not stand in fulfilling relation to them. He has no genuine ties. He passes through the world without being touched. He manipulates it with tongs, wearing sterile gloves. He remains distant and estranged.

A feeling of emptiness haunts him. Most of his work is meaningless, incapable of providing genuine satisfaction. The hours of "leisure" are sickened with boredom and deluged by packaged entertainment. A fretful busyness to "kill time" and restless movement from novelty to novelty bury an ever-present sense of futility and vacuousness. In the midst of his endless achievements, modern man is losing the substance of human life.

LOSS OF NATURE

Man has lost nature—and in the most obvious way, through its removal. The expansion of cities and suburbs has swallowed the land, and man is surrounded by concrete and asphalt. He neither smells the earth nor sees the sky. He knows neither the awakening dawn nor the quiet of evening. He does his utmost to separate routine life from the natural day's rhythm and from the change of season. His animal world has shrunk to pets: the last generation of children who knew even the horse has passed. His world of plants fares little better: what flowers and trees there are in most cities are barely a painful reminder that nature exists.

Modern man knows almost nothing of the fruits of the earth: he lives in total divorce from their nurture and growth; he has not experienced the promise of planting and the fulfillment of harvest; he has not felt the loam with his hands. What little knowledge he has of where things come from and how they live, of their relation to soil and water, to air and sun, is entirely bookish. He scarcely knows how the earth's fruit looks: he sees it frozen and canned, cut and ground, bleached if it had color and dyed if it was pale. Many young wives who live in American cities may never have seen peas in pods or a coffee bean.

An acute manifestation of our separation from all that is nature's bounty and, at the same time, a symbol of our divorce from the world, is the package. Almost everywhere the package receives more attention than its contents. Nothing escapes it in our food stores: what is not hidden in boxes and cans is wrapped in paper and cellophane.

The same divorce from nature is achieved by the modern building. With sealed windows or even entirely without windows, the box in which more and more of us spend the better part of each day is intended to "free" us from every change in the natural environment, from being touched in any way, and it results in tomblike isolation.

Nature today is a thing for manipulation and use. Apart from the way it furthers or obstructs man's economic and other practical aims, it is nothing. Land is space to be built on; rivers are dumps for waste; trees are material for paper. Nature's place in our lives is solely its role in technology: we use and extract, produce and transform, control and discard.

Mountains are leveled for highways, trees felled for parking spaces, and lakes and rivers turned into sewers. We master, subjugate, and exploit—and the bond with nature is dissolved, intimacy disappears, and appreciation fades. Man has lost his awe and his love. He does not care for nature; he does not seek it; he is not close to it. Even when he escapes to it from the sweltering gray of a stifling city, he does not quietly rest in a forest's shade, listening to the rustle of leaves, feeling the earth under him. Instead, he rushes past and through in his car, hugging the highway and glancing at things from a distance as he passes—in the rush of traffic, the smell of exhaust, and the noise of engines.

Feelings of closeness toward nature are often considered outdated, dismissed as mere romanticism. We may have a private longing for nature lurking where it is not exposed to ridicule, but our minds do not support it. Wordsworth and Keats wrote poetry whose imagery is lovely and whose emotional impact is great, but many believe that what it says is not to be taken seriously. (No poetry, indeed, says anything if one accepts the division of language.) The prevailing view of nature, as I have already mentioned, is derived from science, and in the scientific view nature is neutral. It is simply there and ongoing. Its character does not justify our feelings toward it; it is neither bad nor good, awesome nor gentle; its beauty is only a projection of our minds.

The usual consequence of this view is that people's capacity for response to nature is undermined. And this is true even if they know no science, because its outlook has permeated everyone's life. Delight, joy, awe, and the feeling of intimacy are without basis, they are all "in the mind," divorced from their source. And thus divorced, these feelings toward nature wane.

Some may say that this consequence is not inevitable and that although our feelings and attitudes cannot be justified by our intellectual view of nature, this is no reason for their

43

abandonment. They argue that this view forces us to recognize that the justification of feelings lies not in whatever elicits them but solely in themselves and that we must allow our emotional responses to be independent of our knowledge of things.

But this attempt to overcome the neutrality of nature by making our emotions self-supporting has fatal consequences. First, it makes us into schizophrenics: it cleaves our selves into two parts, the feelings and the intellect, and it would have one part of us react to the world in a way the other part judges unwarranted. Second, it hastens the very estrangement from nature that afflicts us: it makes our emotions self-enclosed by isolating the subjective self from the world.

The belief that feelings toward nature are unwarranted combines with a general avoidance of feelings as such. To draw close to nature is to allow one's feelings to become engaged. A spring meadow may tempt one to run and leap, in imagination at least. Autumn, with its fulfillment, clear light, and falling leaves, sometimes brings strange fusions of elation and sorrow. But such feelings, modern man believes, are not to be indulged in. They discomfort and embarrass him and arouse his suspicions. He derides and suppresses them, for they do not fit the climate of modern life.

For most Western people nature has moved into physical and spiritual distance. They do not feel themselves *in* nature, are not aware of its presence, and do not imaginatively hold communion with it. It has ceased to inspire them and to cause them to marvel; it does not nourish their souls.

LOSS OF MAN

Man has lost man. This predicament, because it lies at the very center of our lives, is perhaps the most difficult of all to face. To call attention to it is to risk being accused of exaggeration or of wanting to do away with all that is modern and to return to an illusory past—even though human estrangement has been a central theme, over the last hundred years, of many thinkers and artists who are widely known and praised. Our concern, let me repeat here, is not the past, but the present, and the transformation of the present toward a sounder future. But there is no hope for such a transformation unless we acknowledge the true state of the present.

As our dependence on mechanical devices spreads, the occasions diminish for human meeting. More and more our daily transactions take place with lifeless things. Machines dispense our stamps, cigarettes, and drinks. In the supermarket we serve ourselves from shelves. Correspondence is spoken into the dictaphone. Banking is done by mail. The world of the office is paper and type. In the factory our intercourse is with machines: we watch lights, push buttons, turn levers. When we must deal with a person, we speak to him not face to face, but over the telephone. If he is in the building next door or one floor up or even in the adjoining office, we use the intercom.

And what do we see of another man when our dealings are direct? Usually he is no more to us than an unknown entity who does a job. He is a faceless, anonymous embodiment of a social role. Think of the person who checks your purchase at the supermarket, or the clerk at the five and ten, or the bus driver who changes your coins. You and he hardly see each other's face. On most occasions, men are regarded merely with respect to the way they fit an organization's slots. So habituated have we become to this that few of us can hear the human indifference so blatantly contained in the common phrase, "to use men on a job."

Interaction between individuals tends to take place exclusively in terms of the service they render each other. Beyond that, the man as a man is considered a nuisance: his personality interferes with the routinized process of work and system. This sense of interference is clearly implied when we say—with approbation, of course—that someone knows how to "handle people." He knows, that is, how to neutralize the personal elements that obtrude into the impersonal system: he knows how to "adjust" individual men to fit into functional grooves.

A man—even as nature—is regarded as something to use and manipulate. Nothing, not even the conquest of space, has moved faster than the conquest of men. We are incessantly subjected to the crudest, as well as the most insidious, means of influence and persuasion to make us act in ways desirable to a host of manipulators. These means are omnipresent, pursuing us at work and at leisure, in the office and at home and on the way between. They have entered all areas of life, including even the school and the church, those supposed strongholds of the human personality.

People's conception of the individuals they meet more and more imitates the vision of science. And the vision of science, just as it divorces man from nature, divorces man from man. Therefore its acceptance in the conduct of life brings human alienation.

Our examination of science will make it evident that in any scientific account of man—be it in biology, cybernetics, psychology, or sociology (whenever and in so far as the two latter are, or try to be, scientific)—he is seen merely as a phenomenon connected in definite ways with other phenomena, analogous to a natural phenomenon in physics or chemistry. He is a thing, an object held at arm's length to be observed and scrutinized; a configuration of characteristics ("variables," in scientific terminology) associated in certain ways with other variables describing other neutral entities. He is neither wise nor foolish, truthful nor dishonest, sensitive nor crude. He is not a man who participates in a human relation. He is not a concrete individual who meets another in all his otherness. When we account for another's weeping in terms of glands, we obliterate the person and replace him by a physiological event; the sorrow or joy of tears is not to be found in glandular secretions. When we explain a man as a case of social conditions, we understand not the concrete man, "the brother, the real brother," [1] but the case; and a case, no matter how useful the explanation, is no more than a diagram. When in the manner of behavioral psychology, we approach a man with reinforcement schedules and stimulus conditioning, we may modify his behavior, but we are not in touch with a man. What we explain and act upon is a faceless, nameless, value-free, impersonal example of a scientific generalization.

All this is not, as it stands, an indictment of science. Nor am I at the moment concerned with, or placing in question, the contribution of science to man's life. I am simply describing the kind of vision yielded by science and what results when this vision—or worse, a perversion of it—is brought to the encounter of man with man, as it increasingly is.

The impersonal conception of human individuals is echoed by a more generalized impersonal stance. The emotional side of life, as we have already observed, is often held down and denied. But the human relation engages the self in all its dimensions, including especially the very personal ones. If sensitivity, feeling, and passion are lacking, the relation dries up at its source.

The relation of person with person is dissolved by the nullification of values. Such relation draws its sap from the world in which it has its being. It does not live in isolation, sufficient unto itself, but needs common participation in actual and imagined experience. It has its being in shared esteem of worthy things (other human relations, nature, human creations) and shared knowledge of the denials and hardships, meaning and joy of man's life in the world. We commune with one another as we work for a common purpose; as we silently watch nature; as we enter into dialogue to find truth and struggle with its demands; and as we listen to music and our eyes meet in understanding. None of these things can

47

occur without a community of values. There can be no bond in labor without accord on the worth of its aim. Bonds forged through hope and fulfillment or doubt and despair rest on common acknowledgment of what truly matters. Men meet in spirit in joint recognition of where importance lies.

It becomes extremely difficult to find even a modest number of men with whom to share such recognition when values are widely held to be private preference and when, as is now the case, the multiplicity of things corporeal and spiritual —products of industry and art, customs, ideals, and beliefs— that can serve as objects of preference has grown to astronomical proportions. Nor is there much hope of bringing about a joint recognition of values; for if they are entirely subjective, then there is nothing to point to in the world through encounter with which accord may be sought.

The destruction of language cripples the relation of man with man. Dialogue is the chief instrument of communion. Men face the world together, know one another, and come close to each other in speech. Through language they seek to grasp and convey to one another what they perceive in the universe and feel in their souls. Without discourse that bridges the space between them, men remain strangers.

The language of the great majority of our contemporaries is as feeble an instrument as a brush with five bristles; it hardly suffices to deal with their routine duties. Nor is this state of affairs much better among the "educated," since their main additional acquisition is a technical jargon. When people try to convey to each other an experience that has deeply affected them, to speak of a delicate situation, a moving encounter, a revealing insight—indeed, of anything departing from ordinariness—their speech is fumbling and impotent. The insipidity of commonplace prose and the stark rigidity of technical jargon are unable to deal with those moments of life that are the vital ingredients of human relations. The trite phrases and the platitudes raised to superlatives fail completely. People who therefore sense the inappropriateness of their speech for what they wish to convey remain closed in themselves; or else they vainly hope that saying "You know what I mean" will give wings to their lame words. Even those who really know the value of language and tend it with care are paralyzed and afraid to speak, for they feel that the language that would be needed—from the simplest to the most pregnant utterance of man to man—has become hollow. Abuse has poisoned it with insincerity, and suspicion has taken its validity. Many words that once could invoke a world are mute. What can be conveyed by *bread* or *water, sun* or *sea, happiness* or *love?*

Specialism, which is being pressed without limit today, will be discussed in several connections. For the moment let us note how it contributes to man's loss of man. During work, as we have already seen, men do not meet as individuals who perform jobs—they meet as embodiments of their jobs; they do not transcend as persons the specialized roles they assume —they *are* their roles. (I oversimplify, because as long as men are not quite robots there is something left that is outside their function. Yet the perfect fit is our world's ideal, if not yet its actual achievement.) Away from work a man's minute specialty so stamps him that when he is with anyone who is not a specialist in the same, or a closely related, field, they find little ground for significant meeting. Their interests are different, and they cannot readily find common fulfilling activities; their views of the world and of life often diverge; experiences do not link them, because they tend to approach things in incompatible ways; discourse is impeded because of differing modes of thought and the dearth of topics of which both have understanding; the very instrument of meeting, language, suffers because it is permeated by the specialist's viewpoint.

Estrangement between men due to specialism is evident everywhere. It is especially striking and sad, however, among

49

men devoted to learning, for among them one might hope that common dedication to things of the spirit would provide ample ground for human relation. But nothing could be further from the truth. These men have been driven so far apart that, for example, the connection between scholars in a university is chiefly the administrative apparatus.

Specialism pursued to its current extremity is fatal to the relation of man with man. It cuts us off from one another, leaving as the only link between us the interaction defined by our narrow specialized roles. We touch each other only with the "externally established functional part of the self." [2]

LOSS OF CULTURE

Man has lost his own creations. His knowledge, his learning, and his art (collectively, his culture) largely fail to enhance or sustain his life.[3] The chief reason for this loss is that we no longer look upon culture as some kind of whole that an individual can grasp. It has become a collection of innumerable isolated pursuits of the mind and of their infinity of disconnected products. Connections are lacking because in the realm of the mind they exist only in so far as they are perceived and expressed by individuals. Relations and wholeness come into being when they are apprehended and given shape by a thinker or artist. Just this effort, however, has been abandoned. We no longer attempt to see encompassing connections; we no longer conceive of all the efforts of the mind as constituting any kind of unity. With rare exceptions, men do not pursue their special work within a perspective of a sizable portion of human creation, a perspective that would lend meaning to their efforts and be enriched by them in turn. Whatever connections a pursuit may have with other specialties are solely functional. It may make use of techniques developed elsewhere, or draw on other results; but it is not related in a partnership, in some kind of concord or complementarity.

Of course no pursuit and no piece of work can contain the universe. Every individual thing is what it is by virtue of limitation: physics is not poetry, painting is not biology, and none of these disciplines can include another's range without losing its identity. Creation in every realm requires selection, and in this respect all activity is specialized; the issue is the degree of specialization and the spirit in which it is carried on. Today the degree has reached the most perplexing extremity, and the spirit is to regard each specialty as contained within an isolated cubicle: specialism is enthroned.

Extreme specialization has been forced upon us by the over-powering bulk and complexity of learning and techniques. To acquire a specialist's proficiency in even one of the all but infinite number of specialties existing today is an enormous task. It does not seem that anything other than extreme specialization is possible. But this is only half of the reason for its ascendancy. The other half is that we idolize the specialist's attitude and that this idolization has resulted in, and is adding at an ever-accelerating rate to, the stupendous bulk that makes ever more narrow specialization necessary. We restrict our attention to a narrow focus not primarily because we seem unable to do anything else but just as much, or more, because this has become the standard way, the only way of "really doing something." This way alone is felt to carry conviction and possess reliability. Specialism and the labyrinthine pro-liferation of things are mutual cause and effect. As long as only work done in the modern specialist spirit is esteemed, continued multiplication of specialties is inevitable, since there is no limit to what can be known and to the techniques that can be developed.

Culture is lost to man because he cannot possibly compre-hend more than one or two specialized fields. With each field being accessible only to its specialist practitioners, it cannot contribute to the spiritual life of anyone else. We are rapidly losing the last educated people who have a significant outlook on the totality of human endeavor, and we shall soon have only experts. Men do not breathe the air of a common spiritual atmosphere. Except for the practical applications of the specialist's results—the most obvious being those of science to technology—and the benefit or suffering brought by these applications to nonspecialists, the specialist's work of the mind does not really contribute to others' lives. It does indeed have an influence upon them, and a very pervasive influence, too. This is most evident in the applications just referred to; equally important, though less evident, is the influence wielded through the fact that specialists are teachers, administrators, and professionals of all kinds and that their specialist attitudes, orientation, and modes of thought mold the climate in which everyone lives. But to be influenced thus is not the same as to partake of culture; it does not result in an enhancement of life through the understanding and appreciation of men's creations.

In the sciences it is taken completely for granted that understanding is restricted to experts. Nonscientists, in general, are as ignorant of science as if this fabulous endeavor did not exist. I am in no way contradicting my previous arguments that our whole life—reason, language, emotions, values, attitudes toward nature, and relations among men—has been drastically affected by the scientific enterprise. But hardly any nonscientist understands or appreciates science; almost no one is capable of making its insights, its procedures, and its attitudes a valuable part of his life. With obvious modifications, this holds true even for scientists, for their scope is almost always an extremely narrow specialty, and competence in specialties as practiced today does not in general reach out to anything else beyond. In saying this, I am not primarily thinking of the fact that, for example, even a penetrating knowledge of Newtonian mechanics or Einsteinian relativity leaves one in complete ignorance of, say, animal metabolism; but, rather, that there is a different and most important kind of understanding that competence in a scientific specialty does not ensure. Specialties have been so standardized, so elaborated, and so systematized by established thinking and routine methods that it has become not only possible but very common to make contributions considered important to a special field without truly understanding what one is about and, particularly, without understanding the place of one's own work within a more comprehensive perspective—be it a perspective remaining purely within science or, a fortiori, encompassing other provinces of culture.

The situation might appear to be very different in other fields; indeed it is true that some have not reached the degree of specialization prevalent in science. Nevertheless, the same kind of development is found everywhere. In all fields of learning the research paper, the technical monograph, and the professional journal have become the principal products of thought. Experts speak only to experts; the fruit of each man's work is for a few confreres. Scholars do not carry on their work in a spirit that includes as an integral aim the enlightenment of those outside their profession.

Suppose that by great exertion we succeed in gaining an expert's understanding. Suppose we have the ability, time, and perseverance to get to know some product of the specialists' work, to grasp some part of modern culture. The reward is rarely worth the effort. The knowledge we acquire appears to be completely irrelevant to our lives. Having gained it, we feel as if we ourselves, our lives, had not changed one bit, except that a particle of inert, isolated, though hard to achieve knowledge has been added to our already crammed minds. If we struggle along to gain more of this culture, we feel impelled over and over to ask, "So what?"

Such experiences of futility probably cease for most people not long after their college days. Little time elapses before they abandon, if ever they made, the attempt to understand anything outside their specialty and before they cease to inquire into the human relevance of their own specialized work. But this futility is an experience that many a college student knows. I am not thinking of those who learn only because they are obliged to, because the resulting degree is the requisite for social status or for a means of livelihood; I am thinking of the very best students, those with greatest potential and greatest eagerness to see how learning and art will open the world. They study mathematics and physics, ancient history and Elizabethan poetry; they are steeped in books and manuscripts; they solve problems, do experiments, and write scholarly reports and essays—but they see little meaning in all this work. They may know the satisfaction of a challenge overcome, a difficult problem solved, or curiosity aroused and satisfied. But all this does not raise the import of culture beyond that of a crossword puzzle or a game of bridge. That, indeed, is what culture has become for many of those who devote their lives to it. Not trying or not able to see any greater value, or believing that value is only private preference, they satisfy themselves that culture is fun, or an interesting game to play. Fun is desirable, and games are entertaining; but the sustenance of spiritual life is something else.

The attenuation of the significance of culture is not surprising, given the disjointed character of the products of the mind. As a specialty is driven further and further, and becomes more and more isolated from a larger context, it becomes increasingly irrelevant to man's life. Meaning inheres in connections, in revealing relations. Science, history, and art are significant for us to the extent that they are intertwined with our lives—with the matrix of fact and ideal, of circumstance and possibility of our existence. The specialized work of today has such significance only in very tenuous ways or not at all. With the decay of a feeling of wholeness, the aim of mental work becomes exclusively to push forward the detailed knowledge of a particular area or the refinement of a technique. What is disclosed or discovered and the nature of the insight gained become much less important than the mere fact that new knowledge has been acquired or a method refined. Hence we pay far more attention to cleverness, "originality," and means than to the significance of ends. We are more concerned with solving an intricate problem than with the nature of what we are trying to solve.

When culture is relevant to men's lives, issues and questions are primary and govern the concern with means: there is a darkness before men that they believe it important to penetrate, disorder and confusion surrounding them that they feel an imperious urge to transform into harmony, an inarticulate sense or intuition in their souls that they must apprehend and shape. Today, however, the more usual situation is that an established method obliges us to seek problems to which it can be applied. Having become specialists, we must continue to exercise our skills—no matter on what, with no regard to the significance for man.

Disregard of man in the realm of learning has still another cause: the modern mind believes that only by removing and isolating learning from life can the integrity of learning be guarded. Doubt of reason, distrust of language, and nullification of values all have to do with suspicion of personal elements. Desires, interests, feelings, needs, and hopes, it is feared, easily lead to lapses in logic and neglect of evidence; they give rise to slanted interpretations and prejudiced views. And emotionally charged language may divert one from the truth and sway one to unwarranted beliefs; it may displace the validity of reasoned argument by the impact of persuasive rhetoric. Values—being tied to feelings and being (in the prevalent view) only subjective—are thought to twist one's vision in the direction of merely personal preference and advantage.

Dangers from personal elements do indeed exist, and they increase with the extent to which the field of learning is enmeshed with the rest of life. The more related learning is to the human situation, the more intimately connected with us as individuals—with our concrete existence here and now—the greater the peril. Conversely, the greater the distance between learning and what we are as men—the feelings we have, the predicaments we are in, the convictions we hold, and the commitments that engage us—the less is the threat to our pursuit of learning. We can understand why learning seems to many to require removal from life's concerns: this separation protects its validity; it safeguards objectivity.

The separation is most pronounced in science—and science is the safest, most reliable area of learning. Its approach to its subject matter, the nature of its interest therein, and the kind of knowledge it seeks are as removed from the living concerns of the person as it is possible for a human endeavor to be. Other fields have been emulating science. Psychology, sociology, and anthropology have sought actually to become sciences; history, political science, and philosophy show determined efforts to take science as their model; scholarship in all other areas, including the critical studies of the arts, has been strongly attracted. Reason has become scientific reason, values are eschewed, language is sterilized, interpretations in distinctly human terms—involving desires, feelings, and purposes—are replaced by explanations in terms of impersonal forces, and sympathetic viewing of the human condition gives way to objective analyses. Everything is done to reduce the presence of elements that belong to the living of actual lives.

Thus knowledge is not regarded "as an internal . . . function of life," [4] as Ortega y Gasset insisted it should be. It does not arise from life, is not infused with it, and does not end in it. On the contrary, knowledge is mostly external to life and irrelevant to it. It moves within specialized spheres enclosed within themselves and does not seek to contribute to our existence.

When we leave the areas of learning and turn to art, we often find a similar isolation. Much modern art, and especially that which is prized most highly by those who are acclaimed as experts, is inaccessible to the nonspecialist. Much of it appears to require a medium other than art—the specialized critic's prose interpretation—to bring it within the realm of intelligibility. Much of it seems to necessitate skilled analysis and scholarly research; paradoxically, the necessity for these approaches often seems to exist even when they are contrary to the artist's intent. Whatever the merits of such self-enclosed art, and whatever the reasons for its being so self-enclosed— and they are potent—to the extent that it requires a specialist's interpretation it fails to speak as a work of art.

Even with respect to older art, which people believed they could understand though they were neither artists nor professional critics—and I am speaking of people to whom art truly matters, not of those to whom it is a means of relaxation from "serious" pursuits, or those like Eliot's women who "come and go / Talking of Michelangelo"—even here an analogous loss has set in. We are often told that the layman's response is "mere sentimentalism," that true understanding requires specialized knowledge and skillful critical analysis. If this were true, then all art would be lost to us, for we are not specialists, and we must reject sentimentalism, which is a corruption of sentiment.

There are other important reasons for our loss of art. To give a proper understanding of these reasons I would have to draw upon numerous matters that are taken up in later parts of this book. It must therefore suffice here to give a mere indication and leave the substance of the issues, as well as the justification of my remarks, to the sequel.

The spiritual climate of the contemporary world is poisonous to the arts. (This is true despite their considerable popularity, for this in itself does not imply true understanding, and despite the worship of "creativity," for such worship is a distortion of the arts, of values, of human creation, and of the person.) In the first place, art is charged with emotions, and the emotions are the most distrusted, suppressed, and abused part of the modern personality. The tenor of modern life is an alternation of anesthesia and emotional whipping. The emotional life is dried up, or exploited and corrupted for ulterior purposes. No worse environment is possible for the arts.

In the second place, artistic language has little power in the modern world. Suspicion of language and the enormous influence of technical language have eroded the poetic import of words. The detrimental effect of the cleavage of language has already been mentioned. Our sensitivity to literary language is being dulled by the heedless and corrupting usage that constantly assails us. In this adverse situation writers have felt impelled to manipulate language, sometimes in the most extreme fashion (even to the point of attempting to strip words of their meanings and to rely solely on sound), in the hope of giving it fresh power—with the long-range result of contributing to its infirmity.

The forms of most visual art are in an analogous predicament. Many of us, being constantly assailed by pictures, are not sensitive to the pictorial world of Leonardo da Vinci or Rembrandt, Michelangelo, or Rodin. Modern painting and sculpture have brought extreme distortion and complete rejection of the representational image. Many modern works of this kind have given vivid expression to important elements of human experience generally disregarded in our narrowly pragmatic era, for example, design, color, and texture, as well as spontaneity, imagination, and surprise. Others have manifested the artist's profound insight into, and sometimes desperate struggle with, the predicament of man in our time. But often distortion and rejection of the image have become simply the vogue and have been practiced without respect, concern, and passion for the world—in the belief, even, that they meant liberation from the world, which according to this belief, had merely constrained us. In so far as this has been the case, these approaches, in the long run, have aggravated our predicament. They have done so by belittling one of the principal powers of visual art, representation; by confirming and increasing our separation from nature and man; and most serious of all, by accustoming us to seeing the world, especially man, as deformed, hideous, chaotic, and inhuman. We have become so accustomed to this and so insensitive to the violation of man that the most anguished outcry of many a great artist against the inhumanity of modern life, made through the most terrifying distortion and destruction of form, is often spoken of as being delightful, original, or poetic.

Often disintegration of form in the arts is a manifestation also of another element of our predicament, the nullification of values. The artist, like all of us—or, indeed, more than most because his keener perception makes him more aware— is often confounded by a lack of significant values that could inform his life and his work, and be understood and cherished by others. In this desperate state some artists have sought to do without values, to make art value-neutral like science, objectively to describe or mirror the actual life of our time. Because values are in the very fabric of art, these attempts are bound to fail and easily lead to aberrations such as the hair-raising jumbles that not infrequently assault us as works of art today: such aberrations are not art, but only more instances of the chaos of our frenzied daily experience, ungoverned by humane values. Other artists have adopted the values implicit in science and technology to guide their work, either hoping to build a new vision that could incorporate the dominant schemes and at the same time be fit for man, or else being unconcerned with man. In either case such works, especially in painting and sculpture and most of all in architecture, have generally not succeeded in incorporating these values into a view respectful of man, but rather, through their impersonality, anonymity, and mechanistic rationality, have contributed to the dehumanizing of man.

Still another manifestation of the crisis in values is what seems to be some artists' attempts to begin from the beginning, to create values entirely out of themselves, unnourished—or uncontaminated, some would say—by what men have esteemed in the past and by the world in which man has his being. This, too, is doomed to failure, because no man can create a world out of himself, and no man can utterly isolate himself from his environment, either physical or cultural. He may have any of various relationships to it—being injured or nurtured, being subjected to it unaware or accepting and rejecting facets of it with understanding—but he deludes himself if he thinks he is creator *ex nihilo*, or God.

Finally, the loss of nature and of man attacks the arts at their core. Art in which man's intimate relation with nature or with other men is essential does not reach those who are estranged from the objects of its concern. Many of us do not know the beauty, bounty, destructiveness, or mystery of nature. Our alienation from the individual person as a concrete being, in his integrity and wholeness, is so great that we frequently fail to be touched by art in which concern with this being is paramount.

We are separated from nature and increasingly estranged from man, and culture, the creation of men, does not support us—we have been losing the world and are moving toward existence in a void. This is a condition more terrible by far than any that has caused men in their heart's anguish to speak of meaninglessness and dehumanization. Most of us do not understand these words—we have become inured to the condition they express. We accept vacuity, nothingness, and destruction as unalterable facts and take it for granted that men's emptiness and despair call not for the alteration of these facts, but for the smoother "adjustment" of man. Ceaseless movement and the tranquilizer seem to us to be the answers to man's yearning and unfulfillment. We fail to deplore man's void because we have no sense of the fullness of man's being in the world—of his relation to nature, culture, and above all, man.[5]

Chapter 5 DISSOLUTION OF
THE PERSON

The culmination of our predicaments is the disintegration of the individual man, the dissolution of the whole and unified person. This predicament, in its turn, permeates all others.

BANISHMENT OF THE PERSON

Man's every activity is more and more modeled after the machine—standardized, automatic, and repeatable. In all departments of life unceasing efforts are made to avoid, or render unnecessary, the judgments, decisions, and even the presence of the individual man. Often, it is true, the elimination of his presence is desirable; innumerable jobs exist in which his place has already been reduced to the role of an automaton, and the release of the human from such nonhuman work must be welcomed. But this is not the crux of the matter. The crux is rather that our society is impelled by the single-minded urge to promote automatism everywhere. To mechanize, to automatize, is to "make progress." The belief that whatever is automatic is better is never questioned; nor are the assumptions that the personal factor interferes with all our efforts to accomplish things and that functional efficiency is to be the governing criterion in all realms. Therefore standardized, mechanical, objective procedures are introduced into all activities. The desirability of this within the whole context of human life is not given the least consideration; moreover, even the question of whether the special aims of the original activity are properly fulfilled by the new procedure is ignored: the procedure becomes the Procrustean bed on which these aims are deformed.

This situation is so taken for granted that few are aware of it or can see its true nature. Once recognized, however, its manifestations are found everywhere. Let it be epitomized here by a development that reaches into the core of the person: the ever-spreading assumption that a person's life need not be shaped through his own search, understanding, and decision —aided by the experience and wisdom of others—but is best guided by the results of so-called objective tests, these tests being trusted precisely because they minimize personal judgment.

CONCEPTIONS OF MAN

The exclusion of human elements from everyday life has its counterpart in current intellectual conceptions of man. Earlier we saw how these conceptions divorce us from others. Now we must give more attention to how they ignore, set in doubt, and often explicitly deny most of those attributes that are the foundations of the person. The mechanistic model is the one most commonly used to provide explanations of all facets of man's life. It is so attractive a model and its embodiment, the machine, exercises by its omnipresence such a hold on the mind, that "understanding" a feature of man is generally assumed to mean that one has discovered the "mechanism" by which it is governed. Any variety will do—physical, physiological, biological, psychological, sociological, economic, or political—only it must be a mechanism. Even if mechanism is not insisted upon, however, dehumanizing aspects remain. The disciplines from which increasingly influential conceptions of man are derived are sciences, or studies wishing to be scientific, and these disciplines have no place for many of the attributes without which the person does not exist. Other areas that accord these attributes central positions have lost their power of conviction through the diminution of understanding. One attribute that is not admitted by science, for example, is purpose, and the belief has grown that what is usually meant by this word is illusory or, if not illusory, must be reducible to categories that are scientific—neural impulse, conditioned response, feedback, chance, and so on. Thereby the view has become current that man is a mere result, a product of hereditary and environmental conditions, devoid of anything that warrants being called foresight, purpose, or freedom.

Absolutely opposed to this is another, older belief, basic and indispensable to Western society, that man is in some measure a self-determining being. This belief is presupposed by the most powerful and respected activities of modern times: the purposeful control and exploitation of nature, the planned organization and transformation of economic and social conditions, and the deliberate processes of democratic institutions. It is the greatest irony that one enterprise—science—is largely responsible for the strength of both beliefs in the modern world: it is through technology based on science that the most impressive feats of control and purposeful planning are being accomplished, thereby constantly confirming the conviction that human intelligence and foresight can affect the course of events, and increasingly giving men, as a genus, the feeling of unlimited power and freedom to subdue and remake the world; it is also through science that the reality of self-determination and the existence of action directed toward aims are placed in doubt, thereby making the individual seem to be an impotent phenomenon resulting from the interaction of completely nonpersonal, nonhuman forces.

In their daily lives, of course, people abide by the older belief, because the demands for choice and purposeful action— even though drastically diminished in the present world—

continue to exist. Their lives have been enfeebled, however, and not infrequently even paralyzed by the newer belief. Very few, undoubtedly, have thought about the matter and arrived at the conclusion that what they are and what they do simply happens according to one or another set of scientific laws, without decision, purpose, or the exercise of freedom. If they did think about it, they might become aware of the total contradiction of their two views.

But a feeling of incapacity nevertheless exercises its insidious effect, a gnawing doubt that men can govern their lives or affect the world through their actions. People feel their own selves to be the outcome of physical and psychological inevitabilities, and they regard existing circumstances and prevailing directions of change as determined by inevitable economic, social, and political forces.

Purpose and self-determination are not the only qualities to have suffered dissolution. For just as we seek to reduce all human activity to the mechanical, so we seek intellectually to reduce whatever was once thought to be distinctively human to nonhuman entities. Language, values, thought, creativity, art, religion, love—we are intent on explaining all of them in mechanistic, animalistic, physicochemical, or in any case, nonhuman, terms. These conceptions largely inform our "sciences of man" and, ironically, infect the humanities and arts. The contemporary mind is determined not only, as in earlier times, to rid itself of delusions about man, to reject false estimates of human dignity, to acknowledge man's biological links to the animals, and to recognize the physical, psychological, economical, social, and political forces that impinge upon man, but to leave not a shred of anything distinctively human upon him. Thus, the traditional view that discrimination between good and evil is a fundamental characteristic of man is deprived of its substance by the nullification of values. Man's awareness of a normative realm, of a distinction between what ought to be and what is, his striving toward ideals, and his moral nature are eliminated from the new conceptions—or when considered, are interpreted in ways that negate the essence of their character. The dignity of man cannot even be spoken of, for the language that is required to do it is distrusted and debased.

In discussing man's loss of man we saw the catastrophic effect of modern conceptions of man on our ability to enter into genuine human relations: we confront not the individual person as he appears before us, but the embodiment of our intellectual categories; we get hold of him with our concepts, we "figure him out," we regard him as a result of chemical processes, as a psychological mechanism, a product of conditioning, a sociological case—and we remain estranged. But now we must note that this approach is used not only with others. We ourselves are also men, and so we look at ourselves in the same way. We make depersonalized objects out of ourselves. We appear to ourselves not as a person but as a thing, a thing divested of all those attributes once thought to be the essence of humanness—consciousness, reason, freedom, purpose, responsibility, values, and love. Appearing to ourselves thus, we feel ourselves to be despicable and repulsive, for the older estimate of man refuses to be quite suppressed and, occasionally at least, forces us to recognize our degradation.

The depersonalized and dehumanized thing we observe stands in no intimate relation to the entity that does the observing. We detach, as it were, a thinking part from ourselves that observes and explains us. It figures us out and then manipulates us accordingly. We split ourselves into a part that explains and manipulates and the part that is subjected to explanation and manipulation, whose thoughts, emotions, and desires are all reduced to something other than themselves. We become strangers to ourselves. We destroy our wholeness.

THE INIMICAL ENVIRONMENT

To this intellectual destruction of man and to his suppression by the automatized and impersonal procedures in every area of life, there must be added the disruptive impact of social and political circumstances. In all parts of our life we are constantly confronted with things whose vast scale far exceeds the individual's size and powers. We rarely live or work in a community in which our presence counts and is felt, and in which the circumstances we must confront are of human dimensions. The enormity of all organizations and institutions, the hugeness of the political apparatus, the appalling rush of events, and the unthinkable powers of extermination that constantly hover over us, all threaten to crush us into impotence.

And not only the dimensions but also the impersonality of our environment stifles us. Our cities, highways, houses, offices, implements, furniture, language, social forms, and much of our art, have become more and more stark, impersonal, and stripped of human elements. Our institutions—business, political, professional, and even religious and educational—outdo each other to adopt and imitate the impersonal character of science and technology, thereby leaving less and less room for the person.

We are not given the conditions necessary to define and shape ourselves as persons. Every part of the world is ceaselessly with us, every local change instantly impinges upon us. Newspapers, radios, and television submerge us in reports of murder, rape, and explosion, shattering all steadiness of mind, all spiritual composure and development, and disrupting the very ground of our existence. The whole world about us, its scattered interests and hysterical movements unguided by fundamental values, constantly bombards us with noise, flashes signs and signals, pounds us with opinions, shouts claims and advice at us (all for our good, always for our happiness) day and night wherever we are, jangling, battering, stupefying, and nerve-racking—and then offers tranquilizers as an antidote. It is already, and is becoming still more, a world in which most people can guard their ability to carry on their daily rounds only by anesthesia of their senses and minds so deep that they are not conscious of all these attacks upon their selfhood, nor of the drugged state of their daily existence.

THE EFFECT OF OTHER PREDICAMENTS

The conduct of life demands the making of choices. We repeatedly come to crossroads where we must make decisions concerning goals to attain and means to use, and these decisions depend upon values. We need values to steer our course within the realm of possibilities and limitations, to meet and assess the world, and to act within it. One's unity and strength depend on the harmony of one's valuations and one's confidence in them.

In the absence of convincing values to guide selection and rejection, men's lives become mere sequences, without meaning and purpose, of incoherent sensations, doings, and escapes. Latent desire for meaning is easily smothered by the chaos of modern trivialities to which people are incessantly exposed and in which they often submerge themselves. Whatever might still exist in the encounter with nature, in meetings with other men, and in pursuits of mind and hand that could sustain men, furnish meaning, and become a significant basis for choice and decision is engulfed by the superficial and the banal. Lacking values, men are pulled in a thousand directions by the ceaselessly clamoring world. Their innermost unity is disrupted. They have no center within which to stand, no unified core reconciling disparate demands and desires, and hence no ability to act as integral selves.

That the diminution of understanding and the destruction of language we discussed earlier contribute greatly to the crisis of the person needs little elaboration. Man as a being who can (within limits) decide and act out of his own self, must have an adequate mental grasp of the world if he is not to be reduced to a mindless object impelled from without and within by the impersonal forces of purposeless mechanisms. Without such a grasp of the world he is impotent before the inertia and pressures of the environment. Without an understanding of what is possible and what is inevitable, he can neither envisage what is not yet nor act in the face of what is. His capacity to choose, his liberation from compulsions, and his freedom to participate in the world depend on the insight and perspective he commands of himself and his surroundings. Any injury to his powers of understanding and to language, their main instrument, is an injury to the core of man.

The loss of culture has a similarly detrimental effect. Man's conception of the world, his inspirations and ideals, his sense of the possibilities and limitations of life and of its depth and scope, depend heavily on learning and art. He is undermined when these become incoherent, inaccessible, and irrelevant.

REDUCTION OF THE PERSON BY SPECIALISM

Man increasingly forgoes the effort to gather into a significant whole the multiplicity of things—facts, values, claims, feelings, and desires—that are elements of his life; he forgoes the attempt to think, judge, and decide by himself. Indeed, he often has no real awareness of self, of a oneness of person, but feels himself to be constituted of disunited parts, each of which he surrenders for explanation and for direction to an appropriate specialist. He has little experience of his own identity. He lacks the sense of being an integral I, a complex but whole self with its own center and unity that would enable him to enter into relation with otherness, with the world. He tends instead to become a formless entity, an amorphous conglomerate, a bundle of fragments whose every part and movement is subjected to external forces —either material circumstances and social pressures or the controls proceeding from specialism.

This condition has gone so far that we have extreme difficulty even in envisaging a different state of affairs to help us understand our present catastrophic predicament. As specialism and the individual's dependence on specialists are now generally viewed, the only alternative appears to be the impossible (and entirely undesirable) state of total nondependence, complete self-sufficiency, and isolation—a pseudo individualism that, not surprisingly, is often proclaimed in this time of the individual's dissolution. But this individualism is not the only alternative. It appears so only because our sense of human wholeness is already in an advanced stage of decay. The difference between the condition that is engulfing us and one in which the integral person exists is illustrated by two contrasting ways in which an individual may enlist another's knowledge. On the one hand, he may look to the other for a decision and expect to be told what to think and to do. On the other, he may ask for help and advice, the fruit of the other's experience, and then seek to integrate it with other parts of his self and to make, out of the self so enhanced, his own judgment and decision.

The second way is disappearing. Consider, for example, the failure one so often meets with when requesting explanation from a physician: the doctor assumes that the patient (or the patient's relative) is unable to understand, need not understand, and indeed is best off when he does not try to understand his condition but abandons himself to the knowledge and care of specialists. The way of personal decision requires both that the individual have the capacity to comprehend things relevant to his life's condition and that knowledge relevant to his life's condition, to which he may turn, exist. Generally neither requirement is met. Not only does the view prevail that knowledge must be removed from life, but we idolize specialization and specialist methods and seek nothing else. The whole person and his requirements are abused and neglected, and our confidence in the person—the reasoning, judging, self-governing person—has already shrunk. Indeed, we have so lost sight of wholeness that we hardly know what a whole person is and therefore what to strive for.

Specialization means attention to a restricted set of aims, interests, and techniques. These should derive their value and justification from their service to man. I do not mean that this must necessarily be utilitarian service, such as feeding or clothing him, but that in some way it must contribute to him as a whole human being. Today, however, special interests and pursuits have been elevated above the men of whom they should be a part. We have become their slaves. Their "progress" is the criterion for the desirability of all action: we justify whatever is done by the claim that it is necessary if business is to grow, if time is to be saved, if science is to advance, if art is to flourish, if the economy is to prosper, and a thousand other such "ifs"; but we hardly ever inquire what is necessary for man. We may assert that each of these "ifs" of course implies the unstated conviction that the special aim is good for man. But even if that were so, the conviction is unwarranted. We have no right simply to take for granted that such special aims and methods pursued in isolation from others (and to any extremity) in fact are good for man—many, indeed, are injurious and deadly. The truth is, these "ifs" show to how great an extent special aims and methods have become their own justification: they govern now, not men. The dissolution of values has undermined the process of judgment to which each activity could otherwise be subjected. The lack of concern for the whole human being and for the human community has allowed every pursuit and every special interest—no matter how trivial, how irrelevant, or how injurious to man—to be raised to an absolute value. Indeed, specialization itself has been endowed with absolute goodness. All these things have become deified products of men to which men give blind obedience, and they are men's undoing.

This maiming of man, this displacement of the whole man by a part, is omnipresent—it occurs in all spheres of daily life as well as in learning and art. The special role the individual discharges and his special competence have become more important than his whole self. His specialty not only determines the mode of his work but stamps out the shape of his life. A method, a particular goal, or an institution exercises tyranny over him. Its precepts and demands impose themselves on all his activities. His whole life becomes tightly adjusted to a limited scheme and order. This makes him conform not only in the obvious social behavior it calls for, but also more insidiously, in his very being and in ways he does not recognize, by shaping his language, his view of all things and himself, his life orientation, and his approach to the world. He suppresses or never cultivates values, desires, and ways of meeting the world that do not fit his special role. The whole man becomes subordinated to a man's function in a system.

Such actual reduction of the person stands in a relation of mutual reinforcement to the prevailing ways of viewing men in daily life. It has become customary—as was pointed out in Chapter 4—to look upon individuals exclusively in terms of their specialized social functions. They are regarded as entities defined by the shapes of their special roles. And as these roles have become more automatized, standardized, and emptied of personal elements, the individual has been more and more subordinated to a scheme of standardized, impersonal functionality, and his worth is judged by how well he fits the scheme. Though we may first apply this view of man to others rather than to ourselves, it is inevitable that it should come to affect our own self-assessment. If the other man is not a person, if he only fills a slot in a functional scheme, if, like a vending machine, he has no identity that transcends the service or product he dispenses, then we ourselves become equally deprived of personality.

This fractional view of man derives not only from our daily life, but also from our cultural interpretations of man. The disciplines of biology, physiology, psychology, and sociology each deliberately confines its attention to a very sharply restricted aspect of things and ignores everything else. None provides knowledge that can do justice to the whole man. This simple truth, however, is easily forgotten. Indoctrinated by specialism, we succumb to the habit of thinking in grooves, and we become unable to perceive or imagine anything outside these grooves. Indeed, we are afraid even to try, for fear that our understanding of things may be proved insufficient or erroneous and lest we be forced to recognize the limited scope of the one approach we know and its inadequacy for many important matters, which therefore elude our grasp. Such recognition is profoundly threatening, for it raises the need for a thorough remaking of ourselves. Thus the partial view held by each discipline becomes inflated, sometimes obviously, sometimes imperceptibly, into a total view. Whatever the partial view does not explicitly include becomes slighted or is relegated to nonexistence or declared to be reducible—at least in principle, or in the future if not today—to the categories of the partial view. Accordingly, a man is displaced by a fragmentary man, or by a collection of fragments, each of which on different occasions usurps the place of the whole.

SUPPRESSION OF FEELING AND OF INNER LIFE

There is one dismemberment of the person that is especially prevalent and disastrous. We have seen it throughout our discussion—the splitting off and suppression of an essential range of human capacities. They are the ones that are most intimately involved in human experience, the elements generally called subjective.

It is no exaggeration to say that the mental air we breathe in the major portion of our daily lives is all but destitute of all these elements of human existence. Most of the things we must do to earn our living and to accomplish our tasks have no place for our feelings. The atmosphere of public intercourse is permeated by an animus against everything involving the emotions. Warm, sympathetic participation in the world is discouraged, and the impulse to engage the whole self is denied.

To say that life is entirely destitute of subjective elements, though very close to the truth, would be an oversimplification, for these elements are inevitably the matrix of all experience; but they generally are neither esteemed nor made a vital part of existence. We often fear them, abuse them, or are ashamed of them (and hence of ourselves). Their exclusion and suppression in the everyday world of work, the world of technology, is obvious. They are not needed in the mechanized factory, the routinized office, and the standardized store. There is no place here for sensitivity to the qualities of the surroundings or for sympathy and feeling for men. The attitude required is one geared to the machine and the system —geared to an apparatus whose efficient functioning (efficiency being understood exclusively in terms of the apparatus itself) overrules all other considerations. Men are simply cogs in the system; personal elements would interfere by reducing the smoothness of the standardized process.

The effects of mechanization on our feelings and sensibilities have been deplored for generations, but it is only since World War II that the machine and the machinelike have been approaching complete dominance over our lives. Everywhere man's sole task is to conform to the requirements of the automatic and the uniform. This adjustment of himself is all but universally accepted and admired. Indeed, one can hardly say that it is accepted, for to accept something means to recognize it for what it is and to be able, at least in thought if not in action, to reject it if one chooses to do so. But adjustment has become as automatic as the machine processes themselves. The consequence is the suppression and often the atrophy of the emotional side of life.

An analogous situation exists in the realm of knowledge. The doubt of reason, distrust of language, and nullification of values all involve the splitting off and denigration of a part of man. Sensitivities, emotions, and desires, it is thought, contribute only distortion. Impersonality has been made into an ideal of intellectual life. Personal engagement is regarded as prejudice, passion as irrationalism.

It is impossible not to have some sympathy with this position. Thought is so easily befogged and distorted that to think clearly requires indefatigable watchfulness. Moreover, our century has witnessed the destruction of truth and justice by untrammeled passion and boiling fanaticism. One understands why reasonable men are suspicious of the subjective elements of life. One can appreciate, for example, the motivation of a renowned physicist when he praised "*the objective mode of approach* to international difficulties" and disparaged "sentimental pacificism" as a way to abolish war:

For sentimental pacificism is, after all, but a return to the method of the jungle. It is in the jungle that emotionalism alone determines conduct, and *wherever that is true no other than the law of the jungle is possible.* For the emotion of hate is sure sooner or later to follow the emotion of love, and then there is a spring for the throat. It is altogether obvious that the only quality which really distinguishes man from the brutes is his reason. You may call that an unsafe guide, *but he has absolutely no other* unless he is to turn his face back toward the jungle.[1]

However, once one has understood the aim of this invective against sentiment, emotion, and love, and has acknowledged the element of justice it contains, one must reject it as manifesting a fatally distorted view of man. Man is destroyed when his reason is pitted against his emotions. It is a catastrophic error to believe that scientific rationality should replace love. It is a deadly mistake to suppose that the only alternatives to dispassionateness and impersonality are prejudice and distortion.

There can be no doubt whatever that most men's ability to view things reasonably is not nearly well enough developed. Reason, despite—and partly because of—the incessantly mouthed veneration of it, is extremely rare. Pretense of rationality is the common condition. Sensitivity may be held suspended, sympathy may be scorned, emotion may be suppressed, and the posture of impersonality may be assumed—but all this does not produce the crystal of reason. Most of those who practice valid thought at all practice it only in the narrow area of a highly specialized activity, where it has become routinized and channeled by standard procedures. Outside this area they believe what they like to believe, turn intellectual somersaults to fit truth to wish and knowledge to bias, and they make lacunae in reason to bend its verdict to their favorite doctrine; they avoid any evidence that might change their minds. However, genuine understanding and humane conduct are not achieved by dividing the self. The contrary, I shall try to show, is true: they require a whole man.

Try as we may, we cannot entirely suppress the emotional side of our divided selves. Having banished it from the mainstream of life, we indulge in sentimentality and contrive excitement. We tell ourselves that these sugary feelings and thrills are to be welcomed and freely enjoyed; or else we regret the existence of emotions but recognize them as unavoidable, and to prevent them from intruding on the "important" parts of life, allow them intermittent play. We tolerantly permit, and even encourage, emotional eruptions, such as aggressiveness, and we deliberately arrange "emotional outlets"—as if the emotions were a gaseous by-product of living whose pressure must be periodically relieved. These outlets (also called "safety valves," since it is taken for granted that a steam boiler is an appropriate conceptual model for man) keep emotional pressure from becoming too great—that is, keep it from affecting the impersonal realms that are the principal part of our existence. The entertainment industry, and the deluge of so-called literature and art, and innumerable gadgets and activities provide endless means for purgation. Modern man is divided into insensitive intellect and senseless emotion, into thought uninformed by feeling and feeling un-assisted by thought, into standardized work and escapist excite-ment.

FRAGMENTATION AND THE RULE OF PARTS

All domains of our life are organized on the principle of splitting a special interest from the totality of human interests and elevating it above all other human interests, with the fragmented, or partial, man who follows the special interest taking the place of the whole man. This is how practical activities are carried on, how knowledge is sought, and how art is created. Every enterprise, every innovation, is pursued regardless of everything but the special interest. The man in business is not expected to be concerned with the effect of his business on men's lives. The man in politics is not sup-posed to be troubled by moral issues: to be realistic, it is be-lieved, one must ignore values and ideals. The man who extends a scheme of knowledge is encouraged to be indifferent to its significance for human existence and to the effect it may have on all other domains. The man of art is rewarded for pursu-ing a technique or seeking originality, heedless of all other things.

Human activities are atomized; none is considered in the light of what it does to the remainder of life. The human self is fragmented into faculties and interests that ignore or sup-press each other. Action is separated from moral sense, reason is split from feeling, life is deprived of understanding, and understanding is divorced from life.

Not long ago the world witnessed how persons of intellect, ignoring morality and suppressing sensitivity, subjected men, women, and children to torture and extermination by the application of science and by efficient technology. And people who watched these atrocities frequented the theaters and gossiped and joked at parties.[2] These are aberrations of such unspeakable horror that they may seem to have nothing to do with our own lives. But in fact they are the ultimate extremity of the atomization, the supposed autonomy, of all special aims, and the fragmentation of the self that are everywhere the rule.

The dissolution of the person is the counterpart of man's loss of the world. Divorced from nature and from other men, the individual is estranged and isolated—bereft, despite all activity, of what is essential to becoming and being a whole person. Without the world, there are no values, no meaning, no relation; and hence no whole self: for the self exists and is unified in its commitments to things it values, in its discernment of meanings, and in its relations to an other. Man—not as a product, an embodiment of a function, or a diminished and split-up being, but as one who is truly human and whole —must be in whole relationship with the world.

Part Two: THE PROSAIC
MENTALITY
AND THREE
APPROACHES
TO THE WORLD

Chapter 6 THE PROSAIC MENTALITY

The elements of the dissolution with which I have dealt were seen to be closely interrelated. But there is a deeper relatedness to which we must penetrate. It is an orientation of mind that stamps our civilization, an approach men take to the world that I shall call the *prosaic mentality*. In this chapter I shall describe its basic characteristics, and in succeeding chapters its intricate and pervasive relation to all aspects of our predicament will become clear.

The discussion thus far leads us to expect that the prosaic mentality will be linked to science. And as we consider the characteristics of various approaches to the world and see that this link is, indeed, close, we may even be tempted to suppose that the very substance of the prosaic mentality is science, that this pervading mentality is simply an overwhelming tendency toward the scientific approach. But this is not the case, for despite the overwhelming effect that science has had, very few people are scientific. Few have the reasoning power, the discipline, the respect for truth, and the precision that science demands. A mentality that pervades our civilization must surely have a great deal to do with science, but it is not identical with a scientific attitude. Also, the dissolution we have discussed has many components that spring not from science—at least not directly—but from modern daily life, among them, anti-intellectualism, impoverishment and abuse of language, impersonality and anonymity, alienation from nature and man, specialism, and fragmentation of human existence. The prosaic mentality, therefore, must have to do not only with science but also with our dominant practical pursuits.

The key to the situation is that science and most practical activities, especially the activities that are informed and affected by science—technology in the widest sense—have in common certain interests and attitudes, and they jointly promote a basic orientation, or approach to the world. It is this convergence of the two chief activities of our time that accounts for the nature and dominant position of the prosaic mentality.

PROSAIC INTERESTS

The prosaic mentality is characterized by a cluster of attitudes and interests that it raises to supremacy over others, which are ignored, denied, or suppressed. It is this suppression that constitutes the fallaciousness and perniciousness of the prosaic mentality, and it occurs the moment prosaic interests are given undue stress or brought to inappropriate places.

The prosaic man is interested in abstractions, in groups of properties that can be abstracted from people, objects, events, and so on, and used to deal with them. Often the abstracted properties are what the prosaic man calls facts. To "get all the facts" and to "stick to facts" are typical prosaic requests. The prosaic man believes in facts.

One kind of abstraction, or fact, is of especial interest—that to which numbers can be assigned. Numbers have sureness and clearness: when you have hold of a number you know precisely what you have; it is the most solid and reliable kind of fact. Dates of events, duration of processes, numbers of objects, sizes and weights and speeds of things, since they are countable or measurable, constitute an abstractable property that can be readily and dependably dealt with and so seems especially real.

Another prosaic interest is methods—means, techniques, and procedures. The prosaic man is intent on practicing a method, busy with a procedure, involved in a technique, immersed in a program. He clarifies and systematizes existing methodological schemes, extends and refines them, or develops new means and techniques. Whatever he does, the method, procedure, or program is the center of attention.

The prosaic man is interested in what I shall call clear-cut boundaries. He wishes to have things sharply defined. He wants to know exactly what is meant, exactly what the facts are, exactly what constitutes his rights and duties, and exactly how to proceed. He hates what he calls blurred boundaries and sees them as a source of misunderstanding, confusion, inefficiency, and conflict. He is determined to find out where to "draw the line."

The prosaic man stresses literalness. Whatever is to be understood and communicated he wants to see spelled out in explicit statements. He thinks that stark, literal prose is the only instrument of expression and communication, and sees deviation from such bare, denotative prose as leading to error, miscommunication, and emotionalism.

The prosaic man praises objectivity, regarding it as the essence of reliability and truthfulness. In the preceding chapters we have seen various aspects of objectivity and some of its associations with science. For the prosaic mind, the objective is identical with the factual, and the practice of objectivity is geared to the other prosaic interests: it means concern with clear-cut abstractable properties, especially quantified ones; stress on clear-cut, standard methods, schemes, and programs, all with spelled-out rules; use of sharply drawn lines and divisions and literal, explicit prose. In addition, and most important, it is believed that to be objective means to withhold the feelings and to be detached and impersonal.

The prosaic man does not necessarily carry into effect the interests and attitudes he professes. He may very well neglect facts, his methods may be careless, and the boundaries he imagines to be clear-cut may be blurred. He may make statements that are far from explicit, use language that does not have the virtues of stark, literal prose, and manifest an objectivity that is sorely deficient. Nevertheless, these are the interests he pursues and stresses.

PROPONENTS OF PROSAIC INTERESTS

We shall see later, especially in Chapter 7 and Chapter 10, how central these prosaic interests are to science, even though they do not suffice to make a person scientific and, in fact, by denying other interests may hinder scientific effort. In this section I want to point out the centrality of prosaic interests in the practical world, especially as the world is increasingly dominated by the machine and all the products of applied science, and permeated by quasi- and pseudo-scientific ideas and procedures.

The interest in abstracted properties of things, or in facts, especially quantitative facts, is evidenced in all sorts of behavior, from looking at one's watch to tell the time, to the most complex process of manipulating, producing, or organizing. We deal with objects and situations in terms of a few properties that seem relevant to our aim. These and nothing else are the elements, the facts, to which we pay attention—even if we don't attend very well. We want to know the number of rooms in a house, the size of a shirt, the weight of a parcel, the volume of flour in a recipe, and most important, the price. Interest in quantitative facts is intimately connected with the devotion of the prosaic mind to a particular abstractable property—progress. Whenever achievement can be stated in numbers, then progress is an easily ascertainable fact. Increases in size, speed, precision, production, salary, circulation, and membership are goals the prosaic man pursues, confident that he knows when and how much progress is being made.

The mechanization of most activities through the application of science has given enormous impetus to this stress on a few abstractable properties, especially quantitative ones. The making and use of machinery requires attention to timing, dimensions, speeds, output, power, and efficiency—all quantitative properties. The machine's products also are viewed in terms of a group of quantitative specifications. Thus, interest in time, size, number, and so on becomes ever more dominant as mechanical processes are instituted.

The same tendency arises from the permeation of everyday practical thinking by the scientific approach. A prime instance of this is medicine, with its focus on certain biological and physicochemical properties of the body and the bodily environment. Other instances include the use of tests of intelligence, aptitude, achievement, and an ever-growing number of other psychological factors; polls of every conceivable kind; and statistics gathered in every area of human activity.

Consider also the stress on method. Much daily activity is routine. The best way to get things done is to be methodical. A proven procedure closely adhered to allows us to accomplish things with a minimum of error and confusion. Also, since we are always trying to "save time," "speed up," and "increase efficiency," we are always intent on "improving" and "streamlining" methods and on developing new ones.

Clear-cut boundaries are another chief concern of much of practical life. We want to know whether a certain train runs or doesn't; we want a shoe that is Size 9 to have definite dimensions; we want to know, if we have business with an institution, which department to apply to and which officer has certain responsibilities; we want to know exactly what our insurance premium is and exactly what the company will pay in each clear-cut set of circumstances. Once more, the intertwining of science with practical affairs, both through technology and through the spread of scientific modes of thought, has furthered the prevalence of this element in daily life. Operating an automobile is a far more clear-cut affair than driving a horse and carriage. Preparing a meal from pre-cooked, frozen foods is a much more clear-cut procedure than most real cooking. The duties and activities of a person employed by a modern organization that is steeped in the principles of technical efficiency, "scientific management," applied psychology, sociological surveys, economic analysis, and "human engineering" are infinitely more clearly defined (or are meant to be) than were those of men working in earlier times.

To deal with clear-cut facts and properties, to set out a definite method, to mark sharp boundaries, we need literal prose. We want to avoid all ambiguity, vagueness, and indefiniteness. We want no nonprosaic elements of language to interfere with statements of the facts, rules, methods, regulations, and instructions that occupy our attention. And we especially want to avoid such nonprosaic elements when the statements involve scientific or technical matters.

Lastly, objectivity, also, has a dominant role in the practical world. Here, too, technology, mechanization, and the permeation of practice by science have been enormously influential, increasing the stress on an objective approach to things, especially the element of impersonality.

Prosaic interests are found in other fields than science and daily practical life. History, for example, emphasizes facts; sociology is intent on quantitative abstractions; modern philosophy often stresses bare, literal prose and clear-cut method. But though these and many other fields frequently contribute to the sway of the prosaic mentality, they are not its main supports. For one thing, some of these other fields do not emphasize all the prosaic interests that have been mentioned, or at least not strongly: in history, for example, quantity and clear-cut boundaries are much less often stressed than fact. Also, such strong emphasis on one or more prosaic interests as does obtain in these areas has come to them largely through the influence of science and the science-permeated practical

86

world. The great emphasis on fact, for example, came to history with the growth of "scientific history" in the nineteenth century, and the special emphasis on economic and other "material" facts came from the consequences of the Industrial Revolution and also from the materialistic doctrines to which science as well as industrial economy contributed. The stress on the prosaic elements in philosophy is largely the outcome of the domination of the mental realm by science—directly and through daily life. Scientific influence is especially obvious in all those areas that have deliberately tried to make themselves totally, or as far as possible, into sciences, such as certain branches of psychology, sociology, anthropology, and economics.

In bringing about the actual spread and encouragement of the prosaic mentality in society today, however, the areas that have been influenced by science and the science-permeated practical world are probably far more effective than the model sciences themselves. For example, various branches of the "science of man"—psychology, sociology, and economics—and those endeavors in the humanities and arts that wistfully, grudgingly, or unknowingly imitate the scientific approach strongly affect many more people than do physics and chemistry. The natural sciences by and large remain in the laboratory (except for the applications they lead to), while the other studies directly affect our life.

PROSAIC FALLACIES

Because of the ascendancy of prosaic interests and the resulting suppression and maiming of other interests, the only areas of thought and expression to escape drastic mutilation are the two sources of the prosaic outlook—science and everyday practice. As we shall see in the following chapters, history, philosophy, the arts, and practical thought that goes beyond ordinary activity and technology are unable to flourish in an atmosphere dominated by abstractions, numbers, method, clear-cut boundaries, literalness, and objectivity. Some of the ways in which the prosaic mentality contributes to the general diminution of understanding are indicated in this section, as are some of the other manifestations and consequences of this mentality.

Consider the prosaic interest in facts. Facts are important, but people who harp on them often neglect other things that are equally important—and without which even their notion of facts would be false. For example, they deprecate interpretation because it appears incompatible with fact: fact is what *is*, they think, while interpretation is whatever one makes it; facts are believed to be objective, and interpretation, subjective. Knowledge of facts—no matter how isolated, irrelevant, or minuscule—becomes genuine knowledge; interpretation becomes prejudice. Further, just as interpretation fallaciously appears to these people to be incompatible with fact, so does imagination. Amassing facts is looked on as serious work; imagining, as play. To "stick to the facts" is considered to be the acme of responsibility; to imagine is to indulge in irresponsible fancy. Facts are thought to go with discipline, imagination with disorder.

We shall see that this prosaic discrediting of interpretation and imagination is poisonous to history, philosophy, and the arts. But it will also be evident that it interferes even with good science, for interpretation and imagination—though always far more circumscribed here than in other fields—are the more essential the more removed scientific research is from routine development.

The prosaic interest in literalism also diminishes understanding. The literal mind has a favorite aphorism: "Questions that cannot be answered are meaningless." This aphorism has become one of the ruling truths of many who think of themselves as enlightened and rational. They use it to ridicule all groping and struggling toward things that cannot be pinned down or spelled out—whether in daily life, philosophical thought, or religion. They use it to decry the significance of whatever escapes literalization. For by an answer, they mean an explicit answer, an answer that is a literal and exhaustive statement. Use of the aphorism as a criterion, they believe, cleanses and decontaminates the mind—and sometimes, indeed, it does this to a considerable extent. But the maxim ignores the vast region of our mental life that lies beyond literality —for example, much everyday thought, history, philosophy, and art. It ignores the fact that questions are requests for better understanding, deeper insight, or more adequate apprehension, which is supplied not necessarily by literal answers, but more often by nonliteral means. In this aphorism is crystallized the sweeping anti-intellectualism of the contemporary intellectual.

Specific answers are complemented by specific actions. Hence, in the prosaic mentality the only questions concerning the world that are considered to have meaning are questions that admit of answers leading to, or provided by, clear-cut, definite actions. In the sphere of knowledge this means science and technical thought. The clear-cut, specific actions are experimental procedures for obtaining sense observations of clear-cut, abstracted properties. The aphorism quoted in the preceding paragraph thus contains the core of positivistic thought: questions that do not lead to clear-cut operations in the physical world are meaningless—and this renders meaningless most of our mental life.[1]

Insistence on explicit answers and clear-cut actions has a far-reaching effect on everyday life. It means that one must always have a definite project, a clear program or plan. Hence the prosaic man is forever incapable of considering issues in depth. He stays at the surface; he remains with things that permit readily specifiable action. He entertains no questions with respect to life, man, or society that do not obviously lead to specific things to do. Everything else, it seems to him, is mere words—idealistic, not realistic; sentimental, not practical. Confronted with a difficulty, the prosaic man gets busy: he works at one thing and works at another; he changes, modifies, and manipulates; he institutes projects and programs; he raises funds, erects buildings, forms societies, appoints committees, holds meetings, collects data, writes reports, develops techniques, and makes rules. And he does all this without ever asking a single fundamental question, without ever attending to such basic things as the aims, underlying assumptions, values, or justification of what he is dealing with and what he is doing. Therefore all his busyness—restless, nerve-racking, and exhausting—is at bottom only a tinkering with and an accelerating of what already exists.

His orientation toward the world is epitomized in a question he is always asking: "What's the problem?" And a problem, for him, is something that can be plainly stated, got hold of, and solved. He looks at the world as if he were studying Euclidean geometry, going from problem to problem—either dealing with those that present themselves or, often, looking for new ones to apply his method to. Since he reduces everything in the world to a problem, his awareness is extremely superficial and narrow.

This is related, of course, to other features of the prosaic mentality. For such a mentality the problem corresponds to a group of abstractions from concrete objects and occasions. The prosaic man picks out these facts and thinks he has the entity itself; he puts the entity in a class so that it becomes one case among many, identifies it with a group of numbers, wraps it in a neat little package for clear-cut solution, and disposes of it with labels and jargon.

His concepts, moreover, and his schemes of explanation are meant to be clear-cut and explicit. Nothing is acknowledged that cannot be laid bare, is not literal, or cannot be measured. The prosaic man, therefore, has a proclivity for pseudo-scientific explanations. His literalism, his technical jargon, his desire for neat definitions, his insistence on drawing sharp lines, his clamor for clear-cut rules and criteria, his belief in facts, his use of numbers, his protestations of objectivity—all these lead him to suppose he is being scientific. His belief in facts—even if it is genuine—has no power to help him recognize the inappropriateness of his pseudo-scientific conceptual scheme, because this scheme narrowly funnels the attention he gives to the world. He is aware of nothing but the group of facts with which the scheme deals, and ensconced in his groove of abstractions, he perceives nothing beyond the scheme. Therefore his views are simplistic. Worse, they are simple-minded and infantile, for he insists with the stubbornness of an infant that the world yield to his categories, schemes, methods, and boundaries. All the while he is insisting on facts, on clear-cut method, on literal prose and objectivity, his narrow obsession is obstructing and maiming the thing to be seen.

For the prosaic man each individual thing is basically another instance of something he has met already. None has freshness, uniqueness, or strangeness. When he finds an unfamiliar situation, it is at once assigned to a compartment or category that provides a standard explanation of it. Stock phrases and routine methods are instantly applied, and the thing is done with. Having dealt practically or intellectually with an issue and disposed of it, the prosaic man is ready for the next—and he has remained fundamentally untouched. He is incapable of facing a situation, of encountering what is to be encountered, of seeing what is there. He wants to be *doing* —to have a technique, to be busy with a procedure—and to continue essentially undisturbed.

This is linked with the prosaic stress on objectivity, for in the objective approach we hold things at arm's length. We stand off from the world and seek to control it. In order to exercise intellectual control, the prosaic man wants everything to be explained and settled; he wants it to be reduced to facts, caught in a scheme of abstractions, neatly and securely assigned to categories, pinned down by definitions, and fenced in by clear-cut boundaries. To exercise practical control, he treats the world as a source of potential profit or harm; he looks at it as something to be manipulated to his advantage —to be used, consumed, made over, or discarded. This does not mean, however, that he always recognizes himself to be engaged in this process. Often, indeed, he does not.

The emphasis on control involves aggressiveness. The prosaic man regards all persons and things as objects to be dominated. He tries to subject them to a practical interest or to subdue them with the intellect. The quest for mental domination does not necessarily imply a powerful mind; it means that whatever intellect one has, powerful or weak, is used to attack the object, remove its uniqueness by reducing it to a standard case, and thereby conquer it.

This disposition toward aggression manifests itself in the esteem given to challenge. To say that a job, a book, or a person, is very challenging seems to prosaic man the highest recommendation, and he habitually regards a situation as a challenge. But this means that his attitude is basically aggressive. He wants to assert himself over things, to get them into his grip, to solve, to dominate, to control.

This involves a basic stance of distrust. Often this distrust lies on the surface: faced with a new situation, the prosaic man insists on credentials in the form of facts, schemes, methods, rules, and criteria. He tells himself that there are two kinds of people, his kind being clear-headed, rational, tough-minded, and skeptical; the others, obscurantist, muddled, irrational, sentimental, and gullible. This neat division shows the prosaic predilection for clear-cut schemes. But human life does not fit it. The prosaic skeptic himself, for example, usually manifests, alongside his skepticism, complete gullibility: he dismisses whatever is outside some accepted scheme, but blindly accepts the scheme. Thus it never occurs to him to criticize the underlying assumptions, aims, and methods of activities in which he himself is engaged.

Sometimes, while being aware of his distrust, he does not show it overtly. He regards life as consisting of the alternatives of either controlling or being controlled, of subduing or being subdued. Hence he is constantly on guard, constantly expecting to be victimized or exploited, and he maneuvers—sometimes in clever, hidden ways—to be on top. Often he is not aware that he expects to be used or controlled by another, and on the surface he may act as if he were sympathetic and even trustful, although inwardly he is withdrawn and suspicious.

No single word can fully characterize the mentality we have described, but *prosaic* suggests several of its major features. Most obviously, of course, *prosaic* points to literalism. It also suggests the commonplace and neglect of the imaginative, the spontaneous, and the unfamiliar. Beyond this, it carries intimations of excessive concern with facts, methods, and clear-cut rules, and is able to suggest other, related elements of the mentality that is at the root of our dissolution. As the concept of the prosaic mentality acquires its full meaning in the chapters that follow, we will be able to reach a more effective position from which to overcome this dissolution.

Chapter 7 SCIENCE

Scientific knowledge is intrinsically public. Whatever description or explanation is advanced by anyone in the name of science must be capable of comprehension and verification in each of its parts by any other competent individual. This characteristic is taken for granted by everyone who seeks or communicates scientific knowledge. It is, as we shall see, an integral element of all other essential characteristics of the scientific enterprise.

The central concern of science is the quest for general relationships among particular phenomena and the explanation of particular phenomena as instances of such general relationships. Thus, the statement, "The distance traversed by a body allowed to fall freely from an initial condition of rest is proportional to the square of the time elapsed," is a general principle, or scientific law, relating the elements "distance" and "time," which can be abstracted from all particular instances of falling bodies. The principle provides a rational order linking the innumerable individual occurrences of this phenomenon in different places and at different moments, past and future. By thus consolidating the perceptions of all events of this class, it brings a certain aspect of the universe within the grasp of the mind.

The individual event is particular and transitory and may or may not be observed; the scientific law correlating certain characteristics of all such events is invariable. It is therefore in its very essence an object of public knowledge: it can always be investigated and observationally verified by anyone having the necessary competence.

Science seeks more than the ordering that would be furnished by an accumulation of independent laws applying respectively to separate, limited classes of experience. The mind is urged toward greater generality, toward more encompassing principles that will account for laws of lesser generality and for particular occurrences as special instances of them. So, for example, the space-time relation for freely falling bodies is found to be implied by laws of motion having far wider generality. This implication is a logical one: the relations of lesser generality are the consequence of the more general relations when these are subjected to the specific conditions describing the more limited class of events. The demonstration of this consequence is what is meant by scientific explanation. A theory, or a set of laws, explains a phenomenon if the phenomenon can be shown to be a particular exemplification of it. Thus, the deformation or bursting of a pipe (of specified dimensions and of a material of specified properties) due to the freezing of water contained in it can be explained as a particular manifestation of general laws governing the volume increase of water in the freezing process and of other laws governing the behavior of deformable bodies under applied loads.

The explanatory laws need not be susceptible of immediate verification by sense observation. They state highly abstract relationships between concepts of which some may, and others may not, represent observable elements of phenomena. But from these relationships are derivable by rational processes other relationships between observable entities (usually measurable ones), and at these points of contact between the system of concepts and experiential reality the two must agree. Scientific cognition therefore derives its stability from two sources: first from the conceptual relationships carefully and tightly joined by rational (and wherever possible, mathematical) argument; second from the junctures of this web of ideas with the empirical world. At these junctures are the hard and stubborn facts, respect for which is a cardinal rule of scientific procedure. We may liken this system of cognition to a steel structure consisting of columns and beams: each member—analogous to a conceptual relation—fits internally with other members of the structure, and some members, in addition, make contact with the ground—which corresponds to experiential reality—and conform to its topography. Because of this twofold conformity, the verification of a newly advanced scientific proposition does not always require observational testing, either directly, if this is possible, or indirectly via the derivation of testable consequences. If a theoretical framework already exists into which the proposition must fit and in which we have confidence, it is usually sufficient to demonstrate appropriate internal interconnections.

The demonstration of these connections must be of a public nature. Earlier we saw that scientific cognition is public at every place where a proposition applies to observable data. We now see that it is public also with respect to the theoretical structure, for the derivation of scientific propositions, that is, the demonstration that certain conceptual relationships are the logical consequence of others, once produced, is verifiable by everyone versed in the appropriate reasoning process.

THE GENERAL AND THE PARTICULAR

It is evident that scientific thought is concerned both with particular fact and with abstract generality. The roles of the two are intertwined: the general principles provide systematic coherence for a multiplicity of particular facts. Abstract schemes in themselves have no place in empirical science: they acquire a place only if they can provide a fruitful ordering for particular facts, that is, if they make contact and are in accord with the world of sense experience, with what is seen and heard. Similarly, facts and the establishment of facts in themselves do not constitute science. The scientific aim is to see facts as manifestations of a general scheme.

A particular observation may be regarded in various ways. It may be shown to be explainable in terms of an accepted theory, that is, to constitute an example of acknowledged general principles. It may be considered as an empirical test for a theoretical system the validity of which is to be verified or questioned. Or it may prompt the development of a new system if there is none into which it can fit or if it is not consistent with one into which it was expected to fit. The extent of attention paid to a particular event depends on the nature of the event, on the methods by which it is observed or inferred, and on the degree of confidence in the theory of which it is an exemplification. But no matter what the situation, the scientific view always sees the event, or strives to see it, as an instance of logically coherent abstract generalities. For the very essence of scientific knowledge is to elaborate a rational pattern ordering the circumstances of this ever-shifting world by showing them to be manifestations of a few general principles. The individual fact, the concrete event that is seen and heard, always appears as a particular case of an abstract generalization.

PUBLIC VERIFIABILITY AND SCIENTIFIC OBSERVATION

The criterion of public verifiability imposes very rigorous conditions concerning the kind of experience that can be admitted into the scientific scheme. By far the greatest part of every person's experience is inaccessible to public scrutiny, at least to the strict and complete scrutiny aimed at by the scientific enterprise. The headache I got yesterday evening while working, and my delight with the color and smell of the chrysanthemums standing in my room as I write are of so personal a character that they cannot be made objects of public cognition. Their nature is very different from my perception that when I pushed an object over the edge of a table, it fell. Such an event is completely accessible to everyone wherever and whenever he may wish to observe it himself. He need not have been present when I observed the occurrence, nor need he use the same object or the same table. Another person looking at my chrysanthemums, on the other hand, may not delight in them or may not believe me when I say that I delight in them or may question whether we really mean the same thing when we both claim delight, or if he looks at other chrysanthemums on a different occasion, he may not be delighted by them. We have no such difficulties with an object pushed over the edge of a table; and because we have none, this event is suitable for scientific cognition. It appears to us as what is often called a completely objective event, belonging entirely to the external world of interconnected things that underlies all the perceptions of all people. It is independent of the particular qualities of my sensations or your sensations, and this independence parallels its independence from the particularity of the individual event localized in place and time: it can be observed any number of times and at any number of places.

Public verifiability does not require that the observations of an event made by different individuals or by the same individual at different times be identical. What does matter is that they be consistent with the abstract relations of which the event is an example, for these relations—the general principles governing the course of events—must be the same for all. The situation is analogous to that of different individuals looking at an object, say a house, from different viewpoints. They do not perceive identical images, but the different images are consistent with each other.[1]

REPEATABILITY OF EVENTS

In the preceding section it was pointed out that stress on public verifiability has consequences for the kind of empirical observations that are acceptable. They must be such as to admit the establishment of complete agreement, the more readily and clearly the better. Observations involving the investigator's pleasures or pains, for example, are not suitable; the reading of the position of a pointer on a scale or the numerical count of a group of items is eminently suitable. There is another condition that events studied by science must meet: the search for general laws implies that the conformity of the course of events to these laws can be checked again and again by different observers on different occasions; this requires that the events be repeatable.

No event repeats itself completely in all details of its concrete fullness. The concept of repetition involves an interpretation of events. If one object falls over the edge of a table and then the event is "repeated," there are two separate events involving one or two objects, and possibly two tables, two points in time and place, and two observers. When we speak of repetition in science, it is implied that we are focusing our attention on a group of certain common elements that can be abstracted from different occasions and that are relevant to our purpose of understanding. Nothing is said about, no restrictions are imposed on, any other aspects of the different occasions. Thus, in the preceding example nothing is, nor need be, stipulated concerning the object's shape, color, or chemical composition, or the characteristics of the table. The general principles connecting the common elements abstracted from these events hold irrespective of the other characteristics of the individual events. The independence of the principles from these other characteristics is the very core of scientific cognition: though the individual events may differ in innumerable ways and hence confront us with transience and particularity, they exhibit uniformities with respect to certain common elements. Thus the requirement that events be repeatable with respect to a set of abstracted properties can be stated alternatively as the requirement that, whenever doubt arises as to the validity of certain principles, observations can be made by which these principles may be validated or rejected.

But what happens when observations are made that violate such principles? First of all, the possibility of errors in observation or interpretation will be entertained; and the alternative possibility that the event observed did not, as had been supposed, satisfy all the conditions by virtue of which it would become a manifestation of the principles to be tested. If one of these possibilities appears reasonable, the difficulty is resolved: there is no scientific inconsistency. If not, then perhaps the observations will be repeated. If they are now in accord with the principles, we are likely to assume that some error had been made in the previous observations and that we need no longer worry about them. But suppose that the renewed observations again violate the principles: would we now entertain the possibility that the events we are studying are not repeatable, so that they cannot be brought into the realm of scientific cognition? If we did this, our enterprise might come to a halt every time an inconsistency arose between principles and observations. Alternatively, do we reject the principles and look for new ones? This course might condemn us to so frequent a change of principles that it would be questionable whether any systematic ordering worth the name could be achieved at all.

The discussion of repeatability has implied that a general class of events is selected prior to the attempt to correlate them by scientific abstractions. Thus, to consider a simple example, one might begin with a general class of events called "water freezing in pipes." As a first attempt at the establishment of general principles, let us propose that whenever water freezes in a pipe, the pipe bursts. If repeated observations be made of this event, it will be found that the law does not hold. Sometimes bursting occurs, sometimes it does not. We might now conclude that this event is not repeatable and hence not subject to scientific cognition. But this would simply be waiving the attempt at scientific cognition. We do not give up that easily, for science rests on the conviction that ordering principles *are* possible. Hence we say instead that we must look for a different principle. In the course of our observations we notice that bursting seems to depend on the material of which the pipe is made. Rubber pipes, for example, behave differently from steel pipes. We therefore presume that the principles we seek will not apply indifferently to all materials and that the elements we abstract from the individual events will have to include a suitable characteristic of the material, the variations of which are necessary for systematization of the observed variations of behavior.

Suppose, however, that we do not know how to do this and that we therefore decide, at least as a preliminary step, to look for less general principles, that is, to narrow the class of events from "water freezing in pipes" to "water freezing in steel pipes." Accordingly, we propose that whenever water freezes in a steel pipe, the pipe bursts. We repeat our experiments, but once more we find that the law does not hold. Again, we might conclude that we cannot understand the behavior scientifically. But now we notice that the shape and dimensions of the pipes play an important role, and so we set about seeking relations that will take account of these characteristics. For example, after further limiting ourselves to circular pipes, we look for laws that take account of the dimensions of the inner and outer diameters. They might state, let us say, that the pipe will burst for a certain range of the ratio of these dimensions but not for others. With this version, repeatability of the event no longer requires that the pipe burst; but, rather, that there be observed a systematic relation between the abstracted elements "bursting" and "ratio of diameters."

Repeatability, therefore, is a flexible conception. Since it is required. If we had to change our abstractions and co-ordinattics of events, one can seek to bring it about by proper choice of characteristics. Thus, in the illustration, repeatability of the events requires the inclusion of the dimensions of the pipes. Again, if one wishes to have a theory correlating the larger class of phenomena including pipes of different materials, suitable characterizations of the materials will have to be included among the abstractions. (The rudimentary laws proposed in this illustration do not lend themselves to a very fruitful theory concerning the behavior of deformable bodies; but they are easily grasped, and adequately serve us here to elucidate the scientific process.)

Repeatability, though a flexible concept, is very definitely required. If we had to change our abstractions and co-ordinating principles very often, we would have no scientific knowledge at all with which to systematize and stabilize our perceptions of the universe, since we achieve this only to the extent that firm principles connecting certain abstractions are established and verified by repeated observations. The requirement is flexible only in that, instead of giving up the attempt at scientific cognition when the events of some class are found not to be repeatable, we seek to modify or refine the classification, to alter the abstractions, or to take account of additional abstracted properties through more complicated principles.

Before we leave the question of repeatability it may be useful to note that viewed in a special way, the repeatability of scientific events becomes their predictability. For predictability is simply the view we have of a future repetition of some event known to be repeatable (whether or not the repetition is later observed). The fact that an event can be observed again and again leads us to call it repeatable; the fact that one can say that it will occur leads us to call it predictable.

ABSTRACTIONS AND THE ISOLATED SYSTEM

While the quest for scientific understanding of an event may involve some flexibility in the choice of abstracted properties, each attempt at such understanding involves a definite group of abstracted properties and their interconnections. Furthermore, this group of properties is considered to be free from dependence on all other aspects of the event in its full concreteness. Scientific statements respecting the event, therefore, refer only to this limited system of abstractions. The remainder of the universe is irrelevant in this context.

To illustrate: The behavior of pipes subjected to internal pressure by freezing water is understood in terms of such abstract characteristics as the magnitudes of the diameters, the stress-strain properties of materials, the volume expansion of water during the freezing process, and so on. The color of the pipe, its geographic location, the time of year when the observations are made, the use to which the pipe may later be put, the source of the water used—these and an infinity of other detailed items are regarded as having no effect upon the interconnections of the elements considered. Therefore nothing need be, and by the same token, nothing is, said about them.

If a particular group of abstractions proves inadequate for the explanation of a certain phenomenon, then as has been said, further properties may be taken into account. The effort at comprehension, therefore, need not be abandoned when a theory co-ordinating a given group of abstractions fails to explain a phenomenon, and a new, refined theory may be attempted that takes account of the effect of previously disregarded characteristics. However, every theory deals with a fixed group of abstracted elements, and the system constituted by these elements is considered as isolated within the universe.

The adequacy of a theory is judged in the light of the closeness of fit desired between theory and observations, for the theory is always an idealized structure. This is inherent in the supposition that the system of abstractions is isolated, that is, independent of all other aspects of the universe. In fact, this independence is only partial, and what is disregarded does affect the system; so the judgment that a theory is good really implies that it is good enough—that the influence on the system of disregarded aspects of the universe is small enough not to interfere with one's purpose. A higher degree of fit may be sought by taking account of previously omitted characteristics. Thus, in the illustration, the lengths of the pipes, the ways they are supported, the temperature in the surrounding air, and so on, might have to be included, this new system now again being treated as isolated from the remainder of things.

There are two factors, however, that demand that the number of abstracted characteristics, or variables, be kept as low as possible. First, and more obvious, is the rapid rise of difficulties in every part of the enterprise as the number of variables is increased. Their empirical control in experimentation, as well as the elaboration of the rational principles connecting them, quickly escapes our powers. Second, and really intimately connected with the finiteness of our powers, is the central aim of scientific thought: to see the largest possible number of particular events as manifestations of a few general principles connecting a few abstractable characteristics. It is through such vision that our minds can grasp the vast multitude of baffling particulars. Too great a readiness to increase the number of abstracted elements in order to encompass further particulars within scientific principles is therefore contrary to the very essence of scientific cognition.

EXPLICIT AND EXHAUSTIVE ARTICULATION

Another all-important characteristic of science is the principle of explicit and exhaustive articulation. I mean by this the principle that the entire object of scientific cognition, that is, all that is of interest to scientific thought, must be articulated, and in a clear-cut fashion. Whatever is to be understood must be developed with all its elements apparent. Whatever is to be explained must be laid bare, plain to see, with all connections necessary to secure the explanation completely stated. (Whenever anything is omitted, one assumes that its essential content can be identically supplied by every competent inquirer.)

It should be evident that this principle is intimately linked with the public character of science, for without it the establishment of complete and unanimous agreement would not be possible. Such agreement becomes feasible only when every facet of the cognitive structure can be spelled out and hence completely communicated from person to person. To make certain that the judgments of individual minds are identical, all elements entering into these judgments must be totally accessible to scrutiny. No part of what scientific knowledge seeks to grasp can be allowed to remain unsaid. One must seek to avoid every conceivable possibility of misunderstanding, of difference in interpretation, or of lack of sharpness. The understanding science seeks is completely contained in the statements that are made: they exhaust that which is of interest in any given body of knowledge—the interconnections of a group of abstracted characteristics. Thus, when one is concerned with the time-distance relationship of falling bodies, there is nothing that engages one's interest, nothing one would like to elucidate, nothing one seeks to comprehend, that is not explicitly embodied in the relevant principles. If one wishes to consider other aspects of the phenomenon, such as the resistance of air, the propositions will have to include additional characteristics, but once again, they will leave nothing unsaid which one believes requires saying in order for the new theory to be complete.

This exhaustiveness is possible only because, as has been indicated earlier, every act of scientific cognition confines its interest to a sharply delineated group of abstractions. With respect to these abstractions, one's knowledge is, as it were, of uniform luminosity everywhere; apart from them, there is no illumination at all.

The principle of explicit articulation imposes very strict demands on the language in which scientific cognition is embodied. Each statement is intended to articulate and convey a definite, clear-cut idea. The scientist-writer shuns extraneous intimations and reverberations. He makes a meticulous effort to pin down every key concept and defines technical terms and notations to denote these concepts. Figurative meanings, connotations, and properties of words and notations that depart from the function of unique and unambiguous reference to ideas or things are irrelevant and hence must be disregarded. Therefore, meanings taken over from nonscientific language are, wherever necessary, carefully delineated, modified to suit the scientific purpose of methodical co-ordination, or even so altered as to barely retain a likeness to the original; also, new words and notations are made up whose connection to other realms is slim—and for scientific purposes unnecessary —or nonexistent.

The success of this endeavor is in very large measure dependent upon the use of mathematics and the discovery of measurable characteristics of phenomena. For here the utmost sharpness of observation, thought, and articulation is possible. The co-ordination of objects or events on the basis of numbers attached to a definite group of measurable elements is the most systematic, explicit, and clear-cut ordering of experience we can achieve.

THE SCIENTIFIC ATTITUDE

Corresponding to the peculiar character of scientific knowledge there is a peculiar approach to experience, a certain kind of attitude adopted by the person engaged in a scientific pursuit. In the first place, scientific thought is severely skeptical. It is unwilling to accept any idea that is not clearly provided with appropriate credentials. Of every assertion it asks: How is it substantiated? Of every explanation it inquires: Has it been tested, and by what methods? Science aims to be critical, in the sense of seeing clearly and truly, and in order to do so, it is critical in the harsher sense of seeking out faults.

Whoever studies a scientific work brings to his task a large measure of skepticism. This will vary, of course, with his purpose. A researcher scrutinizing a newly proposed theory or the report of an experiment with unexpected results will be extremely disposed to doubt. The character of the scientific scheme demands that new assertions prove their validity every inch of the way. If the work brings into question a body of knowledge that has heretofore been accepted as valid, the inquirer is likely to remain dubious even if he is unable to detect an error. It is not too much to say that he will confront the work with a captious or censorious spirit, for it is his business to admit nothing that cannot meet the stiff requirements of scientific validity. On the other hand, a beginner attempting to learn a body of scientific knowledge that is thoroughly established will be much less skeptical, for his intention is not to try this knowledge, but to learn it. Even here, however, an attitude of skepticism is essential. Even the learner must ask what the empirical evidence is for the laws and theories that are being affirmed. He must demand to be shown that the body of propositions is properly co-ordinated in a rational pattern. As he moves from one statement to another he must ask: What justification is there for saying this? What evidence supports it? Is the proof airtight?

This propensity to disbelieve rests on the requirement of public communicability and agreement, and the principle of explicit articulation. Everything must be explicit and capable of being completely conveyed to another and commanding his agreement. Hence the entire body of knowledge must be subjected to the minutest scrutiny.

A good scientist must be cautious. He must be tentative in

his assertions as long as complete substantiation is not available. He refrains from conclusions that do not appear to be fully warranted, and he is therefore inclined to suspend judgment until it can be subjected to the test of complete public agreement.

Skepticism, cautiousness, tentativeness, and suspension of judgment imply a second major component of the scientific attitude: the scientist's aloofness from the object of his attention. His aim is inconsistent with an urge for action other than that involved in experimentation and observation. He is in no haste to reach a conclusion that will lead to practical consequences. It is the invariable principles governing the behavior of certain aspects of repeatable events that he cares about, not the immediacy of the particular occasion. He does not try to reach any decision as to conduct except in so far as this conduct has to do with investigation of the general properties of things; such investigation is by its very nature a process whose primary concern is not the here and now but the universal and the permanent. The things that are of interest to him do not run away nor demand that he do something about them.

The scientist, as scientist, is removed from the world he studies, not only with respect to action, but also with respect to feelings and sensibilities. Sympathy and dislike, delight and horror, are out of place in his approach to the world. Desires and sensibilities toward the world are held in abeyance. The reverberations in his inner life of the events he studies are irrelevant.

His attitude, therefore, is one of detachment, of impersonality. He takes up the position of alien observer. He restricts his attention to matters that lie entirely in a public domain. This rules out all those facets of human awareness that are very personal; it rules out the engagement of feeling, sensitivity, and desire, for these cannot be made entirely public—they cannot be given explicit articulation and are not susceptible of complete public agreement.

Usually the achievement of detachment presents no great difficulty to the inquirer, for several reasons. In the first place, the events themselves are generally of such a nature as to excite little interest except as they relate to scientific study—for example, the events the physicist observes when he investigates properties of materials. Secondly, the scientist is concerned not with the particularity, the uniqueness, of an event to which a personal response is made, but with a group of abstractable generic properties. Thus, the realization that a particular child has been struck by poliomyelitis is likely to involve a powerful emotional response; but a scientific study of the statistical correlation of incidence of the disease with children's ages tends to be emotionally neutral. Thirdly, detachment is achieved without difficulty because the abstractable properties to which the scientist attends have generally no immediate import for his personal life: thus, while the weather may excite a strong reaction in a farmer anxious for his crop, the laws governing the pressure, temperature, and velocity of moving air masses are apt to leave the meteorologist who studies them personally quite untouched.

Detachment and impersonality do not imply that the scientific pursuit is entirely stripped of feelings and desires. The scientist is detached from the events he studies, but he may be very much engaged in the study itself. At the center of this engagement is his desire for knowledge, specifically, for knowledge that is scientific. We need not inquire here into the many possible sources of this desire (some of which may be admirable, others not); all we need to recognize is that it is the chief power behind his efforts to meet all the stiff requirements of the scientific scheme; it is what insists that all difficulties and distortions threatening the integrity of his inquiry be overcome.

There are also desires and feelings that may imperil the

scientific pursuit. Thus, the very desire for knowledge or for success that motivates a given inquiry may also be a source of danger. The scientist is anxious to see a theory he has developed verified by experiment; he is distressed if anyone claims that his arguments are erroneous; he is elated when he believes himself within reach of something for which he has labored. Such anxiousness, distress, or elation may lead him astray: it may tempt him to observe fallaciously what he was anxious to observe or to reason himself toward results that would relieve his distress or confirm his elation. Again, pressures to produce knowledge quickly may give rise to impatience; but impatience, whether arising from a personal desire or a social demand to produce, can interfere with the necessary caution. Or occasionally, the thought a scientist pursues is believed by him to have bearing on other realms that he feels are very important. For example, his work may appear to him to have threatening implications for his philosophical or religious views of life, of man, or of God. Usually these views are not directly relevant to the scientific investigation: they are not included in the scheme of abstracted entities with which the investigation is concerned; therefore, any influence that the threat to these views exerts on the investigation may well distort it. The scientist must try to be aware of whatever motions of his inner self may endanger the validity of his work and do his utmost to prevent their doing so. Such prevention, however, is not what I mean by the detachment and impersonality of science, for its importance is by no means peculiar to science. Human life is always full of conflicting aims, desires, and feelings, and therefore every activity requires appropriate watchfulness. By detachment and impersonality I mean the more special attitude that is linked with all the facets of the public character of science. *Public*, indeed, is equivalent to *impersonal* in this context.

Having stressed impersonality, we must now ask if the scientist's personal being is in any way important. How is he, as the individual man he is, present in the scientific pursuit? Is he present the way he would be in searching for a coin known to be lying on the ground? Or is he present more as he would be in discovering something regarded as already in existence but unknown, like an explorer discovering an island? Is he present as he would be in conceiving something that is new but that can be treated according to known principles, as in technological development? Or does his presence involve creativeness, whereby something arises that neither existed beforehand nor could be encompassed by established rules? Does the scientist require imagination, or are good eyes and a clear head all that is wanted? Does he gain his knowledge by intuition or personal insight, or is it the reward of patient advance by standard methods?

To elucidate this issue, it is helpful to differentiate the activity of striving for new knowledge from that of studying what is supposedly established knowledge. I will refer to them as activities of the seeker and the reader respectively, though I do not mean to imply that they are necessarily carried on by different people, or that there is a clear-cut separation between them when carried on by one man. Reading, as distinct from seeking, is most evident in one who is in the process of learning science. In the work of the scientist who is engaged in research, the two activities can be distinguished as two components. When he reads a piece of scientific writing, his principal concern is to understand and perhaps criticize something already accomplished—though in doing so, new ideas may come to his mind. On the other hand, when he is attempting to develop a new theory or to investigate some hitherto unexplained phenomenon, his main occupation is to seek something that is not yet at hand—though while doing so he may have to read others' work.

Laws and theories are not to be found like coins on the floor by anybody with reasonably good eyes. Even what are called facts are not entities that are obvious to anyone who begins to look: there must be some scheme of abstractions, some interpretation, even if inadequate or provisional, to direct the attention. There is an infinite number of things to be observed in connection with any event, and only one who comes to it with some scheme of thought, even if in an inchoate stage, is likely to observe anything very fruitful for scientific understanding. In this he is like an explorer who has certain objectives in mind and does not voyage about aimlessly. Laws correlating abstract entities may perhaps be construed as constituting principles of the universe that are in no way created by the scientist but that only wait to be discovered, like new lands. But even if construed in this way, such laws can be discovered only by the insight of a particular man. No rules exist whose meticulous observance will show the way to a patient plodder. Even more the product of a particular individual's imaginative, intuitive, and logical powers are the extremely general theories (like Newton's theory of gravitation) from which less general principles can be inferred. The choice and identification of entities to be abstracted from phenomena, the idealization, the hypothetical concepts introduced in the construction of a theory, and the general principles of which it consists all involve an individual's creative resources.

Even in the process of deriving consequences from an established body of principles, the scientist's personal contribution enters. The derivation is rarely one of mere deduction according to established rules of thought. It is very likely to contain statements that begin as follows: "Let x be . . ."; or, "Suppose y is . . ."; or, "Assume for the moment that . . ." Such introduction into the thought process of statements that inject new variables or suppose something to be the case or adduce an assumption are usually steps the seeker has imagined, invented, or somehow seen as enabling him to build a bridge from what has been established to what is to be established, the latter sometimes known in advance (one's aim being to construct the derivation), sometimes not yet known (one's aim being to derive consequences that are to be tested by observation or appealed to for explanation). The ability to make such steps can be cultivated by practice and fostered by teaching, but there are no fixed rules that anybody can follow. The process of scientific research cannot be laid out in a how-to book.

Once more, the personal factor is important when an explanation of a phenomenon is sought. In many instances, for example, such an explanation cannot be provided by simply appealing to a very general theory, even though no doubt may exist in anyone's mind that a certain theory is applicable. This is so because the derivation of particular consequences is often a matter of insuperable difficulty unless numerous simplifications, approximations, and assumptions can be made that are judged to be appropriate for the particular circumstance. For example, there is no doubt concerning the general principles that govern the motions and other properties of the air and moisture constituting the earth's atmosphere; yet the application of these principles by meteorologists to the enormous complexity of actual situations becomes feasible only when drastic simplifying assumptions and approximations are made. The judgments as to which simplifications are likely to be appropriate in a given case and when a simplified theory is good enough can only be made by the researcher himself.

Indispensable as the scientist's personal being is in the seeking component of scientific activity, its presence is nevertheless very much circumscribed. We must remember that the central aim of science is to provide a stable, systematic ordering of phenomena by means of principles having the greatest possible generality. Therefore every seeker's extension of knowledge must as far as possible take place within the ordering already established. If an existing scheme is inadequate or is violated by new empirical evidence, he will attempt to provide a new scheme as close as possible to the old one by introducing modifications or extensions of the latter. Instances when a large new realm of phenomena is for the first time subjected to scientific understanding are extremely rare. There cannot be many initiations of knowledge as monumental as those by Galileo and Newton. Similarly, occasions are of necessity extremely rare when a whole established structure of thought is questioned and a fundamentally new one is put forth so as to accomplish not only all the ordering encompassed by the old one but also the extension and refinement of knowledge. There cannot be many Einsteins, not only because men of such genius do not appear often, but also because it is of the very essence of scientific cognition to remain wherever possible within established ways of thought. The overwhelming bulk of scientific work consists of elaboration, refinement, derivation, and development proceeding on the basis of accepted knowledge and procedure. Within these, the extent of creativity, imagination, and intuition brought to research by the individual seeker varies greatly, but always it is strictly contained by the requirement that every new contribution to knowledge be fitted to the old. Science is eminently a social enterprise to which individuals make contributions necessarily having some measure of personal element; this element, however, is restricted by the demands of conformity with established schemes.

Further, entry of the individual's personality into the seeking component is strictly limited by the public character of scientific knowledge. It is undoubtedly true that intuition, imagination, and the ability to entertain novel thought and depart from routine methods is a major part, probably *the* major part, of the difference between a good and a mediocre scientist, but nonetheless, these personal factors move within strict confines. Intuition and imagination inspire and lead research. Flashes of personal insight are like sudden and instantaneous illuminations in surrounding darkness, suggesting a way;

but the scientific work that is their final issue must be amenable to and withstand public testing. Hence whatever is grasped by intuition or discovered by insight or created by imagination has to be cast into a standard, systematic, and verifiable form. Only when the personal apprehension is made entirely explicit and susceptible of complete agreement can it enter into the body of scientific knowledge.

Here we return to what was said earlier concerning detachment as a characteristic feature of the scientific attitude: the individual stands apart from the things he seeks to understand; he analyzes, controls, and observes them in a spirit that eliminates any relation between them and himself other than that of his cognizing a few of their generic properties.

It may be said that this description is not in accord with modern physics, where the role of the individual observer, of the "cognizing subject," has taken on great importance. But it is easy to make too much of this modern idea of subjectivity —and this has been done repeatedly by those to whom this subjectivity appeared as a great blow to man's capacity to gain valid knowledge, as well as by those who saw in it the longed-for reinstatement of the human being with his powers of freedom and creativity, which had been utterly excluded from the earlier materialistic views of reality issuing out of seventeenth-century physics. The modern acknowledgment that one cannot maintain a total separation between the objects of cognition and the cognizing person does not alter the latter's approach toward the objects. He still faces them in a spirit of detachment, attending exclusively to a group of general properties. What is considered to be the subjective element of modern physics in no way alters the public character of physics, the requirement that its mode of cognition be impersonal, weaned away from whatever is not susceptible of explicit articulation, complete communication, and total agreement.

The realization of this fact is important to us. On the one

hand, it protects us against extreme forms of skepticism that result when too much is made of the subjectivity of scientific knowledge. On the other, it cautions us against looking hopefully to modern physics for the re-entry of the previously excluded human elements and against jumping to the tempting and too-easy conclusion that all conflict on this score has vanished. It warns us that it is wrong to restrict one's view of what constitutes a person to his place in the scientific pursuit, because notwithstanding the importance of this place, it is only an irreducible minimum.

The place of the person in the reading component of science is much smaller than in the seeking. Since the knowledge that a scientific work embodies is explicitly articulated, the reader is not called upon to provide any personal insight or interpretation. Since whatever is necessary to convey the knowledge is said completely, since there remains nothing to be understood or suggested that is not exhaustively stated in clear-cut words, terms, and notations, the reader is not required—and indeed, not allowed—to bring a personal response to what he reads. The writer (seeker) has provided a network of paths for thought, and the reader's business is to follow this network: it indicates (or ought to indicate) every step he is to take. He is not allowed to deviate, and he brings to it only those assumptions, ways of inference, and habits of observation that are taken for granted by all scientists and, more particularly, by those familiar with a given field and that therefore need not be explicitly stated. If imaginative steps were introduced in the seeking process, they have been completely spelled out and require nothing of the reader except the competence to follow and verify the path marked by the writer. To say that it is the reader's business to take step after step as indicated is not to say, however, that it is easy. The paths of scientific thought, while clearly marked, may be very steep.

This utmost impersonality of approach on the part of the

reader is the essence of the public character of science. No matter how scientific knowledge was gained, whether or not it required imagination, personal insight, intuition, or what have you, when it is set down, it must be so devoid of any personal element that it is completely communicable to, and capable of commanding the assent of, every competent reader.

Chapter 8 HISTORY

"Whatever can be known," Bertrand Russell has written, "can be known by means of science." [1]

If this is true, then our knowledge of human life and deeds in the past, which we call history, is in fact not knowledge. Or else it is science. The first view need not detain us here, since it will be dealt with implicitly throughout the chapter. As to the second, I believe there are few modern writers who would subscribe to the bald statement that history is science. At present, indeed, history is more immune to science than any other of the social studies.

The credo that history is science was current in the nineteenth century, but has generally been recognized as being too simple-minded. Those who hold it now are apt to state it more guardedly or with more sophistication than their predecessors. One view, for example, holds that certain differences between scientific and historical knowledge must be granted, but that nevertheless the explanation of events offered by history does not differ from the explanations offered by the natural sciences.[2] Another, similar view states that explanation of an event in history, "as well as in any other branch of empirical science . . . aims at showing that the event in question was not 'a matter of chance,' but was to be expected in view of certain antecedent and simultaneous conditions. The expectation referred to is not prophecy or divination, but rational scientific anticipation . . ." [3] Here the explicit reference to history as empirical science, as well as the implication that "prophecy or divination" constitutes the sole alternative to "rational scientific anticipation," discloses the tenor of these modern positivistic positions, which is to deny that there can be extrascientific knowledge and hence to claim that history really is science, even though distinctions between history and science are being allowed. These distinctions, as we shall see, are of various kinds, but they all have in common the notion that history is close to, but less than, science. History leads to knowledge because, and in so far as, it approximates the scientific scheme. The approximation can supposedly be increased but has its limits, and so history becomes essentially an inferior science.

This notion, however, is in sharp conflict with the high estimate of history as a mode of insight into man that has often been voiced by first-rate minds.[4] Many of these have claimed, moreover, that history achieves this insight in a manner unlike that of science. Indeed, Ortega y Gasset, for example, who sees history as the only adequate way of inquiring into man, believes that it is so not at all because it approximates the method of science, but because the very opposite is the case: only because history rejects the mode of thought that is typical of natural science and adopts its own distinctive path, "historical reason," [5] can it reveal the reality of human life.

We would altogether miss the gravity of the issue if we thought that what is involved here is nothing but a dispute over means, a factional quarrel concerning scholarly procedures, or a controversy over nomenclature. For what must not be forgotten is that these means have an aim—to disclose something about man—and that the character of what is disclosed, the nature of the insight, is inextricably intertwined with the approach by which the insight is gained. What is at issue is our idea of man, our vision of human life, and since this vision continually interacts with everything we do and experience, the issue is nothing less than our lives.

All this indicates some of the major reasons for examining history in this inquiry and, more specifically, for examining it in a manner that often juxtaposes it to science. When, in this chapter, I address myself to various deliberately scientific views of history, I do so chiefly because, as the most thought-out and far-reaching assimilations of history to science, they enable us to see various issues most clearly. But the importance of such issues lies not only in their bearing on views that either assert that history is science or chiefly fight this assertion, but in the contribution they make to our understanding of history itself and, beyond that, of many themes that are central to this book. This will often be seen in the present chapter, but it can emerge into full relief only in Part Three.

THE SUBJECT MATTER OF HISTORY

Let us open a history book—Henri Pirenne's *History of Europe:*

> Between the battle of Bouvines at the beginning of the century and the conflict between Philip the Fair and Boniface VIII at its close, the 13th century stands out as an epoch characterized by the double hegemony of the Papacy and France. Whether separately or by common agreement, they determined the course of policy, while both exerted a profound influence over intellectual, moral and social life: the one through the Church which it directed, the other through the superiority of her civilization.[6]

We begin by noting the obvious: the subject matter of history is human deeds and experiences that lie in the past. In these are included, as almost any history would show, features and events of nature to the extent that they have bearing on human affairs.

Examples of such experiences are a particular battle and a

conflict between two specific individuals. These are typical. History, we can say, focuses attention on the particular, the individual, the unique. Open any history and you will find it replete with proper names, dates, and names of specific geographical locations. It establishes, describes, and elucidates definite events. It speaks of Caesar's death, Alaric's entry into Rome, and Philip Augustus' victory at Bouvines.

But what is meant by *particular?* What constitutes the specific event, the individual unit? Certainly the particularity is not the same for the death of the singular individual, Caesar, as for the occupation of the city of Rome by an army of barbarians. Further, when we read, in our example, that "the 13th century stands out as an epoch characterized by the double hegemony of the Papacy and France," we are being told something very general concerning many men's lives in many places and during a considerable period of time. Indeed every particular event the historian speaks of is always viewed as occurring within a more general context. His interest in the individual, Caesar, and in particular events in Caesar's life entails interest in much more general circumstances in Rome, in Italy, and in other parts of the world, before, during, and after the occurrence of these particular events. We must therefore seek further clarification of the statement that history focuses on the particular.

THE PARTICULAR AND THE GENERAL

The particular is always an entity marked out within something larger. Rome is a particular city in the Roman world, the Romans a particular group of people among a much larger population, Caesar a particular individual among Romans, the battle against Ariovistus a particular event in Caesar's life, the tactics of the reserve a particular event within the battle. Thought always proceeds in terms of such units, and historical thought makes use of many kinds. It is concerned with the single incident in the life of a certain individual, with the much larger unit constituted by a particular event such as the Battle of Bouvines, and the still larger unit referred to as the intellectual, moral, and social life of the thirteenth century in Western Europe. How large a unit the historian considers at any given point in his inquiry depends on the things he is then seeking to understand and on the way various units lend themselves to such understanding. And he freely switches from one to another if it will aid his inquiry. At one point he may be interested in Caesar's personal role in a particular battle, at another in the battle as a whole, and at still another in the battle's consequence for a large area and a long span of time.

But however large the particular entity, it is always restricted—albeit rather flexibly—to a certain area and a certain period, and the historian's principal concern is with the circumstances, experiences, and deeds of men who lived there and then. This implies a characteristic of historical thought that can be brought out by comparison with science. The scientist, as we have seen, views every event as a member of a class of innumerable like events, each one exemplifying the same set of general principles. The fall of this apple at this place and this time is a particular example of the universal laws of motion, other examples of which repeatedly occur with other objects at other places and other times. In its function as example, the particular always leads one's attention to the general. The historian, by contrast, stays with the particular event. He does not formulate laws of which the individual happening is an illustration and of which other illustrations have occurred and will occur at other times and other places. His attention is not directed away from the particular event—whatever its nature—to systematizing generalizations; it remains concentrated on the event. At the same time, his knowledge of an event is very different from that of the scientist. The latter views it in terms of a group of abstracted properties; for his purposes, these properties *are* the event. The historian, on the contrary, does not reduce the event to a group of properties, but wants to get at the event itself. This is why history is often said to give knowledge of the concrete, in contrast to science, which is knowledge of the abstract. The concrete event has a richness infinitely beyond any set of abstract statements that can be made about it. And whereas this richness is completely irrelevant to science, it is very important in history. The fullness of events exercises an attraction on the historical consciousness that is completely absent in the scientific.

This view of history as concentrating upon the particular —where *particular* refers to many kinds of entities—is entirely consistent with the characteristic noted earlier, the inclusion in historical knowledge of what we usually call generality; for this is knowledge of certain general characteristics of men and circumstances in a particular period and locality.

HISTORY AND HISTORICAL GEOLOGY

The business of history is to study events of the past, and the past is not accessible to observation. In science, on the contrary, the phenomena we study, we ourselves can observe. We can do so because they are repeatable—not, to be sure, in their unique individuality, but with respect to a relevant group of abstracted elements. Historical actors, however, are dead, and their actions past. The individuals cannot be recalled nor the concrete events repeated. The subject matter of history, therefore, requires an indirect approach. We must reach it through something that *is* accessible to our immediate experience—historical sources.

What path leads us from these sources to the events of the past? We can bring out the aspects of the question that are important for our inquiry by a comparison with historical geology. This discipline also investigates the past and, like history, also seeks knowledge of particular events. The geologist, for example, who is interested in a particular mountain range seeks to establish the stages and transformations that preceded its present state. The present state is all he can observe, and in this it corresponds to the historian's sources. The geologist's "sources" are mountains and plains, oceans and river beds, rocks and fossils; the historian's are written records of all kinds and artifacts like monuments, tools, coins, statues, and paintings. In addition to his observations, the geologist uses theories about physical processes to arrive at knowledge of the past, reasoning that this past must have been such that the processes could lead from it to the state he actually observes.

The observations themselves, of course, cannot be made without thought; the geologist does not go around measuring, weighing, and analyzing at random. He must bring to his observation a considerable amount of knowledge; on the basis of this knowledge he asks himself pertinent questions, the answers to which depend upon observable properties, and these properties are what he looks for. In this respect, the historian proceeds similarly: where one measures the width of a river bed, the other observes the height of a cathedral nave; where one is interested in the chemical properties of a rock, the other investigates the properties of the ink used in a document. But while for the geologist the ascertainment of such observable properties constitutes the total of what he requires the sources themselves to yield, for the historian it is only a fraction; he must confront his sources in an entirely different way, which has no parallel in geology: he must read them, get at their meanings. A document, to be sure, is observable ink marks on paper; but it is more than that: it is an expression of a mind that is saying something, and it is this content that plays the central role in historical knowledge. A letter written by a historical personage is a communication to another of thoughts and feelings, and to them the historian must penetrate. A painting is oil on canvas, and innumerable physical and chemical observations of it may be made; but its principal import for history is the meanings it embodies. Perhaps the most striking way of exhibiting the difference between the historian's and the geologist's confrontation of their sources is to note that what a historical document says may be judged true or false; whereas the properties observed in geology—just as the document's physical properties—may be correctly or incorrectly observed, but are themselves neither true nor false.

The historian must get to the meaning of his sources, because this meaning is intimately related to the knowledge he seeks: sometimes it is itself this knowledge; sometimes it is a clue. When he wants to know, for example, the physical doings of certain historical agents, a possible source for this knowledge may be a document or a historical narrative. In order for the historian to get from the source to such knowledge as that in the course of the occupation of the Roman Empire "the Vandals crossed the Rhine with bands of Suevi," there is a minimum ability he must have. He must understand the language used in the source; he must be able to move from the perception of a collection of written or printed shapes before him to their meaning. If these shapes belong to a language of which he is ignorant, he will gain no knowledge from them. This is so obvious that its crucial importance may be missed, and it is therefore well to recall that no analogous ability is required of the geologist: the shapes of rock or fossil do not constitute a language.

But the centrality of the process of getting to the meaning is not brought out sufficiently by the quotation given in the preceding paragraph, because it makes the process seem simple: if you understand the language, not much of a problem is posed in coming to the knowledge that the Vandals crossed the Rhine with bands of Suevi—provided we assume that the historian has grounds to believe the truth of the account. But now let us expand the quotation: "The Vandals crossed the Rhine with bands of Suevi, passed downwards through Gaul, pillaging as they went . . ." [7] Consider the phrase "pillaging as they went." Here too, it seems, we are concerned with a physical doing. But no sooner do you think about this than you see that much more is involved: pillaging is not nearly so clear-cut an action as crossing the Rhine. The historian who comes across it in a narrative faces a problem that goes beyond the previous one: what constitutes pillage? As a further example, if we read that a victory was scored or a rebellion broke out or a food shortage occurred, how are we to understand these things? The "victory" might have been a Pyrrhic victory; by "rebellion" the writer might have meant something more like a minor uprising. And how are we to understand "food shortage"? A condition that would constitute a food shortage to a twentieth-century American might seem an abundance to the writer of the narrative, and perhaps —if the writer is not himself one of the historical characters who suffered the shortage—something still different to the people whose deprivation he describes. The point is that in all these instances something more than physical action is involved and that, necessarily, the events are related in the light of certain views, experiences, and evaluations; and furthermore, that the meaning intended by the author is expressed through a much more complex and subtle use of language than is the case in a bare record of physical doings. To penetrate to this meaning, the historian will have to confront his source in a different and more complex manner than was required to understand "crossed the Rhine." Also, he must try to determine whether this meaning does justice to the actual historical event.

The problems in interpreting "pillaging" point up a difference between the approach a scientist, specifically a geologist, takes to the objects he observes and the one the historian takes to the sources that are the ground of his knowledge. For the latter, the things he looks at are not only objects to be observed, but the embodiments of human meanings that he must reach by appropriate interpretation.

This feature of historical thinking emerges more clearly in

interpreting "pillaging" than in interpreting "crossed the Rhine," for in the first example the subject matter goes beyond clear-cut physical action. The importance of human meanings appears still more distinctly when we are concerned with historical knowledge whose subject matter even more obviously transcends that "which can be described in terms of bodies and their movements." [8] Pirenne tells us, for example, that the Roman emperor Honorius, "in order to get rid of" the Visigoth Athaulf, who was "passionately desirous of alliance with the Imperial family . . . resigned himself to giving him in marriage his sister Galla Placidia." [9] Here, evidently, the historian has gone far beyond mere physical happenings; he has gained insight into human personalities. His knowledge is not confined to men's outward doings, but includes something of their inner life experience, that is, their thoughts, intentions, and emotions. Moreover—a crucial point that will be elaborated later—it is in terms of this experience that their actions are intelligible. To gain such insight into the inner lives of individuals and into the general ways of life and experience of people in a certain epoch, the historian must elicit from his sources a great deal more than is borne on the face of descriptions or records of conditions and happenings. His sources are expressions of human purposes, thoughts, and emotions. They constitute a "world of symbols" [10] whose essential meaning is accessible only to one who can interpret or appreciate them. This becomes even more evident perhaps when we remember that the historian turns not only to the written word, but also to tools and other artifacts, to paintings and statues, to coins and clothes, to houses, castles, and cathedrals, and that all of them are to him not only material objects whose properties can be perceived and described, but the "precipitates" of human life, whose significance he must understand in order to discover the lives of the men from whom they derive. He must "read and interpret his documents and monuments not only as dead remnants of the past but as living messages from it, messages addressing us in a language of their own."

It is important to explore further history's interest in men's inner life. This is akin to, though not identical with, what Collingwood has called the "inside of an event." According to him the central interest of history is in "actions," and "An action is the unity of the outside and inside of an event." The "outside" is the physical aspect of the action, for example, "the passage of Caesar, accompanied by certain men, across a river called Rubicon at one date, or the spilling of his blood on the floor of the senate-house at another." This is certainly of interest to the historian, but his interest does not end there. He wants to penetrate to the "inside," to what underlies the physical movements and "can only be described in terms of thought." Thus the event whose "outside" is the crossing of the Rubicon has as its "inside" the thoughts that were in Caesar's mind as he engaged in the action, "Caesar's defiance of Republican law." [11] The historian must discern this thought.

I find Collingwood's distinction between "inside" and "outside" very illuminating even though I cannot accept his confinement of the former to strictly intellectual operations, for reasons I explain later. We are most obviously obliged to reach this "inside" of events when we deal with sources in which the matter of historical interest definitely transcends outward happenings. An example already mentioned is the action of the emperor Honorius in giving his sister in marriage to Athaulf. Honorius "resigned himself" to this "in order to get rid of" Athaulf. Here we have the "inside" of Honorius' action in terms of a state of feeling and a purpose. Similarly, Athaulf's action and, more general, "the progressive Romanization of the Barbarians" are seen in the light of Athaulf's being "passionately desirous of alliance with the Imperial family." [12] We have here illustrations of history's interest in the concrete event. We want to gain insight into the lives of persons, and persons live in terms of what they perceive, believe, and desire of the world. Our aim therefore is to discover and apprehend this experience of theirs. We look for the way things appeared to them, the thoughts they entertained, the plans they projected, the beliefs they held, the customs and traditions they followed, the doubts they had, the hopes which moved them, the fears to which they were subjected, and the needs they felt. We also look for the ways in which all this grew out of, and interacted with, their life conditions, the environment in which they moved, the demands it imposed, and the possibilities it afforded. In short, history deals not with abstract properties applying generally to men's lives at any time and any place (or even many times and many places), but with knowledge of concrete lives as actually lived.

THE NATURE OF HISTORICAL KNOWLEDGE

Now we must proceed to ask in what way history provides understanding of concrete events of the past. One contention is that history is social science; specifically, that as in science, knowledge of the individual event in history is based on universal laws.

Let us briefly recall once again that scientific cognition of a phenomenon consists of the subsumption of it within a body of general principles, that is, the demonstration that it constitutes a particular instance of universal laws. From a direct inspection of any history, it must be obvious to even the most ardent advocate of the identity of knowledge and science that this description of cognition does not apply to history. If you look for a set of laws of which particular events are shown to be exemplifications, analogous, say, to the physical laws of conservation of mass, energy, and momentum, you will look in vain. It is quite true that historians have sometimes talked about laws in history and that occasionally some have been stated: even Mommsen, who considered history to be an art,[13] states a law of absorption of immature people by politically more developed and more civilized peoples, which, he says, "is as universally valid . . . as the law of gravity." [14] But—even without questioning the scientific character (and validity) of such laws—if you expect to find derivations from them which explain actual historical occurrences, you will be disappointed.

There may be many who would agree with one modern historian's interpretation of the absence of the scientific mode of explanation in history as an "intellectual anachronism." He contends that historians ought to follow the example of social scientists: they ought to try to build hypothetical generalizations that will account for events; they ought to focus on uniformities rather than on unique features. History pursued in this "spirit of scientific analysis," he claims, will no longer be considered as "a series of important unique acts, thought to symbolize or cause change in society." The historian will probe to a deeper level than that of "conventional historic events," to the "human conditioning factors" and the "underlying social forces," and once he "penetrates to the level of social conditioning factors that produce persons capable of such acts and tries to find the probability of the occurrence of any type of event, the acts themselves become a surface manifestation of more fundamental forces." [15]

Such arguments bear the stamp of their authors' fixation on the enormously attractive scientific method: there is more concern with promoting the method than with the subject matter of which knowledge is to be gained. It is ironical that the failure of historians to adopt this method is called an intellectual anachronism because it is, on the contrary, the exhortation to do so that is anachronistic; though the techniques of investigation that would now be recommended are unquestionably more subtle and developed than those available a hundred years ago, this scientific conception of history is like that advanced by nineteenth-century positivists. But since I do not share the doctrine usually dear to the positivistically inclined that what is old is bad, I do not wish to dispose of this "new" view of history merely by saying that it is old. A more cogent and completely adequate objection to it is that, in an effort to make history more scientific, it simply confuses history with social science. It simply forgets what it is that history tries to do; it forgets that we want to find out about the actual lives of people, that it is precisely the concrete historical events we want to understand, and that it is just the acts of persons that constitute the principal subject matter of history. It confuses history with sociology, behavioral psychology, and economics. Let me illustrate with respect to sociology by quoting Pirenne's distinction between the two fields:

While the sociologist seeks to formulate the laws inherent in its very nature which regulate social existence—or, if one wishes, *in abstracto*—the historian devotes himself to acquiring concrete knowledge of this existence during its span. . . . For him, chance and the deeds of prominent personalities, of which the sociologist cannot take account, constitute the essential data of his subject. In other words, the sociologist seeks to separate the typical and the general, while for the historian the typical and the general are only the canvas upon which life has painted perpetually changing scenes. The former uses facts only with a view to the elaboration of a theory; the latter considers them as the episodes of a great adventure about which he must tell.[16]

It is clear that anyone who is less interested in men's unique acts and in life's "perpetually changing scenes" than in generalizations about social conditioning factors is simply not interested in history. The procedures he advocates might be good for sociology or psychology—whether or not they are is not of concern to us at the moment—but they do not apply to the field which is at issue. Though this objection be conceded, it may be said that it leaves open the possibility that a new discipline, different from history, could provide knowledge of the scientific type by showing the historian's events to be exemplifications of general laws. History would then be allowed to focus on the individual events, while the other discipline would provide their scientific co-ordination. My objection rules out this possibility, but I will not stop to present a full argument here because the matter, I trust, will become completely evident after we have moved further into our discussion.

A second kind of claim that knowledge of the individual event in history is based on general laws derives from very influential contemporary developments of positivistic thought. It places less emphasis on the need to change historical method and more on the argument that much history, indeed all good history, past and present, already conforms to the scientific scheme. To make this argument consistent with the way histories in fact look, that is, with their lack of general laws and derivations from them, it is usually granted that history is not one of the "theoretical or generalizing sciences such as physics, biology, sociology, etc.,"[17] for these sciences make it their business to establish general principles of which specific events are the exemplifications. Rather, history is said to be one of the "applied sciences,"[18] like engineering, medicine, or geology, which do not focus on universal laws, and hence usually do not seek to establish laws, but which make use of such laws derived from other areas in order to establish the occurrence of particular events and to explain them. This means that (contrary to the "social science" view) specifically historical laws are said either not to exist at all[19] or, at most, to constitute one kind of law alongside a great many other kinds necessary for historical knowledge.[20]

The favorite comparison is with geology, for here we have a study that on the one hand seeks knowledge, just as history does, of specific objects and events—events, moreover, that lie in the past (in this it is more relevant than medicine or engineering); on the other hand geology establishes and explains these events on the basis of universal laws, in this case largely derived from the indubitable sciences of physics and chemistry. The denial that history can be a science has often been based on the argument that history gives knowledge of particular events, whereas science deals with the general, and that this constitutes a (or even *the*) fundamental difference between them. Geology erases this difference: it is concerned with particular events but apprehends them scientifically. History, it seems, does, or should do, the same.

One argument against this view is that in saying that history and geology are both interested in particular events we are misleading ourselves. We group these two fields together so as to contrast them to the theoretical sciences, the former focusing on particular events, the latter seeking generalizations. But while there is obvious justification for this, the very obviousness traps us into neglecting to pay attention to the crucial distinction between the particular in history and the particular in geology. It was pointed out in the preceding chapter that theoretical science also pays attention to particular events; indeed, its business is to provide knowledge that correlates such events. To contrast science with history and geology, and thereby to suggest a close link between the latter two is therefore too facile. It is true that historical geology is primarily concerned with gaining knowledge about particular events and that in this respect it is like history. But it differs from history in that the kind of knowledge of the particular it provides is the same as that found in theoretical science: the particular is seen as an instance of general principles. Knowledge of this instance is knowledge of a definite and sharply limited group of abstracted properties that apply to innumerable other instances, hence to instances that are repeatable. Geology provides scientific explanation because the interest it takes in its subject matter is the interest that characterizes scientific cognition. But this is not the interest history takes in its subject matter, for which, as was said earlier, the concrete occurrence, the "inside" of the event, and the fullness of actual lives are of paramount importance. The historical event, in contrast to the scientific, is not repeatable, because repeatability, as we have seen, is possible only when interest is restricted to a sharply delineated group of abstractable properties.[21]

A second argument only recalls what was said earlier concerning the different ways of confronting sources. The explanatory laws used by the geologist make contact with empirical reality—as must all science—through sense observation of the present state of things. History, on the other hand, is based on historical sources, and attention to these involves much more than scientific sense observation: they are primarily man-made rather than the product of natural process, and to make something of them requires reading, appreciation, criticism, and interpretation. To overlook this difference is to overlook what is basic to science and what is basic to history.

A third argument against considering history as an applied science has to do with the place of laws in history. Where are the general laws and where are the rational inferences from them that supposedly establish and explain the course of events? If any laws are obvious in history, it is only because their rarity makes them stand out. Moreover, when after special search one finds some laws and examines them by the standards of science, one must judge them unacceptable. The following example is particularly telling because it is considered by a positivistic writer as one in which the scientific form of explanation is especially clearly visible. The subject is the efforts of government offices to maintain and enlarge themselves:

People who have jobs do not like to lose them; those who are habituated to certain skills do not welcome change; those who have become accustomed to the exercise of a certain kind of power do not like to relinquish their control—if anything they want to develop greater power and correspondingly greater prestige. . . . Thus, government offices and bureaus, once created, in turn institute drives, not only to fortify themselves against assault, but to enlarge the scope of their operations.[22]

Clearly, even in this unusually favorable example the explanatory statements offered in the first part of the quotation are very far from conforming to the rigorous requirements of explicit articulation, verifiability, and susceptibility to public agreement that must be met by scientific principles; nor does what they explain—the activities described in the second part —follow from them in a way a scientific statement about a phenomenon follows from a system of laws. (For example, from the statement that people who have jobs do not like to lose them, or that people who have power want to develop greater power, no scientific derivation leads to the conclusion that they will institute drives to enlarge their operations; a fortiori, no scientific proof is possible that particular people in a particular situation will do so.) But though we do not have a scientific explanation here, it cannot be gainsaid that the ideas expressed make good sense.

The absence of laws in history is sometimes ascribed to history's being a quasi science rather than a science. Thus it is claimed that while the historian, unlike the scientist, seldom explicitly states the laws he uses, he tacitly takes them for granted. One reason for not stating them, it is argued, is that the laws assumed often are not capable of being formulated unambiguously and with precision; this is because of the difficulty or impossibility of confirming that the laws are in agreement with all the relevant evidence available, one source of this impossibility being that the elements of human affairs are not repeatable to the extent to which those of, say, geology are. A second reason for not stating the laws supposedly is that many of them are not taken from fields of scientific research, but are prescientific generalizations of everyday experiences known to everybody (for example, that "men will generally seek their economic advantage" [23]) and hence are often so trivial that they are not worth being formally set out. The view of history as quasi science holds that explanations of historical events are mostly not explanations in the scientific sense, but "explanation sketches" that consist of "a more or less vague indication" of circumstances and laws considered relevant and need " 'filling out' in order to turn into a full-fledged explanation. This filling-out requires further empirical research, for which the sketch suggests the direction." [24]

What sense is there in interpreting the field of history as being quasi-scientific when it so radically fails to satisfy the very requirements that make science what it is? What scientist could be satisfied with an inquiry whose explanatory principles are vague and ambiguous, can not be stated explicitly, are not always in conformity with relevant evidence, and can not be adequately verified? It has been contended, for example, in a comparison of history and geology, that the lack of repeatability of historical elements only means a "difference in degree of verifiability in the two realms." [25] Yet, even if this statement could be accepted, the difference is so great that if history can only be based on scientific verifiability, it is a hopeless subject. Indeed, all this quasi-scientific view does is to make history into so inferior a science that it becomes worthless. Measured by the criteria of science, the historical "explanation sketch" is amorphous, vague, and ungrounded verbiage. What scientific status can be granted to the explanation of a particular revolution "by reference to the growing discontent, on the part of a large part of the population, with certain prevailing conditions," if the "general regularity . . . assumed in this explanation" is admittedly such that "we are hardly in a position to state just what extent and what specific form the discontent has to assume, and what the environmental conditions have to be, to bring about a revolution"? [26] If we try to save the explanation's validity by claiming that it is only a "sketch" that needs "filling out," and that it "suggests the direction" in which further empirical research may supply fuller explanation, then we are compelled to conclude that the greater portion of all histories written so far and capable of being written for a long time to come —and probably forever—are in so embryonic a state that it would be utterly premature to speak of their giving us knowledge. What interest, however, would we have in history if the knowledge with which we hoped it might illumine us must be postponed to an indefinite future? Clearly, there would be no warrant at all for the claim (made by a positivistically inclined thinker!) that we must seek historical knowledge because there is "a pressing need to be answered," because "we want to see the line along which we may progress towards the solution of what we feel, and what we choose, to be our main tasks." [27] Moreover, we cannot even dimly imagine the "filling out" of an "explanation sketch" so as to develop it into "full-fledged explanation," when we have to deal with laws from an enormous variety of fields that have no unifying structure; when many of the uniformities assumed are prescientific, incapable of explicit formulation, and not subject to testing; when a host of trivial laws must be taken for granted whose complete statement one cannot hope to approach—and would not want to approach for fear of plunging the mind into total frustration by setting every historical statement within an endless sequence of explanatory derivations; when, indeed—as even a writer who considers history an applied science himself states—"the host of trivial universal laws . . . are practically without interest, and totally unable to bring order into the subject matter." [28]

The attempt to interpret the nature of historical understanding on the basis of its likeness to science, I conclude, runs itself into defeat. True, history and science have points in common, and to recognize them is very illuminating and important, but to think of history as a science or quasi science is fruitless and misleading, and only succeeds in writing it out of the realm of knowledge. This, of course, is agreeable to many science-fixated minds; but it is self-defeating to others who try to validate history by cutting it to the sole pattern of knowledge they admit.

The only way one can do justice to history is to recognize that it gives knowledge and gives it in a manner different from science. It provides explanations that command assent now, and need not wait for some uncertain and unlikely future when further research will have filled out present vague sketches. It does not seek to understand a particular event as medicine does a case—"the term 'case' does not belong in history at all" [29]—nor as engineering or geology understand particular instances of universal laws, nor by the impossible attempt to state and account for all the properties of the event by means of universal principles. Rather, history provides knowledge by describing circumstances and occurrences in geographical, economic, social, political, cultural, and other fields; by narrating actions with their backgrounds, contexts, motivations, and consequences; by characterizing individuals, groups, and societies; and by commenting, interpreting, and appraising numerous facets of past life. One can best summarize its various elements by saying that history is a telling of the past. But this is appropriate only if one takes telling in its fullest meaning, not if one thinks of it as merely an enumeration of disconnected facts or a surface account of episodes. History is a telling of the past in such a way that one both learns what it was and understands it.

When I say that history uses description, narration, and interpretation, I do not mean to imply that these are necessarily separate parts, following each other in some sequence. Rather, they are components discernible within a unity, one or another standing out more clearly as the occasion warrants, all of them interwoven so as to constitute the whole that

makes known the events of interest. History makes known
a situation or event by displaying various parts of it, by dis-
closing it in several of its aspects, by locating it within a
context of other things, and by exhibiting connections among
its components and between itself and a larger setting. Larger,
more general matters become recognizable and are given substance through the particulars that they contain; particulars
are set forth and given significance by showing ways in which
they belong with each other and to a more general scene.
An account of Renaissance Florence, for example, may set
forth the city's varied political forms and fortunes, its economic conditions, the financial activities of its wealthy fam-
ilies, the relations between social classes, its intellectual and
artistic activity, and the bearing these phenomena had upon
each other. Its peculiar character will be exhibited within the
larger movement of the Italian Renaissance; its relations with
other Italian cities will be discussed; we will hear something
of ancient Greece and Rome and the rebirth of their civiliza-
tions, of relations with France, Spain, and the papacy. Also,
to know Renaissance Florence means to know about Dante,
Savonarola, Lorenzo de' Medici, Machiavelli, Leonardo da
Vinci, and Michelangelo. As one finds out about each of these,
one comes to know Florence; conversely, to understand these
men, one must see them within the larger life of the city.

One way of achieving knowledge of particular objects and
events in history that deserves special mention is comparison.
This is very different from the way we gain knowledge of
individual events in science. Here the individual event is equivalent to a group of properties that define a class of which the
individual is a member and within which it is distinguished
from other members exclusively in terms of variations in these
properties (generally measurable ones), or variables. To give
knowledge of the individual event, one refers it to its class
and pins down its properties. In history, by contrast, the event
is not reducible to a definite group of properties and there is

no one class that will contain it as a particular case. One does, of course, make use of general concepts—it is not possible to do otherwise in language—and this means the momentary treatment of the individual as belonging to a class. Thus one may speak of Renaissance Florence as a city, a republic, a seat of violence, or a center of art. But none of these concepts adequately describes Florence; none can encompass Florence as a case, or an instance. Each one serves to call up some aspect of Florence; each must be given substance by particulars; moreover, some of them will be appropriate only if adapted by modifications, additions, and exceptions. If one thinks this failure to assign the individual to a definite class is simply due to a naïve choice of classes uncritically adopted from everyday life and therefore sets about, in the manner of science, to define a new class that will do the job, he will soon realize that any group of properties selected for the definition is utterly inadequate to account for all the things that make Florence historically interesting. This is simply the consequence of history's concern with the concrete event, in contrast to the reduction of the event in science to a group of abstractable properties.

While satisfactory historical understanding cannot be achieved by tying the individual to membership in a class, a great deal can be done by comparison, a far more flexible method. Its lack of rigidity makes it of preliminary use, at best, in the sharp and rigid scheme of science, but extremely powerful in history and other areas where the "endlessly varied and endlessly complicated"[30] individuality of the subject matter is crucial. The distinguishing characteristics of a situation, a person, or an event can be placed in relief by setting forth resemblances and differences between it and others, by making analogies and pointing to contrasts. This is evident if the entities with which the comparison is made are familiar; but even if they are not, the setting against each other of appropriate entities serves to bring out the likenesses and point up the differences, thereby enhancing knowledge of both. Since comparison does not require that the particular entities be capable of being placed together in sharply and rigidly defined categories—the entity used for comparison being chosen solely because it illuminates some aspects of one's subject or serves as a background against which the subject is set off —it is a versatile and extremely fruitful instrument. Contrasted with the method of classification in science, comparison has less clear-cut definition and more flexibility, less explicitness and more scope.

HOW HISTORY MAKES SENSE

Since historical knowledge manifests a variety of components, we may reasonably expect that there will be no uniform way in which the subject matter of history is understood, that is, in which the things it talks about—situations, events, and people—become intelligible. There is a grave danger for all thought in that one is perpetually tempted to fit things into too simple a mold. For over a hundred years there has been a tendency to interpret history either as being very much like natural science, or as being, on the contrary, entirely opposed to it. Science, imposing enterprise that it is, has so dominated our minds that we have allowed ourselves to be forced into the alternative of either enlisting under its banner or revolting against it.

The subject matter of history is so manifold that we must be prepared to recognize several modes of understanding. Also, just as description, narration, and comparison are not neatly separated, so different ways of understanding history may interpenetrate. There is one thing common to all acts of understanding. When we say we understand something, we mean that in some way it makes sense to us. This may seem banal but is exceedingly important nevertheless. We have varied experiences of making sense of something, of accepting it as intelligible, of feeling that we understand it, of giving it our assent—and many of these, indeed most, cannot be cast into an explicit and adequate set of rules that we can follow step by step on other occasions. As we grow up, we learn many kinds of understanding; we may, if we endeavor and have appropriate guidance, refine them and develop others. To be educated means, among other things, to be able to bring the proper mode of understanding to each occasion. We can talk about these modes, clarify them, develop them, and help others to cultivate them; but they cannot be written up in a book of rules.

Only a prosaic person, I think, will be suspicious of this, and he may point to science to support his position, for in science, it seems, one can say explicitly and precisely what constitutes understanding. The nature of scientific explanation can be (or rather can be to a very considerable extent) spelled out in rules. This, indeed, is a basic characteristic of the scientific enterprise. But there are extrascientific things in the world that need to be understood, and there is no justification whatever for the prosaic insistence that only science or only such modes of understanding as can be equally formalized be admitted to this task. Even in science, principles of explanation cannot be completely spelled out. First of all, one must remember the importance of the person in the seeking component of science: the standardization of scientific understanding applies primarily to the finished product, the completed theory or scientific explanation of an event; its development, the process of seeking understanding, cannot be carried on merely by following a set of rules. Even the product, however, which must meet the very definite and explicit criteria of scientific validity, contains—and is partially evaluated for —elements that are not a matter of rules. Two examples will suffice. One is the entry into science of an element usually thought of as aesthetic. Scientists are likely to refer to it as simplicity, or elegance. They feel that simpler theories or more elegant proofs and demonstrations are more satisfying and that the understanding they give is preferable; they more readily gain assent. Now there are no rules as to what constitutes elegance or simplicity. One can set out rules of scientific explanation, but one cannot set out rules of elegant scientific explanation. Yet a good scientist strives for it and recognizes it when he sees it. The second example is judgment as to which of various types of explanation of an event is desirable. Different groups of properties correlated by different systems of laws may be abstracted to provide scientific cognition, and there is no way of setting out standard principles to govern the choice. Sometimes one type of explanation, sometimes another, will be judged as providing satisfactory, or the most satisfactory, understanding.

Instead of insisting that history conform to an explicitly formalizable scheme, let us try to discern some of the chief ways in which it makes sense of the past. Take a description such as that of a town, village, or building. We are told, for example, the size of a village, its location and delimitation within the surrounding countryside, about the presence of walls, moats, or gates, the number of inhabitants, the location of the houses, and their shape, dimensions, and method of construction. These and numerous other parts of a description make sense in that we can imagine what the objects described and the whole in which they cohere looked like. If we come across further descriptions that do not fit the picture already formed, its intelligibility is disturbed; to restore it, a re-examination of the new data or a revision of the picture, or both, may be required, until a new, coherent, and perhaps more comprehensive conception can be formed.

Another way of understanding is the apprehension of some pattern or order such as is constituted by a routine of daily existence—rising and working schedules, taking of meals, ceremonials—or by the rules and procedures of a social institution or an administrative organization. Here it is the coherence of various elements within an order or scheme that makes them comprehensible. This is related to what was mentioned earlier, the use of general concepts that serve to co-ordinate and make intelligible particular facts, the latter, in turn, giving substance to the concepts. So, for example, the conception of a political unit as a monarchy or republic, a social organization as feudal, or an economic system as capitalist helps to make understandable a great many factors by linking them in a structure. The individual facts cannot be deduced from the concepts in any strict, systematic fashion: capitalism is not a general concept standing for a definite, clear-cut set of specifiable properties defining all particular occasions of it. Rather, the concept refers to the similarities, the overlap of a complex array of manifestations in different individual situations. It serves as a movable beacon lighting up various aspects of a situation and thereby tying them into a pattern within which they make sense.

In the ways of understanding just discussed, the subject matter becomes real to us: we can conceive of the objects, institutions, and customs as real environments and situations of human life. Thus various parts of the physical description of a village fit together to make a recognizable village, a list of daily activities makes up a feasible day's routine, a group of circumstances and practices cohere in something we can conceive of as a republic.

But this view of historical subject matter and its comprehension has so far tended to avoid men's inner experiences. It has directed attention principally to what is close to, though not identical with, Collingwood's "outside" of events. It stresses the kind of things that are amenable to observation by an impersonal spectator, phenomena that are standard, matter-of-fact, and capable of being described quite adequately in terms of rules, activities, or functions connected in some pattern—a routine, a code, or a system of social or economic interconnections. The physical appearance of a village, for example, or the rule of a monastic order, or the system of electing the government in a democracy seems to be intelligible apart from the inner experience of the historical agents to whom it is relevant. This is not true, however, of the greater part of historical subject matter. It is permeated by what people thought and felt, by the plans they pursued, the desires and purposes they had, the pressures and threats they perceived in their environment, and the effects of these on their inner states. Hence, many of the circumstances in which men lived, the things they did, and the events that took place can be understood only in terms of this inner experience. Moreover, if this were omitted, one not only would be unable to understand the greater portion of historical events, but would fail to penetrate to that which is of central importance in human life and hence in history. To use Collingwood's terminology once more, to omit the "inside" of the event makes it impossible to understand the "outside" and also leaves out the very thing that is of greatest interest.

How indispensable the "inside" is to historical understanding becomes evident when one recognizes that even subject matter that seems to be intelligible without it often is so only partially. Several ways of understanding are in fact constantly being drawn upon, with emphasis varying according to the subject matter. Our knowledge of a medieval village, for example, includes the location of its cottages, particularly the fact that they are clustered together, with none, or very few, scattered in the open country. Here is knowledge without reference to inner experience. But it is, to say the least, very partial, and becomes far more satisfactory when one adds that the cottages were clustered in the village because "in most cases it was too dangerous to live far from the hue and cry of one's neighbours." [31] In this light the matter becomes intelligible in terms of human experience. Again, the Benedictine rule for monastic life can be grasped as an orderly scheme for daily routine; but for fuller understanding one must penetrate to the convictions and ideals that it was intended to serve. Similarly, the election procedure of a democratic government, though comprehensible as an organized system of rules, is properly understood only when account is taken of the human purposes it is meant to accomplish.

Inner experience becomes especially prominent when one focuses on activities that clearly involve thought, for example, when one studies any aspect of the history of ideas. The history of social and political thought, of science, or of philosophy is nonexistent without an account of the thoughts entertained by historical personages. Not only is this thought the very subject that is of interest, but also what was done—the "outside" of events—is not understandable without it. The description of a scientific experiment, for example, is incomprehensible without consideration of the thought behind it.

Thinking, however, is not confined to theoretical inquiry and speculation. Since it has a practical as well as a theoretical function, it is an essential ingredient of most human activity. Technology, for example, involves the application of thought to practical problems of human life. Political action requires thinking about prevailing circumstances and about the means that can be used in view of these to achieve envisaged ends. No matter which area of historical events one considers, they always involve thought in some measure. This does not imply that such thought is necessarily careful or appropriate and adequate to its object—or that people always suspend action in order to think before they act; but, rather, that people do think—whether well or badly, carefully or hastily—and that this thinking plays an important role in what they do, so that the concatenation of actions to a large extent lies in their processes of thought.

Two objections to this emphasis on thought must be considered. The first need not detain us at all. It is based on a strictly materialist view of history that sees human affairs as resulting solely from material, especially economic, forces, thus denying all effectiveness to thought. This is a dogmatic position that is patently false to the actuality of man's life. It is false, for example, to itself; for this materialist interpretation is a manifestation of thought—and thought, moreover, that in printed or spoken form influences, and is generally meant to influence, human affairs. The other objection arises from the belief that the claims often made for the role of thought are extravagant. This objection—often maintained by positivistic thinkers whose aversion to rationalism and dedication to empirically observable phenomena lead to great stress on the measurable elements of physical, economic, and social conditions—is partially justified. The arguments are generally directed against positions for which thought looms so large that it comes close to doing away—and sometimes does do away—with everything else. It is important to emphasize, therefore, that there are a host of things in history that are not resolvable into thought. When I said earlier that men's thinking influences their actions, I had in mind—though not exclusively—thinking concerning their physical environment and bodily state; without these factors there is no human life and no history. A drought, for example, may have an enormous effect on men's lives, and it is certainly not the result of thought. Similarly, a plague and its ravages, such as the fourteenth-century Black Death, is a historical event of the greatest importance. All human action takes place within a natural environment that presents obstacles and opportunities. Also, no human action, no matter how thoughtful, can take account of all the factors—natural, economic, social, political, and so on—that might influence it; nor, partially because of this limitation, can it preview all the consequences. Hence the things that happen are never solely the result of thought.

Positivism is right in insisting that there are factors other than thought, but is inconsistent (just as is materialism) when it disregards thought; for positivism pivots about science, and science is nothing without thought. One cannot read a page in any history without having one's attention explicitly directed to men's thinking or, at least, without being told about activities which clearly imply thinking. Most frequently these are activities undertaken for the realization of purposes, such as military exploits, political actions, diplomatic maneuvers, and economic enterprises. All such activities clearly involve thought: ends are conceived (whether single and immediate or complex and far-reaching, whether highly deliberate or quite unreflective), and means are adopted or policies pursued toward the realization of these ends. For example, in the fifth century barbarians were everywhere in the Roman Empire: "Even in Rome, or at the Imperial court, the sons of northern kings were found, who had gone thither to learn the Latin tongue, or to be initiated into the Latin civilization." [32] And in the thirteenth-century Norman empire of southern Italy, the emperor "Frederick's measures . . . are aimed at the complete destruction of the feudal State, at the transformation of the people into a multitude destitute of will and of the means of resistance, but profitable in the utmost to the exchequer." [33] It is obvious that both examples speak of actions that are purposive and involve thought.

So far I have spoken of inner experience only in terms of thinking. However, inner experience consists not only of what is usually called intellect, but also of emotions, sensibilities, and desires; and these also are of great interest to us, and their consideration is necessary for historical understanding, since actions are influenced by them as much as by the intellect. Indeed, the usual complete separation of thought and feeling—as I have argued in Part One and will (on the basis of the intervening discussion) argue again in Part Three—is very misleading. We do not think at one time and feel at another; the distinction of these elements is justified and fruitful, but it is fallacious to treat them as if our consciousness consisted of neatly separated compartments. The nonintellectual parts of inner experience must be attended to in history. Thus, in the example of cottages being clustered in the medieval village because of the danger of living far from one's neighbor, it is evident that fear was effective in influencing action. And the impassioned exhortations of Savonarola and the deeds to which they led were far from being matters only of intellect. Feeling, sensitivity, and emotion are present in all human activity, whether in the realms of art, morality, and religion, or on the battlefield, in elections, in business competition, or in the home.

The fact that men's experience and actions involve thought, feeling, and desire—their inner life—is of paramount importance in history, and we must therefore ask in what way we understand their inner life and the actions of which it is a part. The kind of understanding that must now be added to those previously discussed is the kind considered central by most interpreters of history who take a definitely nonpositivistic stand. To think of it as only one kind of understanding is too simple; it has been viewed in a variety of ways—among them, as re-enactment of past thought, empathy, understanding from within, knowledge by participation, and *Verstehen*. However, it is justifiable in this inquiry to group these views together, inasmuch as they all oppose the assimilation of historical understanding to that of natural science and place emphasis on man's inner life. It is not sufficiently relevant to my purpose and would lead me too far afield to examine the various views and the differences among them. However, there is a basic affinity between all of them, on the one hand, and my own view, on the other, and in developing the latter I shall draw attention to one or two illuminating differences.

SELF-EXTENSION

To understand men's inner lives we must extend ourselves toward their experience of things. We must bring ourselves to them with imagination and sympathy. Drawing on all our resources, all our actual experience, and on understanding previously gained from whatever sources, we try to make present to ourselves and to apprehend others' being in the world: their life situations, their perspectives, their pressures and opportunities, and their desires and purposes. This is what I mean by *self-extension*. In some measure we all do this constantly in daily life. When we want to understand another person or something he did, or when we try to anticipate what he might do, we try to see things through his eyes, to assess them from his outlook, to sense the world as he does. I do this when a friend speaks to me of his life. I do it when a student comes to me for advice. In commonplace and routine situations this extension of oneself to others becomes rudimentary and eventually shades off into the perception of regularities. Thus, the fact that people carry umbrellas when out on a rainy day is understandable to me because I can easily extend myself to their situation—their desire to avoid the unpleasantness of being drenched—but such extension of myself is hardly necessary and is probably rarely, or at most, marginally, experienced: rain and umbrellas are associated so regularly that to see people carry them "makes sense" without any particular effort on my part to understand. Moreover, so many activities are similarly standardized that one is easily trapped into believing that all understanding proceeds in this fashion. But that this is false one can see at once by modifying the example so as to take it out of the realm of routine. If I see someone walking in the rain without an umbrella, I surmise at first that he hadn't expected bad weather. That would make it understandable because the experience is familiar to me—almost standard. But then I begin to extend myself to his situation, I try to imagine what he may be thinking and feeling. If I had no umbrella I would be hurrying along, whereas this man is walking at a leisurely pace. I, too, would be content to walk if I wore a raincoat; but this man has none. I try to see him more fully, and in imagination to experience the situation in which he is. If I were already wet, I think, having been unable to avoid it, I too might resign myself. But just then, when the man's conduct seems to make sense, I see that he is smiling.

All my attempts at understanding the incident have proceeded by extending myself to the other; but the last point, involving an unusual circumstance, may serve to bring this out still more clearly. A very sober and practical person, one who is apt to keep his eyes on the pavement and his thoughts on his bank account or problems of a committee, is not likely to understand this smiling man in the rain. He will probably not be able to grasp the possibility of seeing the world the way the other does, and will hence be unable to make sense out of this apparently senseless conduct. But, by pushing beyond the limits of the usual we can gain new insights, and the man's smile is the clue to the understanding that makes sense of the whole event. It is March, and the rain smells of spring. (I smell it myself now, and I see that the buds have begun to swell.) This man is out in the rain—walking unhurriedly and unmindful of clothes—because he delights in it.

Depending on the situation and our abilities, such a process of coming to understand something of another person and what he does may take a split second or months and years. It may involve thought and inference similar to that in the preceding simple example, or it may proceed with very little deliberate reflection. The more unfamiliar the circumstances and actions, and the more removed other people's beliefs, values, feelings, and experiences from our own, the more difficult it becomes to understand them, and the more capable we must be of extending ourselves to strange territory.

The process I speak of is not one of "losing" oneself in the other person or of trying to be just like him and excluding the experience of one's own being. In the first place, this cannot be done. (Those who appear to change character in accord with the people they are with do not become genuinely like them, but undergo a chameleon-like change of surface or suppress a part of themselves.) Secondly, to be like the other is not necessarily to apprehend him; just as being oneself is not necessarily to understand oneself. (Some people understand themselves far better than others.) Thirdly, if we could be just like another, we would lose the insight we ourselves possess that may be necessary to see and acknowledge things in the other that he himself can not, insight that sometimes enables us to understand him, in some respects, better than he understands himself. Lastly, we would do away with the actual situation in which we and the other meet and in which our being as well as his is included. The process of understanding others by self-extension is the process in which one person turns toward others in full awareness and acknowledgment of their otherness, extends his being toward realms of experience, thought, feeling, and desire that are not his own, perhaps to realms previously unknown to him, and realizes what it is he is doing. To do all this he must also be aware of and acknowledge his own self as it confronts the others; he must, for example, be willing and able to recognize possibilities and limitations in himself of which he was not aware before attentiveness to others brought them into relief.

The core of the process of understanding through self-extension is the same in studying history as in active life. Only, in history one does not confront the people directly; one cannot understand them through actual encounter but has to rely on historical sources, to find a way to them through the precipitates of their lives.

Collingwood, in his interpretation of history, limits the inner life that can be known historically to thought, to strictly intellectual processes. He does so because he believes that the thought of others, specifically of historical personages, can be known completely, whereas other parts of inner life, especially feelings, are wholly irrecoverable and hence unknowable. One comes to know the thoughts of other people, Collingwood argues, by re-enacting them in one's own mind. To discern and know another's thought—a friend's, a neighbor's, or an author's—one must think it for oneself. Similarly, by interpreting the evidence, the historian comes to "re-think and so rediscover the thought of Hammurabi or Solon";[34] he does it in the same way as he discovers the thought of a friend who writes him a letter or a stranger who crosses the street. Every act of thought takes place in a context of emotions and sensations as well as of other, not directly relevant thoughts and is therefore part of an individual's total immediate experience; (for example, as he thinks, he senses the chair he sits on, he feels a pain, he is tired of his work). This immediate experience can never be re-enacted. It is a unique happening in the life of a unique person and as such, Collingwood argues, is irrecoverable and hence unknowable. We shall never know "how Nietzsche felt the wind in his hair as he walked on the mountains; we cannot relive the triumph of Archimedes or the bitterness of Marius." Thought, on the other hand, transcends its own immediacy; it "oversteps the limits of merely local and temporal existence and possesses a significance valid for all men at all times." Though the actual experience of Plato's thinking is unique and not capable of being relived, we can revive and repeat his thought and hence know it; with Collingwood one can say, I "follow it in my own mind by re-arguing it with and for myself." Since thinking always happens in a context, in the setting of some immediate experience, Plato's argument and the re-creation of it in our own minds must exist in different contexts, but so far as we understand him rightly, the process of argument that we go through is Plato's, not only resembling his, but actually Plato's.

This skeletal summary, while very inadequate to the subtlety and penetration of Collingwood's discussion, enables us to bring out a number of important matters. There can be no question that to understand a process of reasoning one must go through it in one's own mind. If, for example, I read the argument of a philosopher that history is an empirical science,

I will not understand what he says without putting myself through the thought process that is articulated in his writing. I must see the problems he raises, his objections to other views, the inconsistencies or inadequacies he points out, his proposals for dealing with them, and his comparisons of thought with practice. Or, if I hear that a grant was made to a university for the purpose of initiating a new educational program, a necessary part of my understanding of this action is to discern what issues the individuals involved faced, what aims they had in mind, what deficiencies they saw in the existing procedures, what alternatives for achieving their goals they might have considered, and why one or another seemed preferable to them. Thus, the thought element of what is said, written, or done is often the heart of the matter that concerns us, and we apprehend it by enacting it in our own minds.

But granting this, I do not see how we can be satisfied with restricting the "inside" of events to thinking. First, men's conduct is never solely the outcome of thinking, but is equally, and often more, the result of feelings, emotions, and desires. Thus, it does not seem adequate to say—as Collingwood does —that when the historian asks why Brutus stabbed Caesar, he means "What did Brutus think, which made him decide to stab Caesar?"[35] It seems equally important to ask what Brutus felt that made him decide to stab Caesar. The singling out of a strictly intellectual aspect of experience implies an exclusivity of connection between it and what men do, and a corresponding divorce between doing and the remainder of consciousness that are inconsistent with experience. Second, we distinguish thinking and feeling within the complex flow of mental life in order to clarify mental life to ourselves. But we err when we suppose that they correspond to a sharp separation within it. To assume such division is an error to which we are frequently tempted in discursive thinking and one that we must therefore be always on guard to avoid, especially in our prosaic atmosphere. To renounce a clear-cut division means

to content oneself with understanding that is less neatly or-
dered but more adequate and truthful. It makes sense to say
that in some activities thought is more heavily accented than
feeling, or vice versa. But the moment we insist on complete
division, on a clear-cut boundary, we are in trouble. This shows
up at once in the disagreements we encounter if we try to
find a consensus as to whether a particular act or piece of
work is the expression of thought or of feeling. We would
probably all accept Collingwood's reference to Euclid's
thought and to our recovery of it, because it has become
common to identify pure thinking with science and mathematics, and because it is the very aim of science to produce
something that is completely independent of men's personal
lives. But when we come to Plato's work, many will insist that it
is not exclusively the expression of thought. Those who believe that philosophic thinking must be modeled on scientific
lines will therefore judge Plato adversely. Others, while agreeing that there is feeling in Plato's philosophy, will claim that
his work would be much poorer without it. The difficulty is
still more evident when we come to Nietzsche. Can we possibly understand him by interpreting his work in strictly
intellectual, impersonal terms? Yet, for Collingwood, there is
no doubt that the writing we have in our hands is "the evidence of what these men thought";[36] and this makes me wonder
whether *thinking* signifies the same thing for Collingwood
as for me, and if he does not perhaps mean to include in it
(though he seems not to) a good deal more than I am disposed
to do in distinguishing it from feeling. The difficulty is aggravated when we speak of the history of art or religion,
because *thinking* alone is certainly unable to do justice to
these realms. Similar remarks apply to political, moral, and
much other experience—just as to Brutus' stabbing of Caesar.

But if we deny the justification of restricting historical
knowledge to men's thinking, we would seem to make this
knowledge impossible. For its very feasibility is maintained

by Collingwood on the grounds that it consists of re-enacting in our own minds others' acts of thinking and that only such acts can be so re-enacted, the other parts of consciousness being unique and irrecoverable. Here, once more, it would prove too long an excursion to enter into Collingwood's argument, and it is only possible to push against it, as it were, in order to develop our own argument, being grateful for his guidance and the demand his cogency makes on us.

Our knowledge of the "inside" of events does not come from a clear-cut process of re-enactment of thought. Such a tidy removal of a train of thought from a person's life and the reliving of it by another person apply at most to certain very restricted areas of inner life, namely, to ideas that can be explicitly and exhaustively articulated and then completely recovered by another from this articulation. This is most nearly the case in science, where everything that pertains to the thought to be conveyed (with the exception of what every competent reader is presumably capable of unambiguously supplying on his own) is explicitly stated. (Even here, though, the process is not always entirely clear-cut, because, for instance, the author may be making unspoken assumptions that a reader is not.) A similar situation is found in other areas, for example, some kinds of philosophical reasoning. Collingwood, in fact, appears to be thinking in terms of this kind of mental life when he mentions Euclid's proofs as examples and when he refers to thought as argument, "simply as itself, starting from these premises and leading through this process to this conclusion." [37]

Most of man's mental life, however, does not fit this pattern. I do not even believe that it holds for Plato, for example, whose thought Collingwood evidently takes to be recoverable; it is probably even less true for Nietzsche. Certainly it does not apply to art and religious expression, nor to most of the things that people have written and made that constitute historical evidence. Rarely do we have an argument "simply as itself," or an explicit articulation of a process of thought that we can completely re-enact. Rarely do we find a thought or argument that can be lifted clear out of all its context to stand by itself, completely statable, self-enclosed, and without essential connection to the rest of inner life.

But from this it does not follow that our knowledge of others' lives is restricted to their scientific, or certain of their philosophic, ideas. It is true that we cannot re-enact other people's actual experience. We cannot actually relive Brutus' experience in deciding to stab Caesar, nor Archimedes' triumph, nor how Nietzsche felt the wind in his hair. Nor do we actually experience medieval villagers' fear of living removed from their neighbors. But this does not mean that all these experiences must remain entirely unknown to us. The precipitates of men's lives that constitute the sources of history —letters and memoirs, documents and inscriptions, essays and pamphlets, houses and furniture, monuments and poems, songs and stories—are avenues not only to arguments like those of Euclid, but also to thought not so bare and explicitly stated (like that of Nietzsche), to feelings and desires, to the rich substance of inner life. We *can* extend ourselves to others; we *can* to some extent see the world as it looks from over there; we *can* reach toward and make sense of others' needs and emotions; we *can* imaginatively recreate and relive some of their experiences, and apprehend them.

For this kind of knowledge, however, we cannot claim the clear-cut definiteness, completeness, and certainty that are more nearly (rarely entirely) ours if we restrict our attention to thought divorced from the rest of life. We are able to penetrate to others, but not completely and never with certainty. The understanding we can gain, however, by acknowledging the whole of man's life is more adequate and more truthful than what we would achieve by clinging to thought, because we do not attempt to isolate a part of life that cannot be so isolated.

The fact that our knowledge of others' inner lives is not clear-cut may appear to some to open the flood gates to historical skepticism. But it does not. Wholesale skepticism rests on a position that allows only two alternatives with respect to knowledge: certainty or ignorance. But this position is not in accord with human experience. Whether or not there are occasions when our knowledge is certain and complete, most of it is not. Yet it would be idle to gainsay that we do have knowledge. We must not sever human experience in order to gain certainty in one fragment of it—a certainty that in fact is illusory precisely because the severance it rests on is unwarranted.

Since there is no clear-cut boundary between thinking and feeling, most of the things men do being the expression or outcome of both, the mode of understanding with which we are here concerned necessarily allows different emphases and shadings appropriate to different occasions. Its essential character, however, is always the extension of oneself to those one wishes to understand. This means envisagement, in so far as seems relevant, of their situation; sympathetic participation in, and apprehension of, their lives; and imagined confrontation of the world with their thoughts, feelings, and desires. By this extension of ourselves, we make sense of aspects of their inner life and of their actions.

GENERAL LAWS AND SELF-EXTENSION

Because of the crucial importance of getting the best possible understanding of the ways by which we apprehend the world and the difficulties that are constantly raised for the modern mind by the prominence of the scientific scheme, I want to consider a few arguments against the view that understanding of men's inner lives comes through extension of the self. Their common burden is that all or much of the understanding that I have asserted to be achieved by self-extension is, after all, secured by quasi-scientific explanation, the claims for which we have previously found wanting.

In order to think as others do, to extend ourselves sympathetically to their lives, we must have a very considerable understanding of the situations in which men find themselves, as well as of what constitutes existence as a human, of what it is to be a man. For example, if we want to understand men's actions in the economic realm, we must know about industry and labor, production and consumption, the market, prices, and profit; in the political scene, about government, local and national interests, mass pressures, prejudices, ideals, rules and their circumvention, and so on. Above all, we must know how people are likely to react to the conditions of their environment; what they are likely to make of, or suffer from, the circumstances that their surroundings and their fellow men present to them. The argument I want to consider holds that such knowledge is simply knowledge of general laws concerning all these matters—that is, science or quasi science—and hence understanding and explanation of actual happenings consists, just as the positivistic interpretation maintains, in the reference of these happenings to general laws.

Another argument comes to the same conclusion from the opposite direction. It does not contend that re-enactment and self-extension rest on general laws, but accepts them on their own and admits that they may be useful, at least occasionally. They are useful, however, so this argument holds, not because they lead to the understanding we want of particular events, but because they sometimes function as a device for suggesting generalizations whose validity as explanatory principles for the events under consideration must then be tested.[38]

Since both these arguments would return historical understanding to the fold of general laws, we must inquire how these laws are supposed to be arrived at by the historian. The second argument allows that some of them could be suggested by sympathetic and imaginative self-extension; but since generalizations so suggested cannot be considered valid until tested (that such tests hardly ever exist has already been pointed out) and since in any case this method of arriving at generalizations is considered to have only minor importance, we must look elsewhere. The most obvious solution is for the historian to turn to the various fields that seek laws concerning human behavior in general and in special kinds of situations. Foremost among the fields would be psychology, sociology, anthropology, and economics.

But leaving aside the important question of whether and to what extent the principles established in these areas are scientific and applicable to the past, it is evident that historians make very little use of these principles. I do not at all wish to contend that the knowledge they provide cannot be useful in history or that more use of them may not be helpful (at least in some areas of historical inquiry), but only that history has been and is being written without much reliance on the generalizations established in these fields. Furthermore, it is clear that these generalizations do not have the unified systematic structure that would permit one, even if one tried, to apply them to the scientific explanation of historical events.

Is there another source of knowledge of general principles? In our daily lives we acquire a great deal of knowledge about how things in the environment behave and about human nature, and this undoubtedly is indispensable for historical understanding. Let us see, therefore, what sort of general principles this experience might furnish. We have already had occasion to mention a few: "People who have jobs do not like to lose them; those who are habituated to certain skills do not welcome change" [39]—"Men generally seek their economic advantage"—"Ambitious generals will get their countries into war"—"Custom . . . controls conduct, but . . . travel, discovery of new lands, or contact with other peoples tends to break down the unquestioning acceptance of custom and tradition." [40] General principles like these, it is claimed, are the basis of historical knowledge. Why then are they so rarely found in actual histories? Because—so the argument goes—they are so commonly known that the historian usually does not bother to state them: it is not necessary, for example, to formulate the trivial truth that "men who undergo great physical privations are for the most part lacking in mental energy," [41] or "the trivial general law that sane persons as a rule act more or less rationally." [42] Such triviality is equally said to account for the fact that laws of a sociological or psychological variety to which the historian appeals are also not stated in his history: for example, the "law of the sociology of military power" that says, "if of two armies which are about equally well armed and led, one has a tremendous superiority in men, then the other never wins"; or the trivial psychological generalizations that explain Caesar's decision to cross the Rubicon by his ambition and energy.

Now it is only necessary to set down these "laws" to see how impossible it is to explain events as particular cases of them. From the point of view of scientific inference, they are so imprecise and indefinite that one can deduce nothing specific from them. Most of them—as is indeed often admitted—are incapable of being tested. Many of them if interpreted as universal laws are false: for example, some people who are habituated to certain skills do welcome change (because they are bored to death with their routine), and travel in new lands often tends to confirm the narrowness of one's own customs. Moreover, the logical status of the "law" is sometimes extremely dubious: for example, there are generals who do not try to get their countries into war; does this violate the law that "ambitious generals will get their countries into war," or shall we say that such generals are not ambitious? In the latter case we do not have a law at all, but a definition of the word ambitious. Further, it is misleading to say that the sociological or psychological laws that are used are "too trivial ever to raise a serious problem for the students of sociology" or to "arouse the attention of a psychologist." [43] I am not so sure about their triviality—in the sense of their being obvious to everybody. But what is more to the point is that no sociologist or psychologist who tried to be scientific would admit them as laws: they are imprecise, ambiguous, untestable, and not susceptible of logical inferences that, through relationship to other propositions or by empirical test, could be shown to be correct or erroneous. In short, for explanation in the scientific manner they are worthless.

In most cases, the "general laws" that are said to explain events are unformulated not because they are so trivial that everybody knows them already, but because they don't exist. When we try to understand or explain events of human life, we do not usually attempt to do so by referring them, explicitly or implicitly, to general laws. The claim that we do misses the principal point of how understanding is achieved in daily life and in history; it is so under the spell of science that it explains everyday knowledge as well as history by explaining them away. It insists that to understand an event means to understand it as an illustration of general principles. But that is simply to deny by decree the main burden of history—as well as of much of our everyday knowledge.

Consider the example of a historian's assertion "that a given ruler acted in a given way because of ambition or from a desire to please his people." [44] The positivistic view holds that, in giving this explanation, the historian has, "of course, assumed that if anyone is ambitious he is likely to act in that way." Now if by this is meant that it was the historian's intention to explain the given act by subsuming it as a case under the known law "Anyone who is ambitious is likely to act in that way," we must demur. The proposition is incapable of functioning as a general law explaining the event, if for no other reason than that the inclusion of the word likely allows the law to be considered true even if the ruler had acted in some other way; statements which cannot possibly be proved false by the facts they are supposed to explain cannot function as explanatory laws. (Moreover, in testing the law, what difficulty would we encounter with the word ambitious!) The historian, in fact, does not have a general proposition concerning ambitious rulers and their actions that he could apply to explain this and other instances.

Perhaps the positivistic contention is to be understood differently; perhaps it means that though the historian may not himself have thought of offering an explanation by inference from a law, his explanation is actually valid only if the general law in question can be asserted. But his explanation is offered though no one has set up, or expects to set up, a general hypothesis the empirical validity of which is to be tested by applying it to the deeds of other ambitious people. The historian has already understood this particular ruler without referring the actions to a general law, and he will do the same with other rulers with whom he may be concerned at some other time. All he has done is to make intelligible this particular act, and there is no reason whatever, and certainly no warrant, for transforming his explanation into a general principle. To insist that whenever something has been explained it must have been done by inference from general principles is to promote a program rather than to affirm a truth. The program requires that laws be exhibited that explain events as particular instances of them; but the laws advanced in support of the program always suffer from one of two fatal drawbacks. One is that a law is so general and so vague as to be incapable of explaining specific events, like the law stating that whenever a large proportion of the population becomes discontent with prevailing conditions, a revolution starts. The other drawback is that to ensure the specific content required for explanation of a particular act, an *ad hoc* law is proffered, tailor-made to fit the act in question—for example, that if anyone is ambitious, he is likely to act in a way that a given ambitious ruler has in fact acted. This, however, is sophistry: it merely carries out the positivist's program by taking (a posteriori) one element of the complete historical account and stating it in the form of a general principle without showing that this principle really is a general principle, that is, that an indefinite number of other events are properly subsumed under it.

There can be no doubt that the historian has to know something of the special areas with which he may be concerned—geography, economics, politics, warfare, and so on —and that he has to have insight into human life. But it is false to suppose that to have knowledge and insight necessarily means to be in possession of general laws. Indeed, he who presupposes this makes it impossible for himself to discover what distinctive features historical knowledge (or any other way of apprehending things) might have, because he starts by ruling them out.

General laws are indubitably one kind of knowledge, and a great many particular happenings are properly understood by reference to them, most obviously those in the realm of the natural sciences. Where general laws are relevant, the historian must appeal to them. Another kind of knowledge, and a very important one, is that which we gather and make use of in our daily lives, the understanding by which we continually orient and guide ourselves. It concerns every realm of our experience: nature, people, and the products of people's work; it has to do with how things are and how people would like them to be, with what is done and what ought to be done, with the conceiving of purposes and the means to realize them, and with the obstacles and opportunities one encounters. The phrase "daily life" is, of course, a very flexible one, since one man's everyday experience differs from another's. Hence the breadth and depth of one's knowledge depends on the range and quality of the daily life one has had. In addition to this, there are a great many areas of human experience not usually included in daily life—for example, those of intellect, art, and religion—from which insight into human life is derived.

It may seem desirable to characterize all this knowledge

more specifically. I have mentioned some of its sources, but what is its form? In what way is it embodied? How is it, or can it be, articulated? These are the questions to which the positivist answers, "General principles." But this, I contend, is false. It is crucial here not to let the prosaic desire for neat conceptual ordering override our attention to reality. The reality is that the nature of men's understanding and insight is not to be seized in a simple formula. Our knowledge of human life, and hence the knowledge required by a historian, is manifold. What some of its modes of embodiment are is a principal concern of our whole inquiry, and it is therefore premature to say much more at this stage. At this point it is essential only to assert that most of this knowledge is not, and can not be, formulated in general principles of the scientific variety. That this is true for the knowledge required not only in history, but in almost every field, is obvious: whenever you say, for example, that someone is an experienced farmer or craftsman or cook or teacher or businessman or artist or critic or scientist or diplomat or general, you credit him with knowledge that far exceeds knowledge of general laws or standard rules.

To understand men's lives and actions, all kinds of experience and knowledge are necessary and helpful, including those found in general principles of the scientific variety and in generalities having to do with daily experience. Among the latter are many of the so-called trivial laws: for example, that people cannot go long without eating, or that they fear death, or that men and women are attracted to each other, or that people generally seek their economic advantage. Besides these, there are general truths stemming from various other nonscientific sources: the truths, for example, that music relies heavily on rhythm, that scientists verify their theories by experiment, and that color is very important in Venetian paintings. Also, there is a great deal of understanding that is not statable in any of these ways.

It is important for us to recognize that most of our knowledge and insight cannot be explicitly articulated in general principles that could be applied to the understanding of a particular historical event without recourse to self-extension. The contrary is often the case: the knowledge we have is the ground, preparation, or instrument for the imaginative extension of ourselves to those we wish to understand. It guides us, provides suggestions, and offers checks. Thus, from the knowledge that someone was ambitious, no specific action can be deduced; but we have some insight into ambition, and this is necessary if we are to extend ourselves to the person involved and imaginatively face the world as he did. We must draw on our knowledge of ambition, derived from whatever source, to aid and guide our effort to penetrate to his desires and beliefs, his being in the world, for it is out of this being that the specific action issues.

Let us return to a previous quotation:

People who have jobs do not like to lose them; those who are habituated to certain skills do not welcome change; those who have become accustomed to the exercise of a certain kind of power do not like to relinquish their control—if anything they want to develop greater power and correspondingly greater prestige. . . . Thus, government offices and bureaus, once created, in turn institute drives, not only to fortify themselves against assault, but to enlarge the scope of their operations.[45]

We have had to reject the contention that the generalizations in the first part of the quotation provide a scientific explanation for the events described in the second part, a fortiori for specific events of this kind. Nevertheless, the account makes sense to us. It does so because it helps us to place ourselves imaginatively in the position of the people involved: the loose generalizations indicate desires, needs, fears, and habits that serve as clues and guides to our self-extension. We ourselves can grasp the fear of losing a job, the force of habit, and the desire for power and prestige.

The claim that re-enactment and sympathetic imagination are only a heuristic device to suggest general laws is false, because such laws serve neither as the sole, nor even as a major, basis of historical knowledge. Indeed, when laws are used, it is often they that serve a heuristic function, just as do the looser generalities in our example, by providing knowledge to help our self-extension. The same is true for many trivial truths and general patterns discerned in various studies, including history. Thus, the generalization that people commonly seek their economic advantage cannot be used to explain in a scientific fashion any specific action, such as certain people casting their votes on the basis of economic interest. The generalization has no specific validity: one can never be sure that it will hold in any particular instance. But it does indicate a tendency, and as such can serve as a guide in the effort to bring oneself to the lives of other people and see the alternatives as they did, and in this way to understand their decisions.

Only thus can one hope to judge whether the tendency held on the particular occasion, because such a judgment requires that one comprehend various aspects of these men's lives, including other motivations that might take precedence over their economic interest. Whatever it was that led to their action (interests, purposes, evaluations, prejudices, or hopes) involved their inner life, the "inside" of events, which must be understood if one is to understand the action. Otherwise the statement of a generality that indicates no more than a tendency of conduct forces the search for evidence and interpretation into conformity with itself. Instead of shouldering the responsibility of trying to understand these particular people and these actions, we squeeze them into a standard pattern whose adequacy to encompass human conduct is not questioned. The actions of men are ignored in favor of exemplifications of general principles. The men themselves are replaced in our studies by nonhuman entities that go through motions correlated by laws in the same way that particles studied by physics do, with no "inside" of events, no experience of thought, feeling, judgment, or will. This is done not because such explanation is warranted by the nature of things, but because it carries out a dogmatic methodology or a specific dogmatic scheme of explanation. We have here a colossal failure of respect for the subject matter, a colossal failure to be truly empirical by those who claim to be using empirical science; for self-extension is the heart of historical knowledge and of its difference from scientific knowledge.

HISTORY AS A WAY OF KNOWING MAN

I have implied earlier that history, in giving us knowledge of men of the past, also gives us knowledge of what constitutes man, such knowledge being an integral part of a history; the historian himself gains much of the knowledge of man he needs for his own inquiry from earlier historical accounts. Yet I have affirmed that knowledge of what it is to be human is a requirement for the study of history, which seems to imply that history itself does not give us knowledge of man, but is only based on, or is only an application of, prior knowledge of man that is nonhistorical. But this would be the case only if historical knowledge consisted of statements about particular events derived from general principles known at the start of the study, that is, if it consisted of deductions entirely suspended from definite beginnings, for such deduced knowledge cannot go beyond what is already contained in the principles. History is not deductive explanation from given principles, however. The historian must have knowledge of man to undertake his work; but as he proceeds and finds out about the past, his knowledge and insight become revised and enriched, and this knowledge raised to a higher level is embodied in the history he gives us; and when we read it, we may, if we read it well and if he is a good historian, gain enrichment ourselves.

We can now resolve a recurrent perplexity. To say that in order to extend ourselves to others we must have some understanding of man implies that men have things in common, for if we had nothing in common with others, we could not re-enact their thoughts or imaginatively see the world as they do. Recognizing the existence of a common humanness at once tempts us to say that our knowledge of it is scientific or quasi-scientific, since the establishment of properties common to particulars is the very purpose of science. But we have seen that this must be rejected as not properly accounting for historical understanding. Also, it is incompatible with the picture of men's lives furnished by actual history, which shows complexity, variability, and individuality of a kind quite foreign to the instances of scientific theory. In a scientific account men must be reduced to a group of abstract properties that obey general laws, and their actions must appear as instances of immutable patterns. Seen this way, men are not beings who, within and upon the matrix of the inevitable and the contingent, shape their own lives by thinking, feeling, imagining, and striving. They are objects going through movements that conform to the fixed regularities of scientific laws rather than agents who can know, judge, decide, and act in the world and who thereby experience lives that can be known historically after they have been lived, but that could not have been predicted by abstract generalizations.

The recognition that a common human nature implied by a scientific formulation is incompatible with history may be thought to deny that there *is* a common humanness—a conclusion that has frequently been drawn in nonscientific views of history, or at least, that may appear to be implied when it is said, for example, that man has no "nature,"[46] no fixed or constant being. However, without a common humanness the self-extension on which historical knowledge depends would be impossible.

The view of history that we have gained removes this perplexity, for it shows that it is false to identify humanness with what can be known about man scientifically. Many common properties, of course, are recognized in scientific laws. But there are other likenesses and affinities among men, other elements that we call human, and they are apprehended and expressed in other ways. History is one of the ways, and the insight into the constancy of man's being that it provides is consistent with variability and change, with human individuality and men's ability (within limits) to shape their own lives. It is this insight that justifies the assertion that history is a powerful instrument for understanding man.

This understanding is not articulated, and can not be articulated in the form of scientific or quasi-scientific generalizations. Its form is description, narration, evaluation, and interpretation of past life. We discover what it is to be man by focusing on particular people and events—ways people have lived, things they have done, difficulties they have encountered and their manner of dealing with them, ideals they have entertained and their realizations and defeats, and what they have thought, felt, wanted, and suffered. In the positivistic interpretation it is assumed that our knowledge of human life must come from sources other than history in order that, on the basis of this knowledge, particular events of the past may be established and explained. But much of our knowledge of man comes from history. In history, the historian's insight becomes articulated. And those who read his history may have their eyes opened to dimensions and possibilities of human life previously unknown to them.

THE HISTORIAN

Our entire discussion of history indicates that it is an enterprise in which the inquirer's personal engagement has a prominent role. The very fact that, in contrast to the natural sciences, history's subject matter is the lives of men makes for an engagement that does not exist with respect to atoms, chemical compounds, or biological cells, for the student of history has an affinity with his subject matter. Dead men, even as we ourselves, bore the joys and burdens of all humans, and we can not be—and dare not try to be—as indifferent to their fate as we are to the collisions of particles or the reactions of compounds.

Furthermore, we attend to particular occasions—*this* war and its suffering and, perhaps, glorious sacrifice; *this* struggle for freedom; and *this* bloodshed—and the concreteness of such occasions engages us in an intimate way. We extend ourselves to the men of the past and to their lives in an actual world, a world where the outcome of events is still unknown, where action can be planned and undertaken to affect the future, and uncertainty, fear, belief, and surprise pulse with actuality.

The historian has no standardized principles, no established system, by which to interpret his subject. He must bring to his study all his knowledge and all his experience from all areas of life. To a very large extent he relies on insight that cannot be explicitly formulated. The depth, range, and subtlety of his personal experience, understanding, and discrimination, therefore, enter in an essential way into his discovery and account of the past. If they are meager, he will not be able to apprehend properly the life whose remnants and records he studies.

Since the historian's interest in his subject matter is directed, not to a definitely limited group of abstractable properties, but to particular occasions, the subject matter is inexhaustible, and every historian, therefore, will discern in it things that his own understanding and concerns lead him, and enable him, to look for. The past discloses itself in accordance with the questions asked of it, and these questions arise out of the present, out of the material, social, and cultural setting to which the historian belongs, and out of his own personality. What the historian himself brings to the study bears not only on the period or even the aspects of the period he chooses to investigate, but also on the way in which his inquiry proceeds. The historian's personal judgment necessarily continues throughout his work—in his selection of what to attend to, in the way he construes things, in the concepts and categories he chooses for interpretation, in his criticism of evidence, and in the perspective he provides for the arrangement and ordering of his subject.

The prominence of the personal element in history is a principal problem for everyone concerned with the nature of historical thought. How, in view of this prominence, can history provide reliable knowledge? The question has often been answered by completely denying the presence of the personal moment. Anxious to protect the validity of history and aware of how often history has been distorted, many writers have asserted that the individuality of the historian need not and must not influence his work. Looking to science and the apparent solidity of scientific facts, they have argued, for example, that history, like science, presents the facts, all the facts, and nothing but the facts. Their arguments, however, stand on quicksand. Science itself does not support their appeal, because it does not give us all the facts and nothing but the facts. And to suppose that the historian can or should present all the facts is simply silly. The facts about any real situation are infinite in number, and no human account can ever contain them. Also, a mere enumeration of facts—even if facts were independent of interpretation, which they are not—without consistent selection, coherent linkage, and evaluation would profit us nothing, but rather add to the ubiquitous confusion that it is a principal task of the mind to combat.

Other writers, cognizant of the indispensability of the historian's personal role and often opposed to the view of history as science, have so emphasized the dependence of every history on the conditions out of which it arises and on the idiosyncrasy and imagination of its creator that one is led to wonder whether history has any valid connection with the past it purports to speak of, whether it is not wholly the product of the fancy of its writer and the preoccupations of his time.

Reflections concerning these matters easily become controlled by the pre-eminence of science, being either unduly attracted by science or repelled by it. History certainly cannot be validated by making it into a science; but this is not a good reason for proclaiming either skepticism or the absolute reign of the imagination. What authority decrees that there can be no knowledge except what passes the tests of science? The aim and subject matter of history rule out the possibility of applying the scientific scheme. The attempt to do so, as we have seen throughout this chapter, fails in two directions: it cannot succeed in placing history on a properly scientific foundation and therefore ends by making it into a second-class, unreliable, quasi science; and it cannot do justice to history, because it does not see, or refuses to grant, history's distinctive character.

But the difference between the two areas does not mean that history is merely subjective or that it shares nothing with science. One of the major motivations of positivistic interpretations is opposition to loose thinking, to vagueness and obscurity, to the bending of evidence for the sake of a thesis, to explanations that are nothing but impressive words, and to the displacement of veracity by sensationalism, chauvinism, or prejudice. These distortions are indeed as subversive in history as in science, but much greater vigilance against them is required by history, because its subject matter makes inveracity more tempting and because it does not proceed within a sharply delineated, explicit, and publicly agreed-upon scheme. The historian therefore bears a much greater burden of personal responsibility for adherence to truth. He shares with the scientist an attitude of painstaking, critical inquiry. He must be respectful of the evidence, scrupulous in his interpretation, and cautious in his conclusions. Also, his work, like the scientist's, must not be influenced by pressure for action. No demand of the moment can be permitted to sway his thought. He must be capable of suspending judgment if he does not believe it warranted by the evidence. History, in this respect, contrasts with judicial procedure. In the establishment or appraisal of an alleged action, it is the court's business to render judgment and to do so as well and as quickly as possible on the basis of the evidence at hand. History must avoid such pressure. Also, the historian must be wary of perhaps the most insidious danger, that of permitting his work to turn into a tool for political activity, which is apt to be governed only by its own interests and is often indifferent or hostile to truth.

In other respects the historian's approach differs from the scientist's, and one must not deny the differences in attempting to overcome whatever difficulties these differences may pose concerning the validity of the enterprise. One cannot establish the validity of history by claiming that it gives knowledge based on verifiable general laws. It is evidence of a misguided yearning for scientific reliability to deny the role of the historian's judgment concerning what to present and what weight to attach to the things he does present. If one tries to eliminate his judgment as a factor by saying that he selects the things he presents not because he himself believes them to be important but, rather, because they actually had important consequences, one simply shifts the problem, because it is still he who must decide what consequences are important, there being no standard set of rules for this. Nor can one sidestep personal assessment by claiming that in accounting for any given situation the historian must present those factors that explain it. This argument eliminates personality only when there is a unified and publicly agreed-upon system of principles of which the particular situation can be shown to be an example. But this is never the case in history. The historian reports the circumstances and events that *he* believes make sense of the situation. Moreover, he is interested in things, not only because they may have had important consequences or because they may explain other things, but because they have importance in themselves. The historian may therefore study aspects that he judges to have been important to the historical persons of the period he is considering or characteristic of it, even though these aspects had no important outward consequences; and he will also select factors that he (standing in his own time and being the man he is) judges to be valuable for his time, or for all time. To discern in the past things that are important for us to know is, after all, a major purpose of history.

All this, however, is no warrant for a doctrine of subjectivism. That the historian selects does not mean that he fancies or concocts—although a bad historian may do so. What he reports must be justified by the evidence. That he stresses certain factors and ties them into a context in the light of his own understanding is no ground for arguing that his account is merely subjective—although it may be. To be valid it must be consistent, must make sense out of the events and situations he exhibits, must be supported by evidence, and, if it disagrees with creditable sources or interpretations, must give cogent reasons for doing so. The fact that we have different pictures of the same period of the past does not necessarily imply that some or all of the pictures are false or that any picture will do. It is a reflection of history's interest in concrete events rather than in a group of abstractions drawn from them. The fullness of reality is beyond any account. All any history can give us is one view of the past, and different views, in so far as they are truthful, are complementary, like sketches of an object made from different angles. This is a major reason why history always has to be rewritten. As men's problems and centers of interest change, so do their views of the past. The questions they ask of it change, and therefore the answers change. All views may indeed be false, but they need not be, and it is the historian's business to see to it that his view is not. The principal danger is the temptation to forget that all human knowledge is limited, to present one's view as if it contained the whole: a view is false if it purports to be more than it is, if it implicitly negates factors not contained in it.

History has one foot in the present and one in the past. We engage in our inquiry as men living now, with our perplexities, interests, concepts, and modes of apprehension; our subject matter, however, is the past. History, therefore, requires twofold validity. On the one hand it must be in accord with the past; it must be an account of what was once real. This is what we usually mean by its truth. On the other hand, history must be effective for the present; it must satisfy our interest in it, illuminate our questions, set our issues in new perspective, or enrich us in some way. The knowledge it gives us is not complete, absolute, or certain; but it is knowledge which is both veracious and valuable.

The personal element in history must be stressed in the interest of truth. A historian who interprets by means of a standard impersonal system distorts the past, since it cannot be fitted into a system. He himself will not discover the ill fit, however, because—unlike the scientist—he cannot appeal to sense observation to verify his thought. His appeal is to historical sources, which require interpretation to yield their meaning, and he may continue to carry on this interpretation within the same ill-fitting system, blind to things beyond it, without discovering its inadequacy. Instead of imposing such a Procrustean scheme, the historian must extend himself with sympathy and imagination to those whom he is trying to understand. Their ways may differ from familiar patterns; to understand their motivations and beliefs may require him to envisage possibilities that he has not encountered before. He must be open to perceive fresh thoughts and feelings underlying works and deeds. A principal aim of history is to free us from the confines of the mere present and from that narrowness of self that results from reliance on the present alone. To understand history is not to reduce the past to concepts and principles dominant in the tiny scope of the here and now; it is, on the contrary, to widen horizons, expand and revise present ideas and ideals, and enlarge oneself by imaginatively experiencing the past. The deeper the historian's personal life, the more adequately he can accomplish this task. To suspend one's feelings and sensibilities is impossible when one is intent upon other men, but even if it were possible, it would be inimical to the acquisition of true understanding.

We tend to think of impersonality as the only attitude with which truth can be sought. But this is not so. The individual's participation with his personal qualities is not in itself an impediment to truth. We are the victims of our use of words in this matter: *impersonality* and *objectivity* have become synonymous with "lack of prejudice" and "respect for evidence," and we therefore infer that a personal attitude inevitably brings prejudice and falsehood. This is unwarranted. What are bad are prejudice, falsification, and distortion of fact. It is the narrow and timorous vision of the prosaic mentality that connects avoidance of these with suspension of feeling, exclusion of emotion, or the absence of sympathy and imagination. It is true that inappropriate emotions may lead to inveracity: emotions connected with pressure for action, for example, may mislead (though even they can be prevented from doing so to a very considerable extent), and such urgency is generally excluded in historical inquiry. It is also true that personal commitments of all kinds—religious, philosophical, economic, and nationalistic—may distort one's vision; but they need not. One cannot avoid such distortion by invoking objectivity and impersonality, for they do not in fact remove one's commitments; indeed they are likely to tempt one to relax incessant watchfulness by fostering the delusion that one has neatly separated his knowledge-seeking self from his personal self.

It is undeniably far more difficult for the historian than for the scientist to prevent beliefs and political or other involvements from undesirably interfering with his work. This is because the objects of the scientist's attention and the kind of interest he takes in them are removed from such involvement. The historian must acknowledge that this is not the case in his enterprise, and he must therefore be constantly on guard. A genuine and sustained openness toward men with other beliefs is as important for achieving veracity in the presence of such involvements as is clear and scrupulous thought. The issue posed for historical truth by the personal element is not resolved by the prosaic expedient of eliminating it or by attempting to make a sharp separation between impersonal thought and personal feelings; the issue can only be met by cultivating the capacity for appropriate feelings—feelings that will allow one to do justice to the lives one is trying to understand. Truth becomes distorted, not because one's inner self is brought to the work, but because one has not cultivated the aspects of the self that are dedicated to truth. In every endeavor man is beset by conflicting interests—and many interests conflict with the interest in truth. The only way to cope with this conflict successfully is to acknowledge it, face it, and hold in balance the tensions to which it gives rise. Sometimes this is extremely difficult. But then, it is too much to ask that truth be easy to reach.

Chapter 9　ART

SELF-EXPRESSION AND REJECTION OF THE WORLD

There have been various views of art. One that is dominant
in our time holds art to be self-expression. We live in a world
that ignores and tramples the human self, a world in which
man's individuality, his autonomy and importance, are jeo-
pardized by mass production and mass consumption, mass
opinion and mass pressure, impersonal process and mechanized
routine. In a world so inimical to the human soul, art has
seemed to many to be the soul's refuge and bastion. In the
act of creation, they believe, the artist can be himself. He is
not forced to suppress his sensitivity and passions, and to
adjust to an automatized, routinized, and depersonalized world.
He can give spontaneous expression to his unfettered self.
One readily understands the attractiveness of this doctrine.

But the doctrine is more than attractive: to many a contemporary mind no other view of art seems valid. One might
suppose that art is chiefly concerned not with the creator's
self but with the world in which the self has its being. After
all, a novel or play presents the lives of other men than the
artist; a poem speaks of earth and water, of sunshine and
clouds; a painting shows people, faces, landscapes, towns.
However, the very idea of an essential connection between
art and the world is anathema to many of our contemporaries,

who maintain that it is not art's aim to make imitations or representations of the world in which we live (especially when this world is felt to be valueless or repulsive, as it so often is today). And in their rejection of representation they reject the world.

But what constitutes representation, especially that representation, or imitation, that is thought to be irrelevant and inimical to art? This is not at all easy to know. The answer would appear to be most evident in those arts in which the work and the world represented are perceived by the same sense, as is the case in the visual arts, in which both a man and a painting of a man are perceived through the eye. Here representation would seem to mean that the painting looks like the object, and the measure of representation would be its fidelity to the way things usually appear to us. If that were so, then the acme of representative art would probably be reached in the photograph. Painting would generally be inferior, because the artist's personality, his impulses and feelings, and his desire for self-expression act as disturbing factors. Moreover, what the camera easily accomplishes in an instant would require very great skill and a very long time for a man to do. Such representation clearly is not the end of visual art. This must be evident to anyone, even if he has only the slimmest appreciation of painting or sculpture: photographic fidelity to what we usually see in life is not what matters. This is true even in such obviously and indisputably representational paintings as those of Leonardo da Vinci, Vermeer, or Courbet.

What about art perceived through a different sense than is the world it represents? What in it constitutes inadmissible representation? No poem, for example, can resemble a rose, the sun, or a face as a painting can. Except for speech, as in a novel or play, no poet can reproduce what his senses perceive. Nevertheless, modern poets also have insisted that connections between their art and the outward world are irrelevant and harmful—indicating that irrelevant connections are possible in poetry even though they cannot take the form of representation in the sense in which they do in painting. This provides a clue to the nature of the connection between art and the world that must be rejected as an aim of painting, poetry, and other arts as well.

We live in constant interaction with the world. We see and hear things; we react to them and use them; we buy, sell, make, and consume them; we perceive them as big or small, cheap or expensive, exciting or boring. In this everyday inter-action we generally regard and treat everything in terms of our immediate practical interests. On a train, for example, the conductor's uniform serves as a signal: we know what to expect of the man; we know what to do when he approaches us, even without seeing the face under his cap. When we look out of our window on a December morning and find that it has snowed heavily, our eyes instantly turn to the street to see whether it has been plowed well enough for driving. When someone directs us to his house, he tells us how many blocks to drive straight before turning, how many traffic lights to pass, to watch for a school on one side and for a garage on the other. Our interest in the world, our awareness of it, and our attention to it are predominantly channeled by tasks to be accomplished and by habitual expectations.

This practical attitude is so ingrained that it is brought not only to daily life but also to art. People commonly approach a work as if its creator's intention were to depict those aspects of the world that ordinarily command their own attention. Their interest is in the recognition of things with a view to their everyday use. They look at a portrait as they do at a passport photograph, whose function is to identify, or at a snapshot that records an instant of their lives. They read the words of a poet as if he meant to describe what they ordinarily see and hear, and to elicit their habitual reaction. In terms of this prosaic approach to art, then, representation is the exhibition of things as they are perceived, dealt with, and reacted to in daily routine.

Clearly such connections with the outward world are possible in the visual arts, and in the verbal arts also, for though words cannot imitate reality in the way a painting can, they can describe it as we customarily perceive it in ordinary life. But such a relation of art to outward things must certainly be rejected: art is not a mere repetition of everyday experience.

The visual arts, in which work and model are perceived through the same sense, are most exposed to this fallacious link with commonplace reality, and it is understandable that in the effort to avoid this link artists and critics have rejected representation and concern with outward things and have espoused the doctrine of self-expression. The spread of photography has played an exceedingly important role in this because for everyone who thinks of the relation of art to things of the world as the representation so readily achieved by the camera, photography makes representational painting obsolete.

In the verbal arts, especially in poetry, the problem is similar, though perhaps not quite so acute. If the reference that words make to the world merely serves to describe it just as it appears to everyday observation, than this reference has no place in poetry; there can be no doubt that poetry's significance must lie elsewhere. And if the world is rejected, then the concern of the poet becomes solely the self. Just as representational elements would then be unnecessary and misleading in the visual arts, so the meanings of words would become irrelevant and a hindrance to poetry, for most of them refer to the world about us.

But this total rejection of the world is unwarranted. It is not necessary, once we have understood that the connection between art and world that is properly rejected is one particular kind of connection, and other connections are possible;

there is more to the world than is perceived by ordinary men in everyday life. This indeed is a principal reason why art is so important: it discloses aspects of the world of which we are generally unaware, aspects that we do not perceive in our daily tasks, pains, and enjoyments.

Another motivation for the rejection of a significant relation between art and world has to do with our attitude toward science and with the fact that our interest in the world is not confined to immediate practical action; we also wish to understand the world, to apprehend it. Is it not possible that art offers a way of apprehending the world, of embodying the artist's vision and understanding of things?

This idea clashes with the notion that science is the sole way of apprehension. What can art have to do in this realm? In the past, it is true, people thought that art articulated men's understanding of the world, that it expressed their discovery and knowledge of reality. But today this belief is widely considered untenable. It is believed that knowledge is the province of science, that art has nothing to contribute to knowledge, and that if it tries, it follows a false path. Art, it is concluded, as far as it is true to itself makes no attempt to apprehend the world. This conclusion usually leads to the rejection of representation, for representation is conceived of as not only a rendition of what we usually perceive, but a rendition characterized by great precision and totality of depiction. Such representation is considered to be the end of scientific knowledge—though this is in fact not the case—and is therefore rejected in art. Thus knowledge and representation are thrown out together as aims of art.

Here, then, is another ground for denying an essential connection between art and the world and for locating art's vital center entirely in the artist's self. The doctrine that art has nothing to do with knowledge commends itself to those whose devotion is to art as well as to the votaries of science. To some of the former it brings—so they believe—emancipation from the objective nature of things, deliverance from bondage to the world of facts, liberation from the duties of the intellect, and freedom of self-expression; to others, who are not happy at this abnegation of the world but feel themselves forced to it by the pre-emption of science, the doctrine vouchsafes a refuge. To the scientifically minded, on the other hand, it appeals as a clear-cut vindication of their claim that science has exclusive possession of the realm of knowledge, for the doctrine assigns to art a purely subjective role devoid of all cognitive power. But though this settlement apparently satisfies both interests and though its neatness is attractive to the antiseptic tendency of conceptual thought, especially prosaic thought, it is a gross oversimplification.

The issue is most acute in the verbal arts because they rely on the same instrument as does science, that is, language. Language refers to things and by virtue of such reference can embody knowledge of them. The literary arts therefore appear to have cognitive content. The belief that they do, however, is just what holders of the doctrine we are considering want to expunge. The rationale for their position is the theory, which was discussed in Chapter 2, that language has two functions: the expressive, or emotive, and the representative, or referential. Linguistic utterances of the representative kind (such as "This book is black") are said to "represent a certain state of affairs; they tell us that something is so and so; they assert something, they predicate something, they judge something": they contain knowledge. This is the function of language in science. Sharply distinguished from this is the expressive function, which is said to be that of most "conscious and unconscious movements" a person makes, "including his linguistic utterances." These movements "express something of his feelings, his present mood, his temporary or permanent dispositions to reaction" and may be taken as "symptoms from which we can infer something about his feelings or his character." Many of these movements, it is said, do not represent anything and hence convey no knowledge. One such expressive movement is a person's laughter: it may be taken as "a symptom of his merry mood." Analogous to laughter, it is held, are the many linguistic utterances that have no representative but only an expressive function: for example, "cries like 'Oh, Oh' or, on a higher level, lyrical verses." [1]

It is hard to imagine a more misguided conception of lyrical verse, of poetry, than one that denies that poetry contains knowledge and so likens it to laughter or exclamation. This conception ignores both poetry itself and what those who write poetry and those who know how to read it take it to be; compare this idea, for example, with Robert Bridges' view that poetry has "the power of concentrating all the far-reaching resources of language on one point, so that a single and apparently effortless expression rejoices the aesthetic imagination at the moment when it is most expectant and exacting, and at the same time astonishes the intellect with a new aspect of truth." [2] The conception of poetry as being expressive in the way laughter is derives, indeed, not from genuine experience of poetry, but from the imposition on poetry of a doctrine —a doctrine, moreover, that is concerned not with poetry but with science and whose chief tenet is the identification of science with knowledge.

We are told that "the aim of a lyrical poem in which occur the words 'sunshine' and 'clouds' is not to inform us of certain meteorological facts . . ." [3] Certainly this is true—we can agree that the poet's aim is not that of the meteorologist. But the writer continues, "A lyrical poem . . . does not contain knowledge." Thus the fact that the aim of the poet is not to tell us meteorological facts is thought to make it self-evident that the poem can have nothing to do with knowledge or with apprehension of the world. Clearly this conclusion rests on the assumption that the only way in which sunshine and clouds can be involved in human understanding is through meteorology or some other science.

Could it be that this assumption is wrong? Could it be that sunshine and clouds may also appear in a different kind of apprehension? The very fact that the assumption leads to an absurd view of art is an argument against it. And so is the recognition that because science is an enterprise with very rigorously delineated aims and methods, there may very well be room for other ways of approaching and interpreting the world. Other ways do indeed exist; history, for example, has cognitive content, yet is not a science.

To summarize the two positions that deny art a meaningful relation to the outward world, the first cedes the world to the commonplace, to practical daily affairs and routine interests and reactions, while the second cedes it to science. Thus severed from the world, art seems to be exclusively an expression of the artist's individual self, of his desires and emotions, and to have the effect of arousing similar emotions in those who contemplate it.

PURE FORM

Before we inquire further into the ways in which the expression of self may be understood, another interpretation must be mentioned. This interpretation, like the doctrine of self-expression, denies art a significant relation to the outward world, but unlike it, denies art's relation to the emotions as well. It insists that art has no essential relation to anything beyond itself, that art is pure form, creation without a link to anything else, utterly autonomous. This thesis is most frequently offered with respect to music, where it seems especially plausible, but in modern times it has also come into favor in the visual arts and poetry.

One reason why advocates of this doctrine reject the expression of emotion in art is that they believe such expression vulgarizes art. They see art used or made for the purpose of arousing the stereotyped feelings that usually accompany the everyday, to induce cheap sentimentality, or to jolt us into vapid and spurious excitement. It is in order to save art from degradation by the vulgar and banal that the pure form view separates art from life and asserts that it has nothing whatever to do with anything beyond itself. This rejection of emotion is analogous to the rejection of the outward world as seen in everyday life.

Another reason for rejecting the expression of emotion in art is to combat the idea that art is a kind of release, or outburst, of the emotions. (This idea of art as an outpouring of emotion is discussed in the following section.)

There is also the fact that viewing art as an emotional expression sometimes tempts the beholder to turn his attention from the work toward the supposed emotions of the artist. The viewer uses the work as a springboard for delving into the artist's private life; he explains the creation in terms of the artist's love affairs or frustrations. But the significance of art is in the structure of words or sounds or colors that the artist has made. This structure is the proper focus of attention in both contemplation and creation, and to ensure that our attention remain there, the pure form doctrine presents the work of art as an aesthetic organization of a sensuous medium without reference to anything external to itself.

The pure form doctrine, as it relates to emotion, is confirmed in the minds of its advocates by their experience of works of art. They assume (fallaciously, as I shall argue) that if a work of art did express emotions, they should be able to describe these emotions, but they find that in fact, every attempt to do so fails. No words—happiness, joy, sorrow, pity —ever seem quite adequate to describe the burden of a particular work. The impossibility of describing the emotions expressed by a work of art proves, it is held, that none is expressed.

TWO VERSIONS OF SELF-EXPRESSION

The thesis that art is the expression of the artist's feelings appears in two versions that are often not clearly distinguished, but that are in fact very different. The first version sees a direct and exclusive connection between the artist's emotions and his art: his emotions are released and poured out in his art. This thesis is very attractive because it appears to do full justice to the highly personal character of artistic creation. It gives free scope to the life of the feelings and insists that these feelings are the very heart of the artist's work. It eliminates all danger of intellectualization or of submitting art to academic rules or empty conventions. For these and allied reasons it has many adherents among those deeply devoted to the arts.

But attractive as the thesis is in these respects, it cannot do justice to art. Indeed, it has much in common with the idea we have already considered, especially with respect to lyrical poetry, that works of art embody no meaning, no cognitive sense, but only allow the beholder to infer something about the feelings of the artist, just as one infers merriment or surprise if a person laughs or cries out. Both laughter and cry are generally the kind of immediate expression of emotion that artistic expression is claimed to be by the view we are now considering. We laugh as we are moved to laugh. We cry out on being startled. Note that we do not, as a rule, laugh in order to express, and convey to another, our mood. The laughter simply comes, and the hearer may infer something from it; the same is true for the cry. In this respect both are analogous to what is usually meant by a symptom—a condition or phenomenon that is an accompaniment or result of something else that can be inferred from the condition or symptom, like the rash from which the physician infers that the patient has measles. It is not surprising, therefore, that a writer who likens lyrical poetry to laughter and exclamation categorizes all three as symptoms. But this grouping obscures more than it clarifies. The same writer also believes that a lyrical poem has an aim, which is "to express certain feelings of the poet and to excite similar feelings in us." [4] And the existence of an aim at once suggests that a poem is a very different kind of entity from laughter and an exclamation.

Their being classed as symptoms obscures this difference. Moreover an expressive symptom—whether purposive or not —from which we can only infer a person's feelings, is not at all the same as a "symptom" that is intended to express his feelings and to excite similar feelings in us. The cry from which I infer a person's pain is not uttered to excite this pain in me. Clearly a conception of expression that does not insist on a difference between artistic expression and the expression represented by a laugh or a cry cannot do justice to art.

The thesis that art is produced by an outpouring of the artist's emotions makes nonsense of the labor of artistic production, the need for skill and discipline, and the modification, rejection, and growth of style. Moreover, it suggests that every man is constantly engaged in activities essentially like artistic creation: every time he "expresses" himself, every time he cries out or laughs, or hits an object in anger, he is doing basically the same thing as Beethoven while composing or Michelangelo while painting.

"To express feelings" is apt to be understood in this untenable interpretation as to vent them, or let them out, that is, as a mechanical process much like the emission of steam from the safety valve of a boiler in which the pressure has become excessive. In this phenomenon consciousness and creativity play no role whatever. In the contrasting version of art as an expression of feeling, other meanings of "to express" move into focus—to set forth, embody, articulate, make known— and with these we really enter the realm of art. A work of art is not simply a concomitant of its creator's feelings, an outburst, or ejaculation. Rather, it must be made, must be shaped so as to be in conformity with the artist's intentions, with the things in his soul to which he strives to give palpable form. The very fact that the artist can judge his work with respect to how well he has succeeded makes it clear that it is not merely an ejaculation or a symptom but is rather an articulation, an embodiment, of something. An ejaculation is whatever it happens to be; an embodiment is adequate or not adequate, genuine or not genuine. This is because the work is not the outcome of the way the artist's succession of feelings happened to issue into some form, but is the outcome of the way form was given by him to something into which he has insight. Hence art as the expression of the artist's feelings implies a factor in addition to that of having these feelings. It implies an awareness of these feelings, a grasping and a comprehension of them. We can readily see this factor in the usual expressions of inner life. When I say, "I am sad," I not only am sad but am capable of recognizing my state for what it is and of finding the appropriate words for it. Often when we try to articulate a feeling, we find that we are not able to do so. We cannot make a shape that captures what is within us, anxious to be born in words. I do not wish to imply here that we first have a complete grasp of what we feel and then look for a way to articulate it, but only that awareness is essential in the articulation of our feelings. The two factors are usually intimately connected in our experience, awareness guiding articulation, articulation clarifying, enhancing, and deepening awareness. Without awareness we could not have the experience of being either more or less satisfied with the expression achieved. Such expression, therefore, is radically different from involuntary movements, physiological phenomena, and many ejaculations. These simply occur as parts of some physical state: they are not formed to articulate something, hence are neither appropriate nor inappropriate and neither succeed nor fail.

The artist, by a process analogous to our usual expression of inner states, tries to give shape to his apprehension. Indeed, the major capability that distinguishes an artist is that he has such command over an expressive medium—words, paint, stone, or sounds—that he can give sensible form to what he feels, whereas others stumble and stammer or must remain mute. It frequently happens that in the contemplation of some work—a poem or painting, for example—we suddenly realize that it is the perfect embodiment of an inner experience of ours to which we have never been able to give form: we recognize in it the motion of our own soul. What was amorphous before is suddenly shaped; what was a vague stirring, an elusive inner movement, is suddenly captured in an artistic structure: we can behold it, we can contemplate it, we can really see it for what it is. Thereafter it may become an instrument of communication between ourselves and others to whom it also speaks. It "says" something. Instead of trying to describe a state or process of our inner life by discursive language—an attempt that very often fails—we refer to the work as its appropriate expression.

Art, then, can express things that plain language cannot—this, indeed, being a principal reason for art's importance. And there is surely nothing surprising in this. Ordinary speech with its words for inner states, like *happiness, sadness,* and *loneliness,* can do no more than mark out certain aspects of experience in a manner more or less adequate for the ordering and communicating necessary in most daily life. These are crude categories that encompass a vast number of individual experiences sufficiently similar to be usefully lumped together for ordinary purposes but otherwise enormously different from each other. Such categories, therefore, convey very little of any particular experience—of its specific quality, shading, tone, or intensity. We cannot expect to find one or several words to characterize properly the complexity, subtlety, variety, depth, and range of any part of our inner life. Words, after all, and even discursive language are not identical with experience, but rather are instruments for ordering, guiding, clarifying, and articulating experience. There is more to experience than can be properly articulated by these instruments. Therefore, the impossibility of adequately stating in plain words the inner life processes expressed in a work of art by no means warrants the conclusion that none is expressed. On the contrary, it is evidence of the enormous importance of art; for without art, with nothing but everyday language, there would be no adequate medium for the expression of most inward life.

APPREHENSION OF INWARDNESS

The observation that a work of art can express and hence reveal to the beholder his own inner experience implies an essential characteristic of art to which so far we have paid no specific attention. In his work the artist sets forth his feelings, impulses, and passions. In this respect it can be said that he expresses his own inner life and that his art is self-expression. But art is more than this. The true artist is not primarily concerned with those aspects of inwardness that are merely incidental in his individual life, and he is not an exhibitionist. Rather, he is concerned with the moments and aspects of his inner life that in some way belong to man as man, that at least potentially and in some measure are a part of everyone's experience. If he sets forth his apprehension of what is only meagerly indicated by the word loneliness, it is indeed his own apprehension rooted in his own personal life; but loneliness is a universal experience, and if the work is good, others will see in it the expression of their own lonely selves. Again, the artist's joy in the rebirth of spring, the expansion of his inner self when once more life bursts forth, is his own joy and is felt, grasped, and meditated on by him in his own life's context; but such joy and such exaltation are not only his, and their embodiment will therefore have significance for others.

The recognition that the artist's work arises from his self and also transcends it, is important but is not enough. It may leave us with the impression that this transcendence rests solely on the fact that human beings resemble each other, so that even though the artist may be absorbed in his own inner states, his revelation of them will necessarily have meaning for others. Surely such meaning is important, though even so the artist must not be too preoccupied with himself lest he so charge his work with what is merely idiosyncratic, merely incidental, that the universal import is obscured—and this may easily happen to a petty artist. But beyond this the genuine artist is actively concerned with penetrating into human life, with fathoming, comprehending, and articulating those aspects of it that he senses are important. He focuses not only on his own life, but on the lives of others. What is embodied in his art is not derived solely from his own actual experience. This is another aspect of the fact that art is not the result of a mere emission of the artist's feelings but is the disclosure of his insight. He gains understanding of other people's feelings, the motions of their impulses and their passions. To do so, he must certainly have rich experiences of his own, for without them he would have no clue to the character of other people's lives; but the human inwardness that he discloses has a range and depth that extend beyond his own firsthand experience of life.

Just as, in artistic creation the work is not simply the symptom or result of the artist's emotions, so, in appreciation the work is not simply a stimulus of emotions. In the first place, to call art simply a stimulus fails to distinguish it from innumerable other emotional stimuli. If, for example, I found a treasured possession wilfully destroyed, I would be thrown into great emotional excitement, but this would not make the perpetrator an artist. In the second place, a good work of art does not simply excite us. The presentation of a scene full of anger or jealousy in a novel or play does not put us into a state of anger or jealousy such as we might experience in an actual human encounter. If it did, we would not grasp the work, for art requires contemplation; it demands a certain kind of repose, a temporary withdrawal from the pressures and burdens of active life. The anger, jealousy, hunger, or fear expressed in art is not ours and is not directed toward us as it would be in actuality: there is nothing we need to do with respect to it, no decision we must make, no responsibility we must immediately assume or reject. We are relieved from the immediate and insistent demands of active encounter and, by virtue of this relief, are enabled to contemplate as we otherwise rarely can. We feel and apprehend the emotions; we behold them illuminated, clarified, and raised to a degree of intensity that we rarely if ever experience in active life and that, when we do experience it, usually makes us quite unable to be aware of what it is that we are living through. There can be no doubt whatever that the contemplation of art is a highly personal and emotional experience; but usual pressures and demands are largely removed, and the imagination plays a dominant role. Our inward life has a freedom to move and expand that it does not usually have, and we see it in this enhanced state, disclosed and made palpable, in the work to which we respond.

In this response our senses come alive, we look and listen keenly. Art offers the occasion for delight in lines and colors, sounds and rhythms. In much of life our senses are lulled by wearisome sameness; or else we are faced by confusion, by a buzz of sensations and disjointedness of events in which we cannot really behold anything because they have no unity or form. In art there is variety and individuality, subtlety and shading, novelty and surprise; there is also structure, order, pattern, and harmony, providing unity and wholeness that we can contemplate and grasp.

In this view of art as the apprehension of inwardness, full justice is done to that essential feature of art it is the central aim and merit of the pure form interpretation to stress. This is the fact that the work of art is a created pattern of sensuous forms, an aesthetic surface, the beholding of which is the heart of art appreciation. But we can recognize and affirm this positive part of the pure form theory without adopting the defensive and untenable claim that art makes no reference to anything beyond itself. The expressiveness of art resides in its aesthetic form, in the specific pattern created within a sensible medium, and the *sine qua non* of contemplation is proper attention to this pattern. Neither in creation nor in contemplation is the work of art a mere correlate of emotions, especially the rather insipid emotions that accompany much of daily life and routine escape from it. Those who think of art in this way do not approach it with the ability and desire to move in a new realm of experience that transcends the commonplace and has extraordinary qualities and levels of feelings and sensibilities. Confrontation of a work of art leaves them fundamentally unchanged. Instead of expanding their selves to reach the work, thus attaining new understanding and sensitivity, they reduce the work in typical prosaic fashion to fit into their usual frame of experience, allowing it to function only as a stimulus of the emotions of everyday life or of the emotions they are unable or afraid to acknowledge in everyday life and therefore suppress. They do not really behold the work itself, they almost ignore its aesthetic surface. Their attention is on the needs and dispositions of their everyday selves rather than on the object of contemplation. They are not sensitive to the pattern of sensuous forms that constitutes the work and through contemplation of which alone its real significance can be grasped.

But we must not combat this false linkage of art and emotions by denying that there is any link at all between art and inwardness. And it is equally unjustified and misleading to postulate an entirely new class of emotions—aesthetic emotions—that are supposed to belong to art and to have nothing whatever to do with the rest of life. Such total separation between art and life does not exist. The fact that the inner experience expressed by art cannot be adequately described by general concepts does not warrant the view that it is totally different and disconnected from other spheres. Each of these solutions—that of no inner experience and that of purely aesthetic emotions—is advanced in opposition to a false approach to art, and in fighting that approach, is shaped by it. Both try to save art by completely denying its links with life. But art has significance only when it relates to life.

APPREHENSION OF MAN'S BEING IN THE WORLD

So far I have spoken of the relation between art and inwardness. In the doctrine of self-expression we have seen an emphasis on art's essential roots in the artist's self. It is true that art is an expression of the self, but art is not only self-expression, and therefore the term is dangerously misleading. Works of art are the articulation of the artist's comprehension of man's inner life.

What about art's relation to outward things, to what we sometimes call the objective world? Must such a relation be ruled out? The interpretation of art as the embodiment of inwardness appears to have no place for it; some of the arts —for example, music, or purely decorative design—whose patterns of sounds or of shapes and colors make no reference to the outward world, seem to fit readily into this interpretation. The validity of the interpretation comes into question, however, as soon as we turn to the verbal arts, which very often refer to the outward world, and to the major part of painting and sculpture, which is pervaded by representational forms. These arts seem to proclaim that a relation to the world is essential. But this relation, as we have seen, is odious to many modern minds, and they therefore interpret these arts in ways that deny, or at least drastically diminish, the significance of the relation.

The extreme position holds that such a relation is completely irrelevant and hence pernicious. The work is a created form with no essential link to anything beyond itself, and therefore the referential power of words and the recognizability of visual shapes are nothing but obstacles to the true nature of art, shackling its proper powers. A more moderate view accords the outer world a certain instrumental role. In this view, whatever else the work may be, it undoubtedly is a very highly organized entity, the very antithesis of mere jumble: structure, order, and form are its core. This is by no means to say that these forms must be simple or that they must be of some given type, but only that without form there is no art. To create is to shape, to give form to a medium. The role of the outward world, so this view holds, is to suggest forms. The world of nature and of man is an inexhaustible source of all kinds of forms and patterns—shapes, movements, sounds, and so on—and the artist uses them (though without in any way being bound by them) as organizational elements of his medium. The sole function of such forms, however, is to provide diversity and unity of aesthetic pattern: the outward world itself that they describe, represent, resemble, or suggest is said to have no relevance to the work.

A greater significance is sometimes accorded to the world once the relation of art to man's inward life is granted, for the artistic use of elements of the outward world is seen not only to provide formal organization but also to express human inwardness. It is obvious that human actions in a play, or the presentation in a novel of events and situations involving people, are at the very heart of the work. And in poetry, painting, and sculpture it is evident that the human figure, the human face, situations and events from active life, man-made objects, animate and inanimate nature, and countless other elements of the outer world have a significant role for the artist as he expands, explores, and reveals the dynamic processes of inner experience.

Even in this interpretation, however, which affirms an important connection between art and the outer world, the outer world occupies a position subsidiary to inwardness, which is the focus of interest. The world about us, the universe in which we have our being, is only an instrument for the articulation of inwardness. The artist looks to what is outside himself only to discern forms in which his inner life can be expressed.[5] The rushing of rivers, the hushed murmur of summer afternoons, the human body, the encounter of lovers, these and the infinity of things around us are alluded to or depicted only in order to give palpable shape to inner life.

Now this, I submit, is a very strained view of art. It supposes a separateness between inwardness and the outer world that is not in accord with human experience. It is as if we had an inner life quite independent of the world, as if our thoughts, feelings, emotions, and desires existed, or could exist, hermetically sealed from the world; and as if (despite this isolation) we could then turn to the world in art in order to express this isolated subjectivity. But surely this is not the case. Our inner life is a part of our being in the world. Fear of death is not something independent of the world: we have seen death; we constantly see it in the decay and dissolution of things. Love is not merely inward, merely subjective: it is a relation of the self to something beyond. Joy and sadness are not sheer inner states divorced from the world: they are movements of the soul toward and away from otherness; they occur with meeting and parting, communion and loss.

Art is the embodiment, not of sheer internality, but of man's being in the world. "For the sake of a single verse, one must see many cities, men and things, one must know the animals, one must feel how the birds fly and know the gesture with which the little flowers open in the morning. One must be able to think back to roads in unknown regions, to unexpected meetings and to partings one had long seen coming; to days of childhood . . . to parents; to childhood illnesses . . . , to days in rooms withdrawn and quiet and to mornings by the sea. . . . One must have memories of many nights of love, . . . of the screams of women in labor. . . . But one must also have been beside the dying, must have sat beside the dead in the room with the open window. . . ."[6] Art is concerned with the outward world as well as the inward. It sees men's faces as well as their affections. It sees nature and the change of seasons; it hears the sound of fading footsteps and the clamor of voices. It sees man's life in the world, in churches and taverns, in toil and feast, sweating and singing.

Art erects no walls between inner and outer. In our prosaic outlook we are used to supposing that there is a sharp division between the two. In science, it seems, it is the outward world we apprehend, separate from the human personality, independent of inwardness. And in ordinary practical activity what we use, control, or avoid appears to be the outer world, entirely separated from us. Yet even here the division is not so simple. What we attend to in practice is relevant to our purpose; we select the aspects we deem important; we co-ordinate and manipulate for the furtherance of our aims. And in science we look to the world with a view to finding a definite order that our minds can grasp. The facts of science do not simply exist by themselves, independent of human consciousness. They are what is disclosed when attention is directed to a given area; they are the content of a field of human interest, the answers to questions.

Nevertheless, while a complete separation does not exist in practical affairs and science, it is true that in them the relationship between inner and outer spheres is very limited. In art, however, to suppose that any cleavage exists is completely mistaken: there is no detachment of the self from the world. While intensely heedful of the outward world, art apprehends it in the light of its import for inwardness; intimately concerned with inwardness, art sees it as infused by the outward world. What matters is the rich and varied human relation to the world, man's whole being in the world: the way he fares in it, and the import, meaning, and significance he sees and feels in it.

The degree of attention to outer and inner spheres, however, varies among the arts and, within a given art form, among styles and individual works; and so does the nature of the relationship between the work and the inner and outer spheres. In music, for example, there is, in general, no direct connection with the external world. Yet the inner life that is expressed in music is the inwardness of men who live in the world. The growth of tensions and their resolutions, the rhythms and repetitions, the interweavings of voices, the breathtaking soaring and the calm repose, the grave procession and the headlong leaps—these are the palpable shape of the inwardness of beings who live in and with and against the world. The painting of a man or a landscape, on the other hand, refers directly to the outer world, depicting its visual shape. Yet these shapes as depicted bear the imprint of inner life, of the pressures and promptings of personal import, of the thoughts, emotions, and visions of a person in his complex relation with external reality. The work of art arises neither from the artist's self alone nor from the world alone, but from his encounter with the world. It presents us with new, intense, and significant ways of being alive—of sensing, thinking, feeling, and acting.

Representation in art does not mean representation of the world as it usually appears to us in everyday life. Nor does it involve giving knowledge of a scientific or quasi-scientific kind. One must not be misled by the fact that artists and writers about art have made contrary assertions. *Science* has not always meant what it generally means today: it used to mean knowledge in the largest sense and not only knowledge gained by the particular method of empirical, or natural, science, whose prototype is physics. Also, the word scientific when used in connection with art has often meant "very attentive to the world as given in perception" or "intent upon correlating art with reality" (in nineteenth-century Realism and Naturalism, for example). With these meanings it may indeed be used without making art into quasi physics (though at the risk of misleading oneself, especially today). The same is true when *scientific* is used to mean "opposed to the idealizing or romanticizing tendencies in art" or "wishing to pierce the ruling pretensions and falsehoods of society and to disclose the commonplace, ignored, and base." But some artists who have claimed that they conceived of their art as scientific have explicitly meant something closer to the more specific phrase "empirical science"—for example, that their art should be pursued as "an enquiry into the laws of nature." [7] However, their actual, often very fine work does not fit their declared intention. This paradox may be resolved by the observation that the intuitive notion of art that informs a good artist's creative activity seems frequently and understandably superior to his philosophical formulations about art.

Vasari's comment that Leonardo was able to paint things just as they look in life does not imply that the ordinary man, or the scientist, for that matter, would usually see them this way. If you looked closely at Mona Lisa's throat, Vasari wrote, "you might imagine that the pulse was beating." [8] But usually we do not see someone's throat with such intense awareness. Nor would we be moved to imagine the pulse by looking closely at an anatomical diagram. The power of artistic representation is that it gives the viewer new and intimate apprehension of the world. Once Leonardo made a painting, according to Vasari, "with some marvelous flowers, the dew upon them seeming actually to be there, so that they looked more real than reality itself" [9]—more real, that is, than they usually seem to be. Why do they usually seem less real? Because we usually live in ignorance of the concrete world; our perceptions are channeled and standardized, and our sensibilities are torpid. The reason we have such desperate difficulty in understanding the import of representation (and have degraded it to something essentially nonartistic) is that we are all but totally divorced from the world. It no longer seems to make sense for man to turn to the world to behold it with rapture and amazement; but such beholding is of the essence of human life. Art heightens our awareness and gives experience the vigor of freshness. It holds and deepens our attention. It invites us to see and to hear, and to respond to what our senses perceive with inner aliveness, with depth and refinement of feeling, intensity of passion, clarity of vision, and unfolding of imagination. It draws us to the world, it calls forth wonder.

THE PARTICULAR AND THE UNIVERSAL

Art is keenly concerned with the particularity and individuality of things on all levels: colors and sounds, shapes and textures, and all their nuances; natural and man-made objects, and men themselves in their complex uniqueness; particular events and situations in the outer world; the infinitely varied configurations of inner experiences—of moods, feelings, images, thoughts, and desires.

Art's individuality is manifested first in the work's specific pattern of sensuous elements. Each good work has its distinctive individuality in which every peculiar feature, striking or subtle, is an important part of the whole. Look at a painting and see how crucial is every large and small element of the composition, how even a tiny area of a certain color is necessary for balance, vitality, or accent. Note how a poem depends on the cadence, the rise and fall of the voice, the repetition of a sound; or how important to a piece of music is a change in tempo, a particular interval, or the ineffable tone quality of the oboe or cello.

The individuality of art manifests itself also in another way. The pattern created by the artist and contemplated by us is the embodiment of a particular apprehension that the artist has gained. It makes palpable a particular way of experiencing the world, a penetration into some of its aspects, or an insight into inner states. Thus poetry can depict the sensory world— a bird's flight, the wind in trees, or the touch of a hand—so that we experience it imaginatively with a clarity, intensity, and intimacy that far exceed our usual experience. A painting can present a branch of a flowering tree, a horse, a garment, a ceremony, or a human body or face with a vividness, a power of presence, that makes us see as we almost never see in active life unless we ourselves know how to be aware of the world with the sensitivity and penetration of the artist. It makes us sense the "thereness" and reality of these things so that, as Vasari said of Leonardo's flowers, they seem more real than reality itself. Music can poignantly express the infinitely varied and intricate undulations of inwardness.

In citing these examples I have spoken as if inner and outer spheres were separate. It is almost impossible to avoid such separation in expository prose. But for art, as I have said, this customary conception of things is not adequate. Thus, a vivid depiction of a bird's flight includes as an inextricable ingredient the event's human significance, the feelings we see embodied in it. A harvest scene is ears of wheat, sun, crows, sky, men scything and men resting in the shade of a tree; at the same time it is everything that harvest means for man's life. The feelings and longings embodied in music have behind them the world that we endure and love. Hence the individuality with which art is concerned is the individuality neither of the outward world alone nor of inwardness isolated from the world, but of a human experience, of a man's concrete being in the world.

It is implied in the foregoing that art, while characterized by particularity, also transcends it. The work is not merely the reflection of a particular moment in the artist's life: it arises from his whole personality, from his experience of many things and many occasions, from his intensive perception and study of aspects of human existence that he deems important, from his entire vision of the world. Even a portrait or biography, whose particularity is perhaps more pervasive than that of any other form of art, extending as it does beyond the work itself to the specific person portrayed, has an essential significance beyond such specific portrayal. In the first place, it is not a recording of an accidental, momentary appearance but an interpretation of a personality, of an individual's self; and secondly, it not only is an image of this particular individual, but it contains the artist's understanding of matters of human import as they peculiarly manifest themselves in this individual. Think, for example, of Rembrandt's "Man with a Golden Helmet."

Complementing this wider significance of the artist's work is the fact that it speaks to many men. The artist's particular view of man and the world, and his understanding and insight become, in some measure, those of the beholder. He gives us the embodiment of experiences that might become more universal. His new and personal vision may become the vision of others. His creation presents a realm of being in which others can share.

It is fundamentally important to realize that this universality, which is essential to art, is obtained without forsaking individuality. The universal is in the particular, and the beholder of art apprehends it only if he attends to the particular with the immediacy and intimacy it invites. Thus, looking at an Impressionist canvas we apprehend the harmony, iridescence, and colorful richness of things bathed in light, by experiencing these qualities in contemplation of that particular work. A tragedy—say, *Hamlet*—shows us the weakness and dignity of man in showing us the weakness and dignity of particular men. Music explores and enhances man's inner life, not by giving us universals removed from individual contexts, but by presenting us with particular occasions of immediate experience. Generic words for experience, such as *affirmation, longing, fulfillment, sadness, exuberance,* and *joy,* are indispensable in the totality of our mental life, but they are only thin, abstract indications of what we can apprehend in music by immediate personal response to a highly individualized, sensuous form. It is permissible to speak of music as being abstract if one means by this that it does not refer to specific objects and events of the world; but it is not at all abstract in the way science or, even more pertinently, mathematics is. A mathematical work completely lacks the powerful and penetrating sensuous value of music. It is not an individualized entity inviting immediate experience; it has no vital effect on us, no personal impact; its words, terms, or written notations, expressing its logical relations, are not interesting in themselves. They do not arrest us. We look through them, so to speak, to the universal meaning they convey. In music, on the other hand, as in all the arts, universality is not seized directly but reverberates within our vital, sentient experience of the individual work. A great artist so shapes the work in all its particularity that its universal significance shines forth and can be grasped by the beholder.

FORM AND MEANING

It is widely believed that wherever expression is given to some meaning, the meaning can be separated from the form into which it is cast. We have already met this belief at various points in this book: what is said is one thing, and the way it is said is another. But however justified this belief is in other areas, it is not appropriate to art. The assumption that it is, is generally conjoined with the further, prosaic assumption that all meanings are susceptible of being expressed in literal propositions of discursive language. Hence, works of art are supposed to have a content that can be extracted from them and stated literally—perhaps a plot, a set of ideas, a social or political view, feelings, moods, moral notions, or religious thought. The work is treated as a kind of container for this message. The purpose of the artistic container is to make the message more convincing, palatable, or accessible, or to provide entertainment and relaxation along with the content. Sometimes the work is prosaically looked at as a problem or a challenge to the intellect, a cryptic rendering of an idea that must be dug out, and intellectual satisfaction is derived from the process of analysis and detection. Sometimes the artistic form is considered an embellishment, a sugar coating, which sterner and more disciplined and sober minds would prefer to do without.

The idea that form and content are separable fits the prosaic view that art represents things as we experience them in ordinary life, for such experience can usually be expressed without art in everyday language; hence art becomes merely another way of saying the usual things. Belief in such separability and the notion that all meanings can be expressed in literal language can also lead, and frequently do lead, to the belief that art has no meaning at all. For if it did have, its meaning could be paraphrased. But how, for example, could one paraphrase the Shakespearean sonnet that begins, "When I have seen by Time's fell hand defaced / The rich proud cost of outworn buried age"? Has time a hand? Can cost be defaced or an age be buried? If these lines are regarded merely as a fanciful way of saying what can also be said straightforwardly, then this rather ordinary meaning would seem not to warrant the fanciful poetic garb. Hence it is concluded that there is no meaning in art, that it is a mistake to expect ideas, insight, or content of any kind, and then either of two interpretations of art that we have already met is embraced. The first of these interpretations assigns art exclusively to the subjective realm and at the same time denies that the expression of inwardness has meaning; the second interpretation concentrates on art as pure form, as a pattern of sensuous shapes without content.

But as we have seen, there is no justification for assuming that if art expresses something, if it has a meaning, we must be able to say what this meaning is. This assumption imposes a set of ideas on a reality that is not in accord with them. Art embodies meanings that cannot be removed from the individual work and put into another form; hence, specifically, art embodies meanings that cannot be paraphrased in plain prose.[10] It is fallacious to approach art as if it had a content that could be extracted from it and stated in a different, especially nonartistic, form, and it is just as fallacious to deny such extracted "meanings" by denying meaning altogether. Such denial deserves our sympathy, because the meanings it declares to be unacceptable—vacuous, vulgar, or unbelievable—are indeed unacceptable. But the denial must nonetheless be rejected, because while recoiling from the consequences of certain presuppositions—separability of form and content, and the all-sufficiency of literal prose—it accepts the presuppositions, which are themselves false.

A work of art is a highly individual entity made by its creator to embody his apprehension of things, and it demands from the beholder a sensitive response. Its form is not merely a convenient, startling, or pleasing wrapping for conveying a meaning; it is the only form, or embodiment, of the meaning. What the work discloses is to be found only in contemplation of the work itself; if we say that it expresses the predicament of human existence, the endlessly varied presence of nature, the mystery and pain of love, or the rise and fall and intertwinings of inner life, we do not mean that these are messages or ideas that can be extracted from the work. These expressions are apprehended in contemplation of the work, in our immediate, imaginative experience of it. As paraphrased ideas, as concepts, they are bare indicators, thin abstractions. In art they are caught alive, they have substance and density. As we experience the work, every one of its elements matters; every aspect enters into our response, aiding or hindering it. Hence no part of the work can be changed, no translation can take place without altering—and if it is a good work, diminishing—its significance.

The danger of looking for messages is most acute in the verbal arts, for in them the temptation to extract meanings in terms of literal statements is greatest. Such extraction of content from the artistic form and its paraphrase in plain prose would seem to be accomplished by simply regarding the words as functioning the way they would in literal statements and ignoring such aspects of the work of art as rhythm, connotations of words and their sound, and imagery and figures of speech as constituting the artistic form and having nothing essential to do with meaning. But the writer has not put into an artistic form a meaning capable of being stated in a non-artistic form, a meaning that the reader or listener must in turn extract if he is to understand the work. Artists have often protested that they do not know what their work means, or that it contains no ideas. Goethe's reply to those who would ask him what idea he sought to embody in his *Faust* was: "As if I myself knew it, and could articulate it." [11] Mallarmé insisted that a poem is made with words, not ideas;[12] and MacLeish has written: "A poem must not mean / But be." [13] I believe that the common significance of these utterances (not necessarily exactly the one that the writers themselves had in mind) is that a meaning cannot be adequately stated independently from the work itself. Goethe did not know what his *Faust* meant in the sense of having written it to embody an explicitly formulizable idea; a poem is not made with ideas in the sense that it is not a container of ideas separately conceived in literal language; a poem does not "mean" in the sense that one can point to a nonpoetic statement and say that this is the poem's meaning.

From all this, however, we are not justified in concluding that literary art has no content or that its content is unimportant. To deny the validity of paraphrased meanings is not to imply the absence of meaning or that art is nothing but emotional ejaculation or a pattern of sensuous forms. To say that a poem containing the words *clouds* and *sunshine* does not aim to convey meteorological knowledge is not to imply that it aims to convey no knowledge at all. *Clouds* and *sunshine* are capable of conveying other than meteorological meanings.

The views of Goethe, Mallarmé, and MacLeish imply stress

on the work itself, its own form. That is where the meaning is to be found. The work is created in its own peculiar shape to express the artist's intentions, and it discloses to the beholder whatever it has to disclose and whatever he may be capable of apprehending through itself, not through some other medium in which an extracted meaning is spelled out.

Poetry, and all literary art, embodies its meaning by drawing upon all the resources of language. The sense of words is flexible and open; it alters with context, has different weights and shadings according to specific occasions. Metaphor, imagery, repetition, rhythm, and sound all interact to produce a work's total significance.

Similar remarks apply to the visual arts, whose representational power is often mistaken as merely serving the prosaic purpose of identification or of description with quasi-practical or quasi-scientific interest—all these supposedly constituting the extractable meaning. But representation in fact functions in intimate conjunction with line, color, texture, and other factors, and the work's meaning is inseparable from them.

The denial of content or meaning in art—which stems, as I have argued, from the mistaken assumption that such meaning is necessarily an extractable idea—is, of course, intimately related to the rejection of a connection between art and anything beyond art; for the connections that are rejected are always connections that belong (or are supposed to belong) to nonartistic realms—ordinary life, practical affairs, and science. They usually involve meanings that can be stated literally (like descriptions of things, verbal or verbalizable, from the standpoint of practical interests), knowledge about things that properly belongs to science (like meteorological facts about sunshine and clouds), or expressions of emotions that correspond to verbal labels. Such prosaic descriptions, knowledge, or expressions, it is true, are not what connects art to the world. The proper connections—those that do belong to art and without which art would lose its significance—reside inextricably in the individual work, which relies on all the resources of its medium and on their complex and fertile interactions.

THE EVOCATIVE POWER OF ART

How does art enable us to grasp concrete individuality? To understand this properly, we must remember that our awareness of individuality depends not only on what confronts us but also on our approach to it. For even when we confront a concrete individual—a person in our daily life, for example —we are very likely not to be aware of him as an individual, but to notice him only for the function he discharges—as service-station attendant or bank clerk; we view him as an embodiment of the abstraction "service-station attendant" or "bank clerk." Because the nature of our approach to the reality before us is crucial, it is essential that the work of art allow and invite the appropriate approach. This requires expression by some means that is very different from strictly literal language, whose very nature is to focus on and make explicit sharply defined abstractable properties of things and whose only approach to individual concreteness is exhaustive compilation of such properties—an impossible endeavor.

Art does not even attempt exhaustive statement; it evokes individuality by educing imaginative response. It does not spell out and lay bare what is to be seen, heard, felt, and understood (that is exactly what is impossible); it elicits concrete experience in the beholder.

To return to Shakespeare's sonnet:

> When I have seen by Time's fell hand defaced
> The rich proud cost of outworn buried age;
> When sometime lofty towers I see down-razed
> And brass eternal slave to mortal rage;
> When I have seen the hungry ocean gain
> Advantage on the kingdom of the shore,
> And the firm soil win of the watery main,
> Increasing store with loss and loss with store;
> When I have seen such interchange of state,
> Or state itself confounded to decay. . . .

The responsive reader will have experienced a vivid image, an immediate and poignant sense of the terrible and inevitable destruction and decay of all things with the passage of time. The poem does not give us a detailed description, a lengthy enumeration of the transient things of this world, or a summary, abstract, and generalized statement such as "nothing lasts," which by itself is a truism that conveys little. Instead, with all the powers of poetic language the poem summons destruction before our imagination and evokes its particulars to our mind's eye and ear. We have the feeling of experiencing it; we are imaginatively in the midst of its fury. The words do not spell out clear-cut properties of the "interchange of state," thereby channeling our attention to elements that are abstracted from the reality. Instead, they make a few selected particulars grow and radiate so that the interchange, in its tumultuous and terrifying actuality, is immediately apprehensible by our imagination. The words are not connected to neatly demarcated areas of reality as though by single threads, as technical terms are. Rather, their denotative meanings are ample, and their connotations draw a host of things into our experience, giving it substance, density, and poignancy, and calling forth reverberations, memories, and feelings; the structure of sounds interacts with meanings to create the very tumult of ceaseless change before our minds. Once more, we are not explicitly told, through a group of abstractions, just what constitutes change and decay, but change and decay are suggested in such a way that our experience is full and concrete.

Imaginative, personal response and the fact that art does not lay hold of its content in an explicit, exhaustive fashion are complementary. Understanding something that is stated explicitly does not permit imaginative, personal response. On the contrary, such understanding requires us to make our minds follow (sometimes not an easy task) in the strict paths that have been set out for us. There is no individualized experience here—only what can be made completely public. Whatever is so expressed and communicated is there, complete and uniformly illuminated in all its facets. Once we understand it, we understand it completely and have nothing further to gain from repeated reading. But in art, where meaning is suggested, not made explicit, imaginative, vivid, and personal response is mandatory. And because the work of art is not an exhaustive articulation of something that can be apprehended completely, we can return again and again (especially if the work is great) and find that it continues to give new insight. There are no strictly delineated paths to a final goal. We cannot be told what to do, we must do it for ourselves, but always in conformity with the art. We must live our personal experience while having all our attention on the work. It calls for our fullest personal engagement.

Art is the source of an experience that reverberates through a person's whole self. Here and there it illuminates our perceptions with a flash of incandescent brightness; or it spreads a penumbra and discloses intimations; sometimes it strikes a penetrating blow or sometimes gives peace like a gentle caress; occasionally it lifts us to sudden and convincing insight that can only be held as a shadow in the memory. Art is concerned with that realm of being in which we sense ourselves filled with what cannot be named, with experiences that are as real as anything else we know—or more so—but fleeting, that are powerful, strange, intimate, and wondrous. It is concerned with the pulsating, variegated, and rich process of human life in which the sharp separations to which conceptual ordering tends to give rise are inadequate, where contrasting states (exaltation and pathos, joy and melancholy, vitality and repose) interpenetrate and are indivisible, where things have fullness and movement.

RESPONSE AND LISTENING

As we read, hear, or look at a work of art, it calls upon us to *respond* to it. Response, as we shall see, is essential not only in art but also in other areas of human life, though its particular form varies. To respond is to relate to a person, object, or situation making a demand upon us. The demand may be in the form of an actual address to us, or it may be inherent in the sheer existence before us of its source. The response may involve an overt answer in words or actions, or only an inner movement. In contemplating art we make no overt answer, and our response has only what may be called a receptive component, not an active one. But receptive response must not be thought of as merely passive; it requires a great deal from us, and it can be very exhausting. The best understanding of it is provided by its manifestation in the realm of hearing: *listening* may be considered a paradigm for all other receptive responding, or for the receptive component of all forms of response. When we really listen to someone or something, we do all we can to enable him or it to reach us. We minimize interfering sounds and remain silent ourselves. We try to hear fully and to be sensitive to the import of what we hear. For this we need inward as well as outward silence, since we are also kept from hearing by the clamor of plans, fears, and other voices of our own selves. Listening at its fullest is like trying to hear a very soft sound, like stilling ourselves and even stopping our breath, the better to hear.

Like listening, responding in general involves the utmost attentiveness. You are aware of an other before you and do all you can to be receptive. Such attentiveness requires that you check all interests and impulses that tend to divert you. It means that your own self must be carefully contained so that it will not obtrude, erect barriers against or obscure what there is to receive, or seek to dispose of it or dominate and control it in any way. You must be able to meet what comes without restlessness and impatience, to quiet any urge to turn away from it or to do something to it. To respond to a work of art, you must actively live yourself into it, imaginatively taking part in its movement, attuning yourself to its vibrations, allowing it to touch your thoughts and affections, faithfully following its suggestions, and tactfully and discerningly giving to it your personal self with all the richness of your experience.

It is important to distinguish the immediate and emotional character of the response to art from the kind of immediacy and emotional engagement that frequently characterize ordinary life. The inner life is not the same in receptive response as it usually is in situations in which the pressures of the world actively impinge upon us. To contemplate the terrible fate of Lear is quite different from being crushed by such a fate ourself. Indeed the ability to contemplate requires the temporary absence, or at least lessening, of the exigencies of nature and society (or the contemplator's ability to hold in abeyance the weight of existing exigencies), and of the thoughts, affections, and desires connected with them. Life situations that have pressing implications for our well-being and that engender the desire to control, use, or avoid things tend to preclude or render very difficult the responsiveness requisite for art. Strong sensations permeating the bodily self with instant pleasure or pain distract attention from the work. Any situation that directs attention chiefly to our own self and hence away from the work of art throws the artistic approach out of balance. Art, even at its most intense and most powerful, must never be so shocking or violent that it drives us away, but must always draw us toward it and permit or even invite our response. The mere indulgence in feeling without sensitive and refined attention is not response, even though it be stimulated by a work of art.

The recognition of this difference between response and the kinds of experience so frequently found in ordinary life is one of the principal reasons for the propounding of "removal theories" of art, which assert that art is a completely autonomous realm removed from the rest of life. In order to appreciate a work of art, it is said, we must forget everything else, we must leave behind the concerns, feelings, and thoughts of life. The emotions that belong to art are aesthetic emotions and have nothing whatever to do with others. "As art becomes purer," Roger Fry has written, "it cuts all the romantic overtones of life which are the usual bait by which men are induced to accept a work of art." [14] The beholding of a work of art supposedly takes place in a realm in which the presence of anything from outside this realm is an intrusion.

This issue is evidently the same as one met earlier, in the discussion of the connections between art and things beyond art. I argued then that the denial of all connections derives from the legitimate rejection of connections inappropriate to art (such as ideas about the world that belong to science or ordinary practical interests, or habitual emotional reactions) and from the mistaken supposition that other connections are unimportant or even impossible. False connections are linked with improper approaches to art, and the removal theories properly reject such approaches.

These theories, however, are most commonly directed against the "ordinary man" [15] whose "aesthetic sensibility" is comparatively weak. Also—since not all works of art are good and many gain their appeal to the aesthetically insensitive public by exciting emotions that most people experience (or would like, but fail or fear, to experience) in ordinary life— the theories are equally directed against artists who, because they are "too feeble to create forms that provoke more than a little aesthetic emotion, will try to eke that little out by suggesting the emotions of life." [16] The objections of these theories to the degradation of art are of the greatest importance; but an interpretation shaped primarily by opposition to the incompetent is bound to be misleading. It places far too much emphasis on matters that ought to be taken for granted, and it thereby gets badly out of balance. Certainly art is not the same as most people's everyday life. There is a difference between the passion and sublimity of a late Beethoven quartet and the feelings evoked by events of practical or sentimental interest. The paintings of Titian or El Greco are not pretty pictures like those in advertisements. Good literature does not, like pulp magazine stories of rape and murder, seek to excite readers into momentary escape from their usual boredom and frustration. But once we realize that people's failure to see the true significance of art is due to their aesthetic insensitivity, to their prosaic approach to art, there is no longer a reason for keeping art away from life; to do so is like keeping a garden from sun and rain in order to discourage weeds.

Each experience of art, to be sure, is unique. What we feel in listening to a symphony is not the same as what we feel on other occasions; the experience of looking at a painting of toiling peasants is not that of toiling ourselves. Not only that: looking at one painting is not the same as looking at another, for each work is unique and can be grasped only in immediate experience. Uniqueness, however, does not imply removal or isolation. Our experiences, awarenesses, and apprehensions interpenetrate, and their mutual relevances are vital to the meaning they have for us. Take a simple example from daily life: there are friends for dinner, and my wife has prepared a fine dish. I enjoy it. I enjoy it because it tastes good, and that in itself is valuable. But there is much more to the enjoyment. The dish not only tastes good, but pleases the eye by being artfully served, and it is preceded, accompanied, and followed by others that together make the harmonious unity of a meal. Moreover, there are the joys of partaking together of the yield of the earth and of conversing, exploring ideas together and reminiscing about similar occasions in the past. Each element has connections with the others. The sensation of taste, for example, is not the same as the feeling of hospitality, but is not therefore isolated from it. If I see a tree in the autumn heavy with fruit, my feeling is not the same as the feeling I had when I saw it in the spring, radiant with blossoms. But they bear upon each other. What I feel in autumn has to do with the fulfillment of the promise of spring and also with spring's passing; what I feel in spring has to do with the anticipated fulfillment in autumn and also with the fact that these blossoms must fade. Again, when I love, I love an individual, and my love for one person is not the same as my love for another. Yet these loves share common ground and affect each other. Also, each love is what it is by virtue of all the experiences that bind me and those I love; and each experience is what it is by virtue of our love.

Similarly, experience of art is connected with all of life. My experience in listening to a Mozart piano concerto (I have purposely adduced an example from music because it is the art for which the removal theory would appear to be most adequate) is certainly an experience associated with that particular piece of music, and in that sense some might say that it is a unique aesthetic emotion. But being aesthetic (associated with a work of art) and unique does not mean being without bonds and connections to anything. The concerto's sunny, dancing themes evoke a response that echoes with feelings from other light-hearted, sunny, and joyous moments. The Olympian grandeur of some parts embodies a mood that I have fleetingly known on other occasions. And the agitated strings, the intimate, serious, yet gentle song of the viola, are the shape of anguish and longing.

The artistic experience is an enhancement and transmutation of our life experience. This indeed is its office. Often, feelings and insights are but latent in active life and emerge into full being only in art. It is as if the life experience were vague, inchoate, and elusive; and needed art to give it form and make it more real to us. Listen to Bach's "Magnificat," and you will come to know what exaltation is, by experiencing it. Moreover, as the experience of art transmutes and enhances our life experience, so the latter is necessary for art. The more deeply we live, the more profound becomes the significance of art; and the greater our understanding of art, the more penetrating may become its enriching effect on the rest of life.

Part Three: WHOLENESS

Chapter 10 UNDERSTANDING AND APPREHENSION

A chief cause of the current diminution of understanding and reason, as discussed in Chapter 1, is the prosaic belief that every effort to know, articulate, and communicate must have certain definite characteristics. These characteristics are inherent in science, though this is not always recognized, and they are not necessarily appropriate to other modes of understanding, which may have different, and often opposing, characteristics. In this chapter I want to examine some major modes of understanding and the wider realm of apprehension in terms of a number of basic characteristics, making use of the conceptions of science, history, and art developed in Part Two. Several of the issues that are important in this chapter have been examined at length in those earlier chapters, and I shall only recall them, as a rule, for my intention here is to place them in a synoptic view that I hope will provide new clarity, stress, and meaning. Other important matters were only implied or touched on earlier and will be amplified here. At the beginning of our study, in Chapter 1, the concepts understanding and reason pointed to the realm with which we are concerned. This realm will now be indicated more adequately by the concept *apprehension*.

MODES OF APPREHENSION

Knowledge, Ortega y Gasset properly insisted, is an integral function of life.[1] Man finds himself in the world and seeks to grasp it. Only by drawing its baffling complexity into some kind of order can he orient himself, act, and live. Moreover, man feels that the apprehension of reality is essential to meaningful existence. He finds himself placed in the universe—a part of it yet somehow apart from it—an entity surrounded by other entities that have their own natures and that issue a compelling call to him to seek them out. In the midst of an inexhaustible and perplexing world, living by it, against it, and with it, he strives for apprehension. This striving has no one encompassing and exclusive path to follow; different kinds of apprehension are appropriate to different parts of life.

Because a contrary view is so prevalent today—that one way of apprehension, science, is the best or even the only way—it is essential to understand why other ways are necessary. This can be made clear by an example from everyday life. Suppose that you are a scientist and that you made a trip to London last week. Suppose that someone asks you why you made the trip and you reply that you went to give a lecture at a congress of scientists. Your reply probably constitutes a perfectly good and truthful explanation: it provides the inquirer with some knowledge about your action. But this knowledge is neither scientific nor quasi-scientific. (It belongs to no branch of science; it is not derived from any system of scientifically verifiable principles; nor is the event it concerns repeatable.) Indeed, the major portion of the knowledge and thought by which we conduct our lives is not of the scientific variety.

The objection may be raised, however, that the knowledge I have adduced as illustration is not really knowledge; that it may indeed have its uses—at least now "when science is not yet sufficiently far advanced" to deal with all events—but that real knowledge about your trip would have to come from science, and that such knowledge is possible, at least in principle. I will later consider the question of whether events of the kind I have mentioned are indeed explainable, even in principle, by scientific method. But at the moment I want to inquire more generally into what constitutes knowledge. The objector might claim that the explanation of your trip could be obtained scientifically—in principle at least—once all the relevant biological, psychological, sociological, and other laws had been found and brought into a coherent theory; or perhaps he might say that your going to London could—in principle—be accounted for by physiology, or perhaps even by atomic physics. Let us grant this claim for the moment. But when will this claim be realized? When will we have this scientific knowledge? Will it be ten years from now or a thousand years or never? Anyone who knows the vast difficulties encountered in scientific explanations, even in situations that are infinitely simpler, will bet on the last. Therefore, what relevance has this claim to the reality of your life? Clearly, none whatever. Such claims for science manifest obsession with one approach to knowledge, an obsession by which the very purpose of this approach and of knowledge in general are eclipsed and suppressed. For knowledge is an integral part of life. An event such as the one we are considering must be understood as well as it can be *now*, while those whom it concerns are still concerned. The knowledge of it that science is claimed to be able to discover in principle is no knowledge at all. It does not serve a human purpose; it has no place within human life.

This is not to deny the legitimate requirement that existing gaps in truly scientific knowledge be accepted until they can be bridged properly. If scientific judgments are rushed, the result is likely to be pseudo explanations that, besides being scientifically untenable, may stop the search for scientifically valid explanations. In the situation we are considering, however, there is no question of inappropriately completing incomplete scientific knowledge. It is instead a matter of providing a different kind of knowledge, a knowledge that is relevant to human life as it is actually lived.

There is a second way in which the claim to scientific knowledge of such an event of everyday life neglects the very purpose of knowledge—and of science as well. The task of the mind is to comprehend, to seek meaning and order in the staggering complexity of the world, to apprehend reality, and to illuminate man's condition as best it can. The kind of illumination one seeks must depend on the purpose at hand and on the life context in which the mind does its work. There is no absolute system of knowledge to which one must conform at all times. Knowledge-seeking is a human activity, and man must direct it in the light of his whole condition. Even if scientific knowledge of an event in someone's life were possible in principle, and even if the relevant theories were no longer in the realm of principle but were already in existence, and even if the applications of these theories to the particular event were feasible—even if all this were the case (and in fact none of it can be taken for granted)—the explanation of the event by this "scientific" scheme would be so unspeakably complicated that, far from furnishing our minds with order and comprehension of what calls for understanding, it would plunge us into total chaos. A "scientific" explanation in terms of the huge, practically unimaginable number of variables that would have to be brought to bear (from such disciplines as physics, biology, psychology, sociology, anthropology, and economics) would be no explanation at all, and certainly it would not be scientific—even if the question of how scientific each of the disciplines involved is, were ignored. Scientific explanation is not achieved by piling variable upon variable. The essential character of science is eroded if one abandons the subsumption of events within a small and sharply delimited group of abstractions. Science seeks a uniform, systematic, and elegant ordering of things. A "scientific" explanation of an event of everyday life, such as the hypothetical trip to London, would not provide the mind with order but rather would threaten it with insanity.

Why should we be compelled to seek to understand everything in terms of the schemes and categories of the empirical sciences even when these schemes are not suitable? After all, the ultimate criterion of any mode of apprehension is that it satisfy our minds. This satisfaction of the mind, of course, must not result from easy, undisciplined, or uncultivated acquiescence. I certainly do not mean to imply that whatever comforts us is knowledge. The satisfaction of the mind must include cognizance of the hazards to which knowledge is subject and attention to appropriate safeguards. In the example that we have considered, the mode of explanation normally used in the conduct of everyday life satisfies the demand for understanding; science does not. Science and what may be called everyday understanding are distinct ways of grasping reality. Everyday understanding (a term similar to "common sense" but more appropriate to my purpose) is not merely—as is often maintained—crude or obsolete science. It may, and should, profit from science, but it has its own character and place. Often it resembles history more than science—though generally life's urgency forbids the application of all the cautions and safeguards of historical inquiry. Hence the question that was postponed earlier, whether science could even in principle explain events of the kind we considered, must be answered in the negative. Just as history cannot, even in principle, be made into science, so everyday thought cannot be.

THE ROLE OF METHOD

Modes of apprehension differ with respect to the importance given to method. I use *method* in a large sense, to mean a systematic procedure, an over-all scheme. As such, method occupies a pre-eminent position in science. In comparison with it, the subject matter, the object investigated, is secondary. The object is of interest in so far, and only in so far, as it submits to the method. Adherence to rigorous method makes science what it is, gives it its peculiar function and power.

But pre-eminence of method is not appropriate to all apprehension, and to make method pre-eminent everywhere is a prosaic distortion. In areas other than science there is relatively greater emphasis on what is to be grasped, and therefore the way it is grasped must remain flexible. The way must be adapted to the subject matter. Both history and philosophy, for example, have this character. We are pulled between what we seek to grasp and the means of doing it. Both are important, and neither can be neglected; but the thing we want to comprehend takes precedence. Thus, the way to a historical understanding of the general social or economic circumstances of a period is not the same as the way to an understanding of unique events, of personalities and their actions, or of religious and moral experience. Thus, symbolic logic and philosophical elucidation of the character of science properly proceed in a manner much closer to scientific thought than can philosophical reflection on art or values or man. In the arts the approach is still more flexible and the very notion of method can easily be misleading.

The advantage of flexibility is obvious. We do not subject ourselves to a rigid scheme, but do our utmost in each new situation, in each meeting with something in the world, to grasp what confronts us, to penetrate it, express it as justly, truly, and adequately as possible. But flexibility also exacts a price. The apprehension achieved does not have the rigidly systematic coherence of science, and the reliability of an established and tested method is to a greater or lesser extent forgone. Recognition of this price is very important. It has a sobering influence, which combats the dangers of carelessness and distortion. But we have also to know that flexibility is worth the price.

Science, hence scientific method, is characterized in all its facets by clear-cut boundaries. The subject matter is sharply delimited; attention is restricted to a definite group of abstracted properties; the phenomena under consideration are regarded as separated, indeed isolated, from the rest of the universe. Whatever is known is sharply divided from what is not known, each bit of knowledge constituting, as it were, a smooth-surfaced block. Whatever is of interest is stated explicitly—what is said, and nothing else, is what is meant; technical concepts pin down rigorously defined ideas; the meaning of terms is closed and rigidly delineated. The goal of science is always uniform and sharply bounded illumination.

Clear-cut boundaries are so important in human life and hold such enormous attraction that it is extremely tempting for many of us to adopt the prosaic insistence on them, and extremely difficult to admit that there are other valid and necessary ways of approaching the world. But there are.

Consider first the question of subject matter. We cannot delimit historical subject matter by clear-cut boundaries. We cannot treat any period of the past as if it were isolated from other periods, or a locality as if it were isolated from other localities. We cannot sharply separate one or more aspects of a historical situation—economic, political, social, intellectual, or religious—from other aspects. We cannot confine historical knowledge to a sharply defined group of abstractions without either turning away from what is of historical interest or falsifying it.

Philosophy is similar. Reflection on any one subject reaches out to other subjects. An inquiry into the character of history, for example, requires attention to such matters as science, art, language, values, freedom, purpose, and human nature. We can stress one matter or another, but we cannot isolate it. Indeed, we understand each one better and better as we elicit revealing relations to others.

In art, we are even further from the scheme of science. Whatever is expressed, portrayed, or shown reverberates with innumerable experiences and reaches out to them by a wealth of suggestions and evocations. No sharp boundaries exist between what is relevant and what is not relevant, what the work is concerned with and what it is not concerned with.

Consider next the ways various realms are structured. Scientific knowledge is piecemeal knowledge par excellence. We go step by step and add piece to piece. Each piece, like a smooth-surfaced block, is sharply demarcated, and it is connected to other pieces solely by a definite set of clear-cut links. We know where each argument starts, what precisely it accepts from other blocks of knowledge or else postulates as hypothesis, and we proceed with it in the way we draw a line from one point to another. It is easy to know when a piece of knowledge is finished, when everything has been said that needs to be said. We know (or we think we know, for sometimes there are assumptions or limitations of which we are not aware) just exactly what we have. In this way scientific knowledge achieves security and approaches a kind of completeness and perfection.

To have experienced the clarity and security of a step-by-step advance, to have learned to appreciate its perfection, is extremely important, for it teaches us to reject desultory and muddleheaded thought. But it is very tempting to demand the same procedure in all realms of mind, to refuse recognition to any other apprehension of the world. To yield to this temptation is to solve a predicament of human existence by ignoring existence, by playing ostrich.

As we live, we again and again require understanding. We sense a tension between ourselves and what we want to apprehend, and we strive to apprehend it by whatever ways we can find. Often this striving cannot end in a tidy, clear-cut piece of knowledge. Often the tension cannot be resolved neatly and completely as it can in a problem of geometry with its Q.E.D. Often, indeed, we do not have a sharply bounded problem that can be solved. If we insist on a tidy resolution of the tension, we maim what we wish to know by reducing it in prosaic fashion to a clear-cut problem with clear-cut answers reachable by clear-cut steps. Or if, instead of imposing a piecemeal scheme, we admit that there are things outside its scope, but embrace the antiseptic doctrine that these things cannot be apprehended at all, then we turn away from the reality of human existence: we seek escape from the inexhaustible, uncertain sea of life within the secure boundaries of a pool.

The clear-cut boundaries of science, we must remember, are not simply inherent in the world that science studies. We must not suppose that science has discovered this tidy order and that other human enterprises still flounder because they have not heeded the news. The blocklike scheme, the step-by-step advance, are a method. Science is an enterprise in which men *choose* to seek piecemeal knowledge—and it is a successful effort. But this does not mean that everything can be comprehended in the same way or that what cannot be so comprehended cannot be comprehended at all. Clear-cutness, security, and piecemeal perfection are possible because everything refractory to them is deliberately excluded. Other modes that are less concerned with a definite method and more with what is to be apprehended do not permit the successive addition of smooth blocks of knowledge. Instead of resembling a mechanism with its separated, clearly defined elements, they are more like an organism, the members of which interpenetrate. Instead of achieving relatively complete and neatly bounded pieces of understanding, they seek to enhance and deepen understanding. Instead of advance by discrete steps, there is gradual growth and enrichment, as various aspects, relations, and ramifications unfold. Instead of the continuity of linear argumentation and exposition, there is illumination of one thing and then of another and another. Instead of single demonstrations, there are approaches along various directions, from which patterns emerge. Instead of dealing with piece after piece, each complete as far as it goes, we return to look at the same topics with different stress and from various vantage points; we see foreshadowings that may later acquire more substance; we recall ideas that yield new significance because of a difference in context or by virtue of intervening disclosures.

History does not have a mechanical structure. Its various parts do not constitute separate, clear-cut elements, but interweave with other parts, each being what it is by reason of its presence in a context and becoming imbalanced or distorted if removed for isolated inspection. The portions of a historical exposition—sentences, paragraphs, and chapters—reflect upon each other, require each other, and work together in mutual support, modification, and amplification, radiating their import to each other. Thus the historian may speak first about political conditions, then about the economy, then social organization, then family life, and so on; but in doing so he must be mindful that what he deals with in each part interacts with every other part, that what he wants to say about political life, for example, must be understood in the light of economic conditions and family life, and that therefore the area indicated by the flexible concept "political life" must be made known by referring to it in various places in different contexts. A section marked "political conditions" signifies emphasis rather than clear-cut demarcation; other sections with different emphases also cast their light on political conditions and provide fuller and more valid understanding. By the same token, any one historical account enhances our knowledge of a period but is not complete or final. Again, our exploration and understanding of the past draws upon, and is permeated by, our understanding of all of life, while at the same time it enlarges this understanding. Each penetrates the other; each enriches the other; each gradually grows and develops.

A similarly organic structure is found in philosophy. The piecemeal, stepwise advance of science is generally not appropriate. The subject matter of philosophical inquiry cannot as a rule be lined up neatly like beads on a string. There are so many relevant issues—so many matters whose bearings upon each other, whose cross-connections, are important—that no straight-line sequence is adequate. Linguistic expression is one-dimensional: one must say one thing after another. But the straight-line connections between adjacent statements alone cannot possibly do justice to the complexity of the subject and to the manifold relationships to be discerned. In science, essentially one-dimensional arguments are possible because we choose to look for, and restrict ourselves to, this kind of coherence: we abide by this method and apprehend whatever can be apprehended in this way. In other areas, where we wish to understand other things, we must create other patterns to grasp them as well as we can. So, for example, philosophical inquiry sometimes begins with a summary statement that is bare and skeletal; then the inquiry begins to unfold. It moves in one direction and then another; it raises objections and explores them; it adduces examples; it amplifies; it exhibits implications; it elaborates connections with things said earlier; it modifies earlier ideas in view of intervening thought. Gradually, our understanding acquires substance and density.

Just as parts of an inquiry require other parts, so the understanding of most philosophical thought requires some prior experience with the subject. We must know something of what the philosophical exploration will enable us to know better. The exploration does not add a sharply bounded piece of knowledge; it enlarges, corrects, refines, and deepens our knowledge. The better our knowledge when we begin to read a philosophical work, the better we are able to understand what the writer has to say. Hence we may return to the same work at various times and derive from it insight we had failed to gain earlier. This is quite unlike science, where the understanding of a proof, a theory, or an explanation is a much more clear-cut affair. We understand or we do not. Once we understand the matter, there is nothing more to be understood by a later return. In science, knowledge is added to piece by piece; in philosophy, it unfolds, grows, and matures.

The arts are even further from piecemeal structure than are history and philosophy. Whatever it is that may be distinguished as a part of a work of art belongs intimately with the other parts. All parts are full of mutual interpenetrations and reflections. Each is permeated by the presence of the others. Each is itself, possesses its own nature, and makes its contribution only within the whole. This becomes especially evident when we consider those parts of a work of art that have the greatest measure of self-containment, or separation from others: for example, the acts of a play, the chapters of a novel, the stanzas of a poem, the movements in a sonata, or the objects or regions represented in a painting. Even here, the very identity of each part reaches its fulfillment through its relations to other parts of the whole.

Again, the meaning of a work of art is not something that can be placed within definite boundaries. It is not, as in science, something we can get hold of completely, so that the work has nothing further to give us. The richness of a great work of art is inexhaustible. What we perceive on any given occasion depends inextricably on what we bring to it. Each new experience, each return, may permeate our whole vision and grasp of things, give them new depth, and transmute them.

In trying, as I am doing, to elucidate the structures of non-scientific modes, I realize how difficult it is to conceptualize them and hence to make a place in our thinking for anything other than piecemeal, blocklike structure. The moment we hear of the parts of anything we tend to think of independent pieces or blocks that can be separated from other pieces or blocks without losing their identity. We tend to form concepts that are rigidly closed and to project these closed concepts onto the reality that is to be grasped by them. Thus a part becomes a smoothly bounded piece in a set of pieces—like a part of a mechanism. Thus the relations between parts of a work of history, philosophy, or art become clear-cut links, like lines in a diagram or connecting rods in a machine. The only kind of order and pattern we are then inclined to allow is the kind that, in the mental world, reaches its acme in science and, in the material world, in the machine.

This difficulty of conceptualization is a special instance of the limitation of a mode of apprehension, here, of a certain kind of conceptual thought. The limitation becomes especially constraining if we permit this thought and the language in which it is embodied to be too strongly attracted by qualities that characterize science, that is, if we insist on thinking of things in clear-cut and explicit terms. The difference in structure of various modes of apprehension is analogous to the difference in structure of various languages. The ordering and understanding of things we achieve varies with the language. Each has different capacities to seize and express man's experience. Each has limitations. What one language does well, another may do poorly. To learn a new language is to gain access to new aspects of the world. Anyone who knows more than one language sufficiently well can verify this for himself. A change in language is a change in a way of life—a change in how we see things and how we understand. It is a change in the order and patterns we discern, the things that can be said and conveyed and thereby given a place in our life, the subtleties of distinctions that are possible, the objects and processes that are perceived. Different languages are different instruments of comprehension and expression and have different potentials and weaknesses.[2]

Our difficulty in conceptualizing what I have called organic structures is connected with the structure of English. There is a strong tendency in Indo-European languages to conceive of things in terms of isolated parts, of clear-cut objects with clear-cut relations. The structure of these languages is said to be more mechanical than those of other languages that are characterized as being more like a chemical compound or even a painting.[3] The very language we use, therefore, disposes us to interpret all structure and order as if they were like mechanical order—to assume that they consist of separate elements connected by clear-cut links, are of blocklike construction, and proceed step by step.

But English, like all languages, can be used in various ways. It works differently in science, in history, in philosophy, and in poetry. The difficulty encountered in conceptually grasping the structures of history, philosophy, and art is due not simply to the nature of English, but to the prevalent tendency to use English in a way that is similar to the way it is used in science, to insist on blocklike, analytical order. Increasingly the poetic resources of English, those which would make for a structure more like a painting than a mechanism, are being discarded. To this extremely important issue we shall return in the following chapter.

EMBODIMENT OF APPREHENSION

An important characteristic of science that is closely linked with its clear-cut boundaries is explicit articulation. Explicitness is not appropriate to all areas, and the prosaic insistence on literal, explicit statements results in a crippling confinement of apprehension. Yet an appreciation of the virtues of explicit articulation is much to be desired: in areas in which it is not proper the danger of amorphousness and obscurity are greater, and awareness of these dangers will militate against them. If science alone provided all our understanding, explicit articulation would probably be habitual, as it generally is with scientists in their scientific work, and a conscious appreciation of its virtues would not be so important. But we have other modes of understanding (and must have them, though they are modes more exposed to danger), and in these modes an awareness of the benefits of explicit articulation can have a vital sobering and balancing function.

Our everyday thought about events, objects, and people would be paralyzed if we always tried to be explicit. The ordering we need requires loose generalizations, flexible classifications, comparison, analogy, and metaphor. These are not explicit forms; they cannot be cast into closed and clear-cut concepts, but make use of other linguistic resources. Of these, only a few are required in much of our practical activity, but if we wish to explore, express, and communicate more personal matters—thoughts, feelings, hopes—we are severely handicapped if we do not command richer, more poetic powers of language.

History is close to active life in this respect, and understandably so, since history's subject matter is the lives of men. Rigid and explicit categorization is generally impossible. If we tried to grasp the material in clear-cut concepts and propositions, we would be unable to write history. As we saw in Chapter 8, the attempt to provide technical definitions of such general concepts as food shortage, victory, rebellion, and republic would make these concepts useless. Suppose we pinned down "food shortage" as the condition obtaining when at least 85 per cent of the population has a daily ration of no more than 800 calories for a period of two weeks or more. The sole achievement of such a definition would be to make it impossible for us to use the term in historical presentation. And if, thinking this to be a commendable removal of vagueness, we proceeded similarly to pin down word after word, we would gradually condemn ourselves to total muteness. History does not use technical concepts because it does not make the futile attempt to grasp individual events by an infinite addition of abstracted properties that correspond to such concepts. It uses language that is capable of making vividly present to us concrete occasions, language fit for narration, interpretation, and appraisal—in short, literary language. To enable us to grasp the richness and variety of unique events, words must make us see, must evoke things rather than pin them down, and must indicate meanings rather than fence them in. Even if a specific historical term such as Middle Ages is used, it is made to function not as a technical term does in science, but so that, as the historian Huizinga wrote, it "could assume so specific a flavor, could conjure up a picture as full of life as history is able to confer." [4] This cannot be done by explicit articulation. Such a picture or flavor must be adumbrated, suggested, or "conjured up."

In philosophy, as in history, the subject matter has priority over method. There is something we want to apprehend, and we must find the best way to do it. Sometimes explicit statement is the most suitable way, at other times what we are concerned with must be brought out by some other means. Of the key issues of philosophical thought—among them knowledge, truth, value, freedom, reason, emotion, essence, existence, man, consciousness, and reality—none can be given clear-cut definition, none can be seized in explicit statement. The business of philosophy, indeed, is to explore them, to elucidate them, to improve our understanding of them. One must be as explicit as the subject will allow. "Our discussion will be adequate," Aristotle said, "if it has as much clearness as the subject matter admits of." [5]

The prosaic attempt to provide rigid definitions in philosophy, with the aim of bringing it closer to the scheme of science, generally does not clarify the issues that baffle the mind, but throws them aside. To attempt such definitions is not to think clearly, but to refuse to think. Consider, for instance, the belief that both science and art give some kind of knowledge. This belief certainly encounters objections and obstacles. Holding the belief and facing objections, we can seek clarification through philosophical thought. If our belief is erroneous, we may discover our error and in the process of discovery greatly enhance our understanding of both fields. If our initial belief is not entirely mistaken, but partial and inchoate, philosophical exploration will modify and clarify it and give it depth and substance. But suppose that, instead of embarking on exploration, we solve the difficulties by explicitly defining knowledge in such a way that it becomes the exclusive province of science. Then we have simply refused to face the issue. Instead of shouldering our task of seeking the best understanding we can attain within the complexity of our situation, we have withdrawn into a safe place. Philosophical thought must never relax the effort toward clearness, but its business is to address itself to what baffles us. The philosopher who sticks to clearness but refuses to answer man's needs serves mankind ill. Furthermore, his idea of clearness is too limited, for it extends only to a method. Its narrowness prevents him from realizing that by his simple and neat solutions he gives a fallacious view of things.

In many areas the philosopher must accept a tension between achieving clarity and doing justice to his subject matter; the same is true for the historian and for everyone engaged in the comprehension of events and people in daily life. Stepwise advance, clear-cut boundaries, and explicitness attract them—the historian more forcibly than the ordinary person, and the philosopher perhaps even more than the historian, because it is the philosopher's peculiar task always to question himself—but they all must do justice to their subject matter and they must not ignore it just because it does not submit to an explicit scheme. This tension is difficult to bear; hence there is constant temptation to escape it. There are historians who are so concerned with making the past come alive that they do not heed the virtues of clear-cut and explicit method, and write pseudo history. There are others who are so obsessed with being clear-cut and explicit that they maim their subject matter. There are philosophers so impressed by the inadequacy of explicit articulation that in avoiding it they become obscure—and perhaps even court obscurity. There are others who so idolize explicitness that they give up inquiring into most things of importance or reduce them to husks. Each approach in pressing an extreme calls attention to something vital, but each forsakes the far more difficult task that is the burden of philosophy.

In history, philosophy, and everyday life, the virtue of explicit and exhaustive articulation should be like a magnet, capable of pulling thought and expression toward explicitness and complete articulation. Sometimes the magnet must be brought up close, so that its influence will be great, sometimes it must be removed to a distance. In art, by contrast, apprehension cannot be explicit and exhaustive. Art suggests, intimates, and gives veiled disclosure. It conveys a sense of the fullness of things by the very fact that it makes one aware of their inexhaustibility.

Science enables us to orient ourselves in the world as a road map helps us find our way. But a map tells us nothing about the country through which the roads pass—ploughed fields, ripe grain, vibrant poppies, sparkling water, the smell of the earth. Science substitutes for the things of the world a set of concepts and places them in systematic and explicit order. Art turns to the things themselves to provide a more intense and intimate grasp. Science is an "abbreviation" [6] of reality; art furnishes a fuller experience of it. It has been said that science provides knowledge *about*, and art knowledge *of*, reality. I would not wish to impose this distinction upon functions of the human mind with stringency, thereby making a sharp and complete division, a kind of division that almost never corresponds to reality; but if it is regarded as pointing to a difference in emphasis, rather than as distinguishing a pair of closed concepts explicitly stating the character of things, then it is useful. "Knowledge about" gives order among certain general aspects of things, but removal from the things themselves; "knowledge of" is a more intimate apprehension of their fullness.

Awareness of inexhaustibility is of the utmost importance for human life, for it is the complement of a sense of wonder. This sense may be liberated when realization of man's enormous capacity to apprehend the world in a variety of ways is accompanied by awareness that no one way, nor all of them together, can get hold of the world, encapsule it, exhaust it. Such wonder is like the marvel of a child who first discovers the world, but is deeper. It is all but absent in our prosaic time, and this absence leaves life thin and hollow.

In its use of language, literary art, especially poetry, stands at the greatest distance from science. The words of poetry do not carry a fixed, clear-cut sense as do technical terms, but function as elements of a living and moving language; their meanings are flexible and evocative, and combine with sounds to call forth in the imagination experiences, thoughts, feelings, and perceptions, so that the total pattern embodies the poem's intent.

History and philosophy lie between science and poetry in the use of language, their distance from each depending on the particular nature of the subject. The sharp light that characterizes explicitness must never disappear completely, but the mode of expression must be shaped to embody the meaning. Strict, rigid denotation generally will not suffice. The resources of language that may be called poetic, in contradistinction to scientific, are necessary to do justice to the subject.

ABSTRACT AND CONCRETE, GENERAL AND INDIVIDUAL

Modes of apprehension differ with respect to their interest in the concrete and the individual on the one hand, and in the abstract and the general on the other. At first glance it might appear that a clear-cut division exists—the individual being found in history and art, the general in science and philosophy. On this basis some writers have spoken of two kinds of studies: nomothetic, whose aim is to establish abstract general principles among an indefinite number of events, and idiographic, which are concerned with the understanding of the individual and the unique.[7] The two kinds of studies are said to have different structures of thought and procedure corresponding to their different aims.

The views of science, history, and art that I have presented clearly recognize and stress the issues underlying this division, but they do not endorse it. They emphasize a very important difference that is properly illuminated by the distinctions between the concrete and the abstract, the individual and the general, and the particular and the universal, but they do not admit that these distinctions constitute a sharp separation of modes of apprehension. They reject such a separation because both the particular and the universal have a place in each of the modes. A distinction, however, is valid and necessary, because it draws attention to the very different nature of this place in the different realms.

In science, the individual is present in the grounding of abstract thought in empirical observation. Observations have to be made of concrete individual events localized in space and time. This fact is a principal cause of that scientific opposition to rationalism, or purely abstract speculation not anchored in observation of concrete instances, to which I drew attention in Chapter 1.

Historians also have repeatedly protested that a rationalistic, purely abstract conceptual system does not do justice to individual historical occurrences, indeed, pays no real attention to them. But history's attention to individual occurrences differs radically from that of science, and it is this difference that justifies the distinction between history and science as being principally concerned with the individual and with the general, respectively. I have discussed this at length, and it will be sufficient here merely to recall the core of the differences: for science, the individual event becomes reduced to a sharply delineated group of properties abstractable from an indefinite number of events; for history, the individual is the unique and endlessly variegated episode in the nonrepeatable process of human life. Science is not interested in the unique-ness and concreteness of the individual, the center of its con-cern being abstract principles in which the particular must be subsumed; history explores the particular's inexhaustible fullness.

The failure of pure rationalism is inadequately understood by many of our contemporaries who see it solely from the scientific perspective. Their opposition to rationalism is that of positivism—valid but inadequate. Their view fails to take any account of approaches to the world that differ from sci-ence: it displaces the individual by a group of abstractions and would therefore narrow man's scope of apprehension and reduce the world he sees. The opposition to rationalism implied by history is more like the kinds of opposition found in ro-manticism and existentialism, though it encompasses positivism as well. Here the concrete individual, the particular in all its fullness rather than a skeletal group of abstractions from the particular, moves into the center of concern.

There are historians who do not understand this position. Their thought is in prosaic subjection to science, and they consequently succumb to one of two fallacies. The first is to seek understanding of the past by the more or less deliberate and consistent use of general principles similar to those of science. This involves essentially the same error as rational-istic history: the actual events are ignored in favor of an abstract scheme; the very purpose of history is lost; the in-dividual occurrences are mutilated and explained away. The second fallacy is less obvious and more prevalent today: the historian retains his interest in particular events (sometimes because he believes that history has not yet arrived or never can arrive at the stage of using or formulating scientific principles and that it must therefore abstain from all interpretation), but he treats these events as if they were scientific, by reducing them to something he likes to call "facts," an accumulation of lifeless properties and endless details abstracted from the "outside" of events. The result is neither history nor science.

Although history focuses on individual events, it also includes generality, a generality, however, that also differs from that of science. It applies not to an indefinite number of events, but to things belonging within one flexibly defined interval of space and time. In history, as we have seen, particular and general are complementary: in exploring the particular event that is the French Revolution, conditions are described that apply generally to many particular events of smaller scope. Moreover, the generalizations and the concepts by which they are expounded—such as the state, war, food shortage, and uprising—are very different from scientific generalizations and corresponding concepts. They are open and flexible, and the substance of their meaning depends on the particulars that complement them.

Though history keeps the particular in the foreground of attention, it has universal significance for the understanding of man's existence. But this is not, and cannot be, made fully explicit. If explicit lessons of universal applicability can be extracted from history they will have to be extracted cautiously and wisely—and the minimum requirement for this is that they refer to the fundamentals of human life and not to specific events—but even such lessons cannot be more than indications to help our thinking: they cannot replace the universal significance of the history itself. In history we deepen our understanding of man, not through abstract principles, but through seeing the actual forms of his life.

Art is interested in the concrete and particular, and thereby resembles history. But in art this interest is even more concentrated. In its description of the economic, social, political, or cultural conditions of a period, history makes use of a certain amount of generalized description. Art as a rule stays away from such description. The novelist and poet aim to create particular people, situations, experiences, and moods. Instead of talking about general qualities of a way of life, they present this life to us. I do not wish in this respect to oppose the artist to the historian. On the contrary, the novelist's and the historian's common aim to present vividly particular occasions in human life is a major and valid reason for the frequent comparison of history to art. But the artist's particularization is pushed further. Whereas in a novel, for example, more attention is directed to particular persons than to society, the reverse is often true in history. In its attention to general and particular, history stands between science and art.

These relative positions are also manifest in the kind of language used in the three fields: the language of history lies between that of science and art. Strictly explicit language and technical terminology can deal only with those aspects of an individual that can be abstracted in clear-cut fashion from many individuals and subsumed in generalizations. This is the individuality of science, a skeletal individuality. Art, most intent on concrete individuality, evokes it by drawing on all the resources of language. History—focusing on the particular, but less intensely than does art, including generality, but a generality more tied to the concrete particular than that of science—uses literary language, but language that tends away from the poetic language of art to the explicit language of science.

Art and history resemble each other with respect to their universal significance. In neither does the universal appear in abstract and explicit form; in both it is inseparable from the concrete and is recognized within an immediate experience. While it would not be just to say that the element of universality is greater in art than in history—this depends on the particular works compared—a tendency in that direction exists in one important respect. The historian wants to know what actually happened, and he is therefore bound to pay attention to many things that are relevant even if their more universal significance seems slim. The artist has more freedom to select; he is not obliged to stay with specific actual situations. On the contrary, he creates by drawing on aspects of many life situations he has experienced, by imagining new ones, by modifying the emphasis of things in actual occasions, and by adding and omitting. He does all this both in the interest of more vital and immediate particularity and for the sake of the universal significance he senses. For this greater freedom, of course, art pays a price. There is a weighty substance to actuality that is relinquished by the imaginary. Moreover, the very bond of history to things that are limited to a particular time and place itself discloses something fundamental and universal, that is, the importance in human life of the unpredictable, the unsystematic, and the singularity of individual occasions.

In history and art one's direct concern is with concrete particularity: universal import transpires, shines through, or is alluded to. In philosophy, as in science, one seeks to discern and articulate universals: the particular is of interest only as an example. But in saying this I am in danger of placing philosophy closer to science than is appropriate, though such closeness is proper in some realms of philosophy, and to some extent permeates all of it. The philosopher's interest in things, however, is hardly ever restricted to a definite group of abstractions and to their rigidly systematic connections. His aim is to explore, clarify, and relate, and to do this he must proceed in whatever ways appear most fruitful. Many matters that it is important to understand and that can be illuminated powerfully by philosophical inquiry elude discussion that is exclusively abstract and generic. Often what we wish to explore are things of concrete experience. True, in philosophical thought we are primarily concerned not with the particular but with its generic features. On the other hand, what one wants to clarify is the thing itself, not a reduction of it. For example, an inquiry into art requires elucidation of the work of art itself and of contemplation of the work, and the concrete reality of the work and of the act of contemplating it cannot be grasped in abstract, generic, explicit terms. The same is true for freedom, morality, or justice. To the philosopher, an abstract view of an entity as obtained in science is not enough.

Science-dominated and prosaic thinkers (as we observed in connection with history) identify the concrete particular with the particular as observed by science. To pay attention to the world, they think, necessarily means to do what the scientist does. But in fact this is a very special and limited attention. The world is not to be exhausted by a set of scientific abstractions and corresponding sense observations. The philosopher must often aim toward full concreteness. Philosophical thought must mediate between the two kinds of attention to the particular and concrete that I spoke of earlier—the historical and existentialist on the one hand, and the scientific and positivistic on the other—and take up positions appropriate to the subject. Whenever it leans toward the historical and existential, it leans toward art, for in art the particular is most fully grasped. Instead of talking generally about a class of particulars, philosophy then seeks to make a representative particular present to our minds. Thus it frequently gives illustrations and makes them as immediate and concrete as it can and as seems necessary.

But the philosopher has to do something that the artist does not. He cannot stay with the particular: the particular for him —as for the scientist—is an example, albeit a vivid one; he must discern and elaborate connections between particulars of the same and of different kinds, he must insist on generic qualities and exhibit their relations. He is concerned, for instance, not with a particular act of the imagination, but with the nature and role of imagination in science, history, and art, with its relation to matter-of-factness, its place in human action, and its tendency to lure us from the implacability of reality. All this pulls his enterprise toward abstract and explicit conceptualization.

Much philosophic thought therefore is under tension between the spirit of art and the spirit of science. Hence many have claimed that philosophy sets itself an impossible task, that it tries to state universals about things that can only be experienced in their ineffable particularity. But in fact, philosophy (and philosophical thought in general, since philosophy as such is continuous with, and a refinement and intensification of, philosophical thought in every man's life) is an enterprise that must hold conflicting demands in a sometimes precarious balance. Philosophical thought is to a large extent abstract reflection upon things that must be experienced in immediacy. The philosopher who talks about art or justice or responsibility or love without concrete experience of them can have no fruitful thought. If he has had such experience, however, then his thought, largely abstract but availing itself of the concrete, can provide understanding—and in returning to immediate experience, will inform and enhance experience.

ATTITUDES

Impersonality and Responsive Engagement

Different modes of apprehension call for different attitudes. In science detachment, or impersonality, rules. Science, of course, is not extrahuman—neither superhuman nor subhuman. The scientist acts neither like a god capable of scrutinizing the world while maintaining himself totally aloof from it nor like an insentient data-processing machine. But in science the range of participation of the personality is narrower than in all other modes, because the product of scientific activity is designed to be as public, as impersonal, as possible. The internal rational structure of science looks as if it were entirely self-contained, as if it had a reality of its own that had no need of human discernment to come into being. The same holds for the correspondence of the rational structure to the phenomena it orders. This correspondence involves a very small number of abstractable properties, such as can be represented in a table of data, and its establishment calls for minimal human engagement: observation of the numbers, positions, and dimensions of things—the pointer readings of measuring instruments. Art stands at the opposite pole: it demands very personal, intimate engagement. This is true for the creative experience as well as for the contemplation of art, which I have described as listening and response.

In general, there is relatively little room in art for a fruitful separation, analogous to that in science, of internal pattern from the relation of this pattern to things beyond. This is because the parts of the work itself (words, colors, sounds) are not made to fit into an explicit, standard structure. The innumerable and complex ways in which the parts hang together emerge only in the process of each individual's personal experience and are not susceptible of explicit statement except in the most skeletal fashion. To speak, for example, of the unity of a Leonardo painting as "triangular structure" is wholly misleading unless it is fully understood that this statement is but the barest, thinnest abstraction from something else, something to which this abstraction can point but something that must be experienced in response to the work of art. If its strictly limited character is understood, the abstraction may help to make one more aware and hence may lead to the intimate vision, the direct experience, of stability, harmony, and unity (qualities, we must not forget, that embrace tension, movement, and variety entirely lacking in a triangle); but the abstraction is not itself the thing that matters. And if the abstraction's limited character is not understood—as unfortunately is often the case—it will distract one from the proper experience; it will prosaically reduce something that can only be grasped anew in each new encounter, in true response, to an explicit, lifeless, and meaningless husk. And what is true for the triangle in this example is true for every explicitly statable structure of the elements of any work.

The intensely personal experience of art is grounded in (and in turn bears on) the person's experience of the world—all that he has felt, thought, seen, heard, touched, and desired. The relation between the work of art and the world is not, therefore, anything that is explicitly statable with clear-cut references to definite aspects of things and that is susceptible of impersonal discernment. Such an explicit relation exists for a photograph taken for scientific purposes but not for a painting, including representational paintings and even portraits. If the attempt were made to introduce such a relation into art, it would make art pseudoscientific: it would turn a novel into lifeless biography or pseudo sociology and a symphony into banally imitative program music.

Science and art provide a polar contrast. Other modes stand in between. Contrary to prosaic belief, history and philosophy should not seek the extreme impersonality of science. Nor, on the other hand, should they seek the intensely personal responsiveness of art. They must move between these poles; they involve a tension and balance, a flexible and often delicate complementarity. Occasionally they may have to approach the extremes quite closely.

In neither history nor philosophy do we apprehend things by means of an explicit, standard system. In each the engagement of a variable range of personal elements is required. Each is similar to art and unlike science in that it does not usually allow us to make a clear-cut separation between an internal structure, on the one hand, and its relations to the things apprehended, on the other. Generally these relations are not at discrete points of the work and are not clear-cut correspondences susceptible of impersonal discernment and explicit statement. They are far more continuous, rich, and intricate. History is a telling of the past through description, narration, and interpretation; and the relations between the past and these historical forms are inseparable from the cohesion and structure of the telling itself. Philosophy explores, interprets, and illuminates, and to do so it must be in touch with what it explores not only here and there, as if providing tabulatable data, but throughout its process of thought.

To make sense, therefore, of history or philosophy, the individual must engage himself in a way that is more or less personal, depending on the subject matter. The actions of men in the past often can be grasped only if they reach the sounding board of the individual's entire experience. His self-extension, which is crucial for historical understanding, involves many and sometimes all his resources. In philosophy, discourse makes sense only as it is continually grounded in appropriate experience.

If we try to gain philosophical understanding, for example, of the character of scientific knowledge, the inquiry must always remain in contact with our own experience of science, or else we will not know what we are talking about. If we inquire into art, our thought must constantly be grounded in response and sometimes in creation; otherwise, our thought will not do justice to the reality. If we argue (or follow an argument) that values are the expression of individual taste and emotion and have no warrant or justification, we must continually bring to bear our personal experience of taste and emotion, as well as of value, justification, and expression. A positivistic thinker, for example, will see justification in terms of his experience with science. A thinker who believes that this notion of justification is too narrow will have to draw on such other areas of experience as he thinks also involve justification in order to clarify for himself what this justification is (or fails to be) and how it is related to that of science. The positivistic thinker, confronted with this position, will have to see if he has any experience of the kind to which the other refers in order that he may understand what is being said. If he cannot recognize such an experience in himself, he has the choice of ignoring the divergent view or acknowledging that his experience may be too narrow and seeking to enlarge it appropriately. The second alternative may be very difficult—and perhaps threatening. The philosopher is likely to be tempted to choose the first, telling himself that the other person is deluded or in some way incompetent. He may be correct, but such a conclusion should not be drawn too hastily, for it is possible that the other's view is better and that it cannot be understood without an experience that our hypothetical philosopher lacks.

Relation of philosophical discourse to its object, moreover, consists not only in the continual grounding of discourse in experience; it also involves the influencing of experience by discourse. Reflection, having drawn on experience, may guide and deepen further experience. Neither interpretation nor experience is fixed. They inform, check, and improve each other. Sometimes, reflection and experience interpenetrate each other so as to become all but indistinguishable: a person may stand in front of a painting, for example, at one moment engaged in an immediate experience, and at the next, drawing upon this experience in reflection about art and perhaps modifying his philosophical conception of it, then once more returning to direct experience—now, let us hope, enabled to see more fully, more justly, more intensely, than before.

Skepticism and Receptiveness

The scientific attitude, we have seen, is characterized by doubt and skepticism. Everything must show its credentials; everything must prove itself before it is accepted. Whatever is unusual, whatever departs from established schemes and systems, meets with incredulity and distrust. In art, responsiveness is called for, and we must approach the work with sympathy, not with doubt. We must live ourselves into a work of art, being willing and ready to enter its world. There are no fixed rules or systems by which the work has to justify itself. To see it for what it is, we must not call it to account but must bring ourselves to it, must be receptive to it.

This is not to imply that we can understand science by constantly saying "No," or that on the other hand, the critical element has no place in art. For we must follow a scientific argument if we are to know whether it is correct or faulty; and we assess the quality of a work of art—this assessment, indeed, being almost inseparable from our experience of it. But the balance of receptiveness and criticism is very different in the two modes. The skeptical attitude hardly ever leaves us as we read a piece of science. If any step not already part of an established system is accepted, it is accepted only temporarily—as an assumption or hypothesis. Also, it must show itself plainly so that we may know just exactly what it is that we are accepting for the moment. A work of science must justify itself step by step. It must win our grudging assent.

A work of art approached in this reluctant way escapes. We cannot prosaically dissect it bit by bit and part by part to assess its worth. We will see nothing unless we can first meet it receptively, ready for the possibility that there is something worth seeing. We will not hear it unless we are capable of listening to its own individual voice. An important quality of a work of art, therefore, is its power to make us listen and to draw us into its world. There are, then, two factors operative in the encounter with art: the beholder's capacity to approach it receptively and the power of the work. It may be that a work is not worth responding to; it may be that for some reason we will judge it adversely. What I say here about responsiveness is certainly not meant to imply that art cannot or must not be judged, or that adverse judgment is always a manifestation of the judge's inability to appreciate the greatness that is really there. (These are absurd notions put forth by many defenders of modern art in order to justify works they praise as original and creative, no matter what their actual quality.) But art requires that we approach it with a response like that of listening. The critical element in our attitude toward art must never be skeptical. Not every work has much to yield, but only if we are receptive to it will it yield whatever it does have. "Works of art are of an infinite loneliness and with nothing so little to be reached as with criticism. Only love can grasp and hold and be just toward them." [8]

Like the scientist, the historian does not simply assent to every opinion and interpretation he meets with in his work. He derives his own interpretations from his sources. A document, for example, may be turned into useful evidence, even though what it says may be untrue: the historian subjects it to critical questioning; he tries to ascertain what the motives for writing it were and weighs various factors that may bear on its validity, confronting evidence with evidence, belief with belief. Through questioning, doubting, and evaluating he elicits knowledge from the document.

At the same time, history calls for the attitude that is central in art—responsiveness. Without it, we can understand neither historical sources nor the lives of men in the past. The historian tries to extend himself to these lives and does so through historical sources. These sources are usually not explicit; they do not lay bare the knowledge he wants. A letter, an essay, a diary, a biography, or an official document is an expression of things he must try to reach, and he cannot reach them by approaching his sources with suspicion. History itself (which also serves the historian as source) is not an explicit articulation of definite, clear-cut knowledge, although it may contain such knowledge. It narrates, describes, presents, and suggests. It evokes the past and seeks to make it alive to the reader's imagination. The reader cannot, therefore, understand a history by approaching it primarily with doubt and by dissecting it. He has to be receptive to the picture it portrays, to be willing and able to respond to it. Since the concepts that history uses are flexible, the reader must not demand clear-cut definitions. He must allow concepts to do their work in context and must try to grasp their changing or expanding or deepening meanings. Literary language demands an approach in the spirit of literature. The reader of history must be responsive to the complex resources of language; a distrustful, prosaic approach can render them ineffective. He must not relinquish the critical faculty but neither must he allow it to interfere with his response.

The element of doubt is clearly essential to philosophy. The whole enterprise is rooted in the disposition to question. Whatever view the philosopher inclines to has to be confronted with objections. In philosophical activity we are constantly engaged in critical examination of our own positions: "What about this belief that I hold? Is it justified? Is it consistent with other beliefs of mine? Is it adequate to what it concerns? Does it do justice to relevant experience? Is the experience on which it is based sufficient? Am I clear enough as to what this belief of mine is? How does it stand up to the views of others? In what ways and for what reasons might I be deluding myself?" Hesitation to accept, critical questioning, and exacting scrutiny are the cleansing fire through which every argument and conviction must pass. But the purpose of doubt in philosophy is to improve belief. The point of seeing through things is to see what is behind them. We reject an idea in order to find a better one. We are reluctant to agree because we want to strengthen the validity of what we are agreeing to. We must therefore be ready and willing to assent.

The philosophical thought of another person cannot be understood unless it is met receptively. We must not approach it with distrust, expecting it to show complete credentials at every step. What is said or written in philosophy is not the explicit articulation of a sharply bounded piece of knowledge. The thinker has striven to understand something. He has found himself wondering and troubled, confronted by fallacies and conflicts. He has tried to resolve them and has looked for conceptions and relations that would make sense of things. He has labored for better understanding and for its most adequate embodiment in the words he has written. The reader must approach these words desiring to comprehend what the author has sought to embody. He must try to reach the author's meaning, to appreciate the difficulties the author faced, and enter into his attempt to overcome them. Unless the reader is willing and able to participate personally in this experience of philosophical inquiry to which the writer has given shape, he will not understand what is being said. He will be critical, not of the work, but of his own distortion of the work. He must not allow obtrusion of his own ideas to hide the author's, but must allow the patterns and revealing interconnections to emerge as the writer has seen and expressed them; he must let the language speak the way it has been intended to speak —whether veering toward the literal or toward the poetic.

Nothing is surer to blind a reader than a skeptical or captious, prosaic approach. Instead of listening to the author's words he is led by such an attitude to attack them and to dismiss or demolish the work without comprehending its import. He is not really willing to entertain the author's ideas but keeps them away from himself by maneuvers that protect the position he already occupies.

Inability to be receptive to another's thought is generally the complement of inability to entertain sufficient doubt with respect to our own ideas. Our prime business in reading philosophical thought is to try to understand—not to cavil and quibble—and to see if the other's ideas can improve our own. In this process, doubt is necessarily included: the other's views have been hammered out by critical questioning and can only be understood if we now think through this questioning ourselves; also, his views must be confronted with our own, so that by critical assessment and resolution of discords a better apprehension of things may be achieved. We cannot doubt, however, without understanding what we are doubting, and we cannot understand a philosophical position without genuinely desiring and attempting to do so. We must be prepared to admit that we may have to be led to a place we have not seen and be willing, indeed eager, to be led. All this implies that while the philosopher has to be critical, he must also be capable of true response.

COMMUNICATION

The impersonality of science, viewed from a different angle, is its ideal of total communicability and agreement. From this ideal, we recall, stem most of its principal features. Total communicability is not a part of all realms. Art, for example, does not seek it. This does not mean that there is no communication in art or that art is strictly idiosyncratic and without potential for human sharing and accord. The opposite is true. However, art is not explicit: whatever it grasps is not, and cannot be, articulated exhaustively or spelled out so as to be completely accessible to the impersonal perception of any beholder. On the contrary, everything depends on imaginative, personal response. Therefore communication in art is much wider, deeper, and subtler than in science, and accord involves much more of the entire person. Art far more than science is an instrument of intimate human meeting, a way to bridge the gap between man and man. Communicability and accord in art are not total, not because they are less important than in science, but because what is to be communicated is infinitely richer; it is, indeed, inexhaustible.

In science we seek to realize total communicability by insisting on a method that is designed to bring it about. We can state things exhaustively because we ignore whatever cannot be so stated. In art, on the other hand, communication cannot be complete because meanings cannot be wrapped in a tidy package and handed from person to person. They are in the fabric of the work and require response. In science we define technical terms and then use them to carry the assigned meanings, that is, we use them after prior agreement as to just what their meanings are to be. In art we cannot first assign meanings to separate elements of the work and then use these elements, because their significance depends on the context. Totality of communication is achievable only when the aim is strictly limited. In art, therefore, communication is much more uncertain than in science. Its realization depends on the particular work and on each approach of each beholder. Similarly, lack of accord is much more prevalent in art, because on the one hand, communication may actually fail, and because on the other, meanings reach beyond clear-cut limits, so that different meanings may justifiably be grasped by different individuals (and even by the same individual on different occasions). Such discord among beholders is not, however, a final, ineluctable fact, but can be discussed and diminished if the possibility of a failure to respond is recognized and responsiveness is cultivated.

Today the place of communication and accord in art is frequently denied. This denial stems partly from the notion—fallacious, as I have argued—that art apprehends nothing, that it is either exclusively a manifestation of the artist's emotions or else pure form, unrelated to anything else. In this view, since art has no meanings, no content, there can be no such thing as communication. Artist and beholders must remain entirely enclosed within their own selves. Denial of the existence of communication in art stems also from the unwarranted assumptions, conscious or unconscious, of the prosaic mentality that communication requires literal language and that communication is hampered by the entry of personal elements. These assumptions imply that the scheme of science is accepted as the model of communication. The assertion that there is communication in art is countered with the prosaic challenge to say exactly what is communicated, to spell it out in literal, explicit language. Any failure of communication or lack of accord on the meanings of a work is taken as evidence that neither meaning nor communication exists, rather than as evidence that art cannot seek total communicability and that therefore the risk of failure must always be faced.

Here again, history and philosophy stand somewhere between science and art, as they do with respect to the associated characteristics of personal engagement and explicitness. What is communicated is not simply contained in a box that can be unlocked by anybody who is handed a key. The contents are reachable only by personal acts of self-extension and response. If a reader of a philosophical work refuses or is unable to enter the personal experience to which the author invites him, he is failing to do his part in the process of communication. For the author it is tempting to try to avoid such failure of communication by modeling philosophic thought on scientific thought. But for philosophy to seek the security of science, however tempting, is fatal.

Our everyday life with other men involves many kinds of communication. Sometimes what we have to communicate is bare and thin and we want it to be communicated totally and surely, like the departure time of a plane or the location of a building. Sometimes what we have to communicate is charged and ineffable—ineffable, that is, in literal prose—like the glory of a morning or disillusionment with a friend. Then we need the scope and power of art: poetic language, visual image, sound of voice, bodily movement, gesture, or reference to works of art known to each person—though such communication cannot be total and involves more risk.

THE NATURE OF EXPERIENCE

A chief motivation for the science-centered restriction of reason is the unacceptability of pure rationalism. The world cannot be known by abstract thought alone. No matter how strong and excellent a structure of ideas may be, it may fail to correspond to the world. Knowledge must include experience; the structure of thought must be correlated with what is to be apprehended. Science satisfies this demand: the scientist ties his thought to what his senses observe.

Theories of knowledge often take it for granted that there are two clear-cut elements—pure thought, on the one hand, and experience, which is seen as sense contact with fact, on the other—and assume that all knowledge must consist of one of these or of both. The cogency of this view of knowledge in modern times derives largely from the fact that it accounts for empirical science, mathematics, and the role of mathematics in empirical science. Pure thought produces mathematics; the combination of mathematics and sense perception produces empirical science.

This view of knowledge, however, is too narrow. Its clear-cut division into two elements applies only to science. In other areas, as we have seen, it is impossible to isolate a structure of meanings on the one hand and clear-cut connections between such a structure and what is apprehended on the other. It cannot be done, for example, in history or in philosophy. (This has been a principal reason why so many modern philosophers, uncritically accepting a notion of knowledge modeled on science, have had to deny that philosophy can give knowledge and have therefore felt themselves obliged to abdicate the better portion of the traditional philosophical endeavor.)

The fact that nonscientific knowledge cannot be divided into two separate elements is linked with the character of nonscientific experience. It is false to suppose that experience can only mean sense observations as they exist in science. In history, for example, there is nothing so clear-cut as scientific sense perception, nothing like pointer readings. But this does not mean that the historian spins a web of pure thought: he looks to his sources and all his understanding of human life to gain knowledge of actual events. Nor does the philosopher interpret the moral realm, for example, without paying attention to actual existence. He needs experience of moral dilemmas, decisions, and actions. This is not mere sense observation of people's behavior. Art, too, is concerned with man's life in the world; it is apprehension; it embodies awareness, perception, and insight. The artist's work is most certainly connected, as is the scientist's, "with what his eyes see and his ears hear and his fingers feel" [9]—but it is a very different connection.

We could go a long way toward liberating ourselves from the crisis of the modern mind if we would recognize the inadequacy of the prosaic view we have imbibed concerning the nature of experience that enters into apprehension. This experience has been equated with counting or measuring abstractable properties of things, and the result is a disastrous curtailment of our attention to the world. Apprehension must draw on the fullness and variety of human experience.

SOCIAL AND PERSONAL CONTEXTS

We have seen that another major cause of the doubt of reason is the belief that only in science can the individual avoid the distortion of knowledge due to such peculiarities of his social environment as language, ideas, and values, and to elements of his own personality. This belief is understandable but not justified. Language, ideas, and values present in the environment are indeed potent in shaping the knowledge we gain: in history and philosophy, for example, they affect what we can understand and how we understand it. But we need not be their prisoners. We can learn more than one language and thereby gain new perspectives on things, and access to new spheres of experience and apprehension. We can cultivate our values by looking to other societies, past and present, and to expressions of values in many realms, by questioning the values we hold at any particular stage and seeking to

259

improve them. Indeed a principal reason for the importance of history is that it can liberate us from the parochial confines of the suppositions prevalent in our own society.

It is true, of course, that our very study of history is affected by our initial position; but this does not mean that we are confined to that position forever. (Such confinement is quite possible, however, and frequently happens—in history and elsewhere—to those who do not know how to extend themselves and do not genuinely seek to enhance their understanding but prosaically squeeze everything they meet into the views they already have.) A person who brings himself to history receptively emerges a somewhat different man, with horizons enlarged and understanding deepened. The notion that we are forever bound to our starting point—in history, philosophy, and other areas—comes from the idea that every mental process is structured like science. The importance of the starting point derives especially from the structure of mathematical deductions. We begin a deduction from a definite place, and where we end up depends essentially on where we began. Nothing really new can be arrived at in this way. The relations we find at the end were already implied (though not necessarily known) in those with which we began. But while this total dependence of the end on the beginning is true for mathematical deduction, it is not true for other activities of the mind. It is not true, for example, for the realm of language. Of course our beginning steps with a new language proceed largely in terms of the language we know; we cannot, at first, think in the new language, but can only translate old thoughts into more or less equivalent new forms, for our mental scope is bound to the old. But we are not condemned to this forever: indeed the finest fruit that learning bears is a new way to see, to think, and to feel—to live. The fact that we begin with the old language in learning the new does not mean that our new power always depends on the old in the way that a picture hangs with its whole weight from a nail or that the conclusion of a mathematical argument depends on its starting point.

Studying history and learning languages are not the only ways to move beyond parochial confines. Philosophical thought also can help us to transcend the limits of a particular society. By questioning ideas, beliefs, values, and presuppositions we see their limits or their invalidity; attend to other beliefs, values, and presuppositions; and struggle toward a more consistent, valid, and adequate view of things.

Peculiarities of our social environment may, but need not, distort understanding; the same is true of personal elements. Our dreadful fear of emotion and everything personal, and our idolatry of impersonal activities have led us to the absurd belief, typical of the prosaic mentality, that a man with emotions, convictions, and desires cannot possibly see straight. (As well believe that to step into water is to drown, because nonswimmers sometimes do.) To have emotions is not necessarily to be in the clutches of emotion. To have desires is not the same as to be driven by desire. We neglect these crucial distinctions. To apprehend the world truly, a person must become aware of the ever-present danger that his feelings, hopes, fears, and impulses may obstruct and warp his apprehension, and he must do his utmost, in ways appropriate to the occasion, to avoid such distortion. Let no one seek by quoting Freud to convince us that this distortion is unavoidable, that desires and impulses operating from the seething cauldron of the id inevitably impose themselves on everything we see, making reason merely rationalization. The principal aim of Freud's work was to bring the chaotic forces under control, and he took it for granted that these forces can be grasped and bridled by reason, that reason can discover rationalization and displace it. To believe that it is impossible to liberate the understanding from distortion by passions and desires would be to deny the whole basis of Freud's work. And not only Freud's: this belief would implicitly deny the validity of all beliefs, including itself; for how could *it* be valid unless it were freed from emotional contamination? That it is far easier to avoid such contamination in science than in other areas is true. But the difficulty of avoiding contamination in any mode of apprehension is not a very good argument against the validity of that mode.

It is not enough, moreover, to grant that it is possible to achieve knowledge *despite* the pressures of social and personal factors. It is misleading to regard these factors solely as sources of inveracity and limitation. They are, rather, the only finite ground upon which mental life can exist at all. They are not merely confining but also enabling conditions. To recognize this at once alters our whole outlook on the character of human understanding. We cease to dissolve it into mere relativity or subjectivity. A particular language, for example, with its particular characteristics, is acknowledged as the very instrument by which a particular kind of understanding can be achieved. A different language has different potentialities. A "superlanguage," free from the particularities of any one language, would not be superior, for it would be reduced to a code. At best it would be the kind of language one uses in science—free from the particular characteristics of a society and a person, and therefore dry and abstract; potent with respect to a clear-cut group of abstractable properties, and potent there precisely because it is impotent elsewhere. We avoid imprisonment in one language, not by attempting to discard the inherent limitations of language, but by learning other languages.

Again, consider the influence of the present on historical understanding. It is misleading to suppose that history is simply made relative by this influence. History is the evocation of the past of which *this* historian in *this* time and *this* place is capable. Without the questions of the present, without his views and his values and his feelings, there would be no history at all. Again, the knowledge we require in our daily life is knowledge needed here and now. It is possible that what we believe to be true is false, or largely so; but there are ways of removing error and delusion. The knowledge by which we live most of our life is not simply limited and biased by being inextricably tied with this person at this time in this place: this person and this life circumstance are also its soil and water and air. The soil and water and air may be barren and polluted, but they can be cleansed and enriched—and without them there is nothing. And consider philosophy. The philosopher's thought takes shape in a given spiritual and material surrounding. He addresses himself to the issues and perplexities of his time and his mind. If he inquires into the justification of values, it is because his time confronts him with the issue of values and he himself has experienced the predicament. If values were an unshaken reality, they would never occur to him as an issue. If he has not experienced it in his own life, he will not know what the issue is, but will be tinkering with its surface and never penetrate to the core.

Knowledge belongs to human life. It has no purpose except as a part of life, and it can never be wholly separated from life. It arises from desires, beliefs, values, doubts, customs, and languages, and lives in them. It cannot be detached from society and individuals any more than a tree can live without its roots.

The personal element is a necessary condition of all apprehending, though its nature and intensity differ in different modes. Emotions and desires may distort, but we cannot deal with this danger by eliminating or suppressing them. It is fallacious to believe that such sterilization serves truth. The imposition in inappropriate areas of a method allowing scant participation of the personality brings distortion, not truth. It leads to atrophy, reduction, and superficiality. A person who insists on such an imposition, indeed, is not free from the influence of emotions and desires, as he may seem to be. On the contrary, he simply fails to acknowledge emotion, for emotions impel him to insist on this impersonal method, and emotions prevent him from examining other modes. Rather than being unemotional, he has allowed certain of the emotions to tyrannize his entire emotional life. It is futile and, indeed, fatal to one's being to try to deal with conflict within oneself by denying a part of oneself, by seeking to isolate or suppress it. The attempt is futile because the suppressed and isolated part asserts itself in undercover ways. Who can continue to maintain a belief in the existence of pure, disembodied intellect after the advent of the psychoanalytic movement and the century-long emphasis in the arts on the passions and desires? It is futile to deny them. But more than that, it is also fatal, because there are essential human apprehensions that are impossible without engagement of the whole personality; the attempt at detachment yields a distorted view. We complacently imagine that we have achieved objective understanding when in fact an unsuitable approach has obscured our understanding.

The fact that reason is exercised within a social and individual matrix need not in itself lead to distortion, but failure to acknowledge this matrix is very likely to do so. We can guard against being misled by feelings and desires only if we acknowledge their presence. To suppose that we are entirely aloof from the world, unaffected by desire, value, or interest, is a sure way to contaminate reason. To take for granted that the language, methods, and concepts prevalent in one social context can apprehend everything that can be apprehended is a sure way to untruth.

Each approach to apprehension has its powers and its dangers and limits. Therefore it is of the utmost importance that we be capable of more than one mode of approach. Only thus can we gain sufficient awareness of the limits and dangers, and therefore the true scope, of any one mode. Only thus can we gain the perspective that enables us to combat distortions that may arise from the conditions of each act of apprehension, and so arrive at genuine confidence in our apprehension —confidence as contrasted to ignorant complacence.

THE DESIRE FOR CERTAINTY

Reason has been confined by the prosaic mentality to scientific reason and quasi-scientific, technical reason because it has seemed that only they deserve confidence. Clear-cut boundaries, definite method, explicit articulation, total communicability, and piecemeal advance give science an appearance of certainty, or absoluteness, that other modes lack.

To see the fallaciousness of this confinement of reason to science, it is important first to recognize that scientific knowledge is in fact not absolute. It is the best ordering of various properties of a range of phenomena that men have been able to achieve at any given stage. It is subject to rejection, correction, modification, and improvement. Despite their general disavowal of absoluteness—a disavowal largely due to science —men yet continue to desire it and to feel that it is found in science, though not elsewhere. They think that science gives certainty, while history shifts from interpretation to interpretation, infested—unless it is made scientific—by subjectivity. Philosophy they see as a series of doctrines, none of which stands—unless made scientific—as a final body of knowledge. These seekers after absoluteness see their everyday thought concerning themselves and others, the matters most relevant to life, as relative, subjective, and unreliable.

We must recognize that no human endeavor, including science, yields anything absolute. We must acknowledge man's finiteness and his inability to achieve certainty and perfection. And we must do this whether or not we recognize the Absolute of religion, for those who do not, admit no absolute, and those who do never dare imagine that they can "take refuge in the certainty that the temple of God is in their midst." [10] Once we no longer dismiss a realm because it cannot give us perfect and certain understanding, we become more ready to see it and judge it for what it does give us and to value it accordingly. Nothing men do, no place they reach, is absolute, but this does not mean that everything is totally shifting, or merely relative. We constantly commit the fallacy of supposing that absoluteness and complete uncertainty are the sole alternatives. But here, as elsewhere, we have allowed ourselves to be imprisoned by our instruments; we are the victims of a simple-minded ordering of things, of the erroneous assumption that a pair of neat concepts exhausts reality.

Man is capable of gaining understanding in a variety of ways, and of improving his understanding. The question is never whether his understanding is absolute but how valid, penetrating, comprehensive, and important it is. Science has security that other modes lack. Where there is uncertainty, there is risk, and the risk in science is smaller than elsewhere. But the price of this security is ignorance concerning all that cannot be learned by the scientific method. We cannot limit our exercise of reason by the criterion of minimal risk. Although histories are rewritten, philosophical views change, and everyday knowledge is revised, while science shows the relatively clear-cut progress admired by the prosaic mind, this does not mean that history, philosophy, and everyday knowledge are worthless. What they are concerned with cannot, in general, be grasped exhaustively. Each effort constitutes one view, gives some understanding. It provides illuminations and insights that leave room for countless others, each more or less good, each prompted, more intimately than science, by the social and personal conditions in which it arises. The progress of science is possible because in science interest is confined within clear-cut boundaries and everything of interest is explicitly and exhaustively stated. When a step is completed, the scientist moves on; there is piecemeal, clear-cut progress. In other areas, we do not move on in this way. In each individual's life as well as in the passage of generations the search returns again and again to the same or similar questions, which must be faced again and again, in terms of the new conditions and perspectives. Improvement is not progress, as it is in science, but correction, clarification, and deeper penetration leading to fuller, more comprehensive, and unified understanding.

THE SCOPE OF REASON

We have seen that reason is much more than scientific reason, that it operates in many ways and cannot be pinned down to a method (indeed, sometimes its task is to question method). But we must now ask if the concept of reason includes the whole sphere of knowledge, expression, and communication that has been suggested here. Perhaps not. In the first place, the concept suggests a distinction between reason and emotion. We have rejected the idea of two mutually exclusive domains, with each human activity belonging either to reason or to emotion. But though reason and emotion cannot be sharply separated (nor always considered antagonistic), they are not therefore indistinguishable, and it makes sense to say that one or another is more basic in a given activity, as emotion is in art, reason in science. If we said that every activity, including art, is an activity of reason—prompted perhaps by a higher esteem for reason than for emotion—we would be in danger of so enlarging the domain of reason that the concept would lose much of its usefulness. Though it is fallacious to isolate reason from emotion and to assign them to separate activities, it would also be fallacious to ignore the profound tensions and conflicts that their traditional antinomy reflects, by simply including art in the domain of reason.

Also, we must ask if reason is bound to language and not to language as such, in any form, but to a definite kind of prose. This is very generally thought to be the case. It does not seem justifiable, however. First of all, we must reject the current assumption that prose, if it is to be compatible with reason, must be modeled on scientific prose and be literal, bareboned, technical, explicit; for this is just the prosaic crippling of reason that must be transcended: neither history nor philosophy uses such language, yet we must surely grant that they manifest reason. Next, if we attempt to delimit a range of prose to include both scientific prose and the more literary prose of history and philosophy, and if we claim that this is the range with which reason is compatible, we will also have to allow, I believe, that reason is compatible with the prose of art forms such as the novel, for there is no barrier between the two latter kinds of prose that would permit one to say that reason can only operate on one side of it. But once the prose of an art form is admitted, I cannot see what would justify the exclusion of the language of poetry: there is no sense in asserting, for example, that reason can be manifested in a novel but not in a poem. Anyone, indeed, who believes that only a very definite form of language is compatible with reason would have to ask himself the perplexing question of whether this form can be found in all languages, and since different languages have different structures, and order and grasp things differently, he may well be led to the view that only those who speak a particular language are capable of reason. Finally, if we admit that reason is not incompatible with the language of art forms, including poetry, we shall also have to admit that it is not incompatible with the lines and colors of painting, the shapes of sculpture, the sounds of music, and the other forms of art, for there is too pervasive a bond among the arts to allow us to divide them into those that manifest reason and those that do not.

I conclude that there is no way of restricting reason to embodiment of a particular kind, either a definite form of prose or language as a whole. Those who take it for granted that reason is restricted to prose usually assume without question that it is also sharply divided from emotion. This gives them a means, they believe, of specifying the kind of prose that is appropriate for reason: it must be referential or cognitive, not expressive or emotive. But this is an unacceptable cleavage of language (to which we return in the chapter on symbols) that corresponds to the equally unacceptable cleavage between reason and emotion.

We have then to consider whether reason admits all forms of embodiment. It has been claimed that the whole realm of art belongs to reason.[11] But this view runs into difficulty. We have already seen that it can hardly do justice to the reason-emotion distinction. And there is another objection. Art often gives so central a place to the sense of wonder and of the mysterious, to the awareness of unfathomable fullness, that one cannot properly speak of it as a form of reason. Reason itself, to be sure, does not always strive to lay bare and reduce and seize hold of in explicit terms, and it is able to acknowledge wonder, mystery, and fullness, but to say that reason can encompass them as they exist in art would lead to more confusion than understanding, for the desire for clear-cut boundaries and explicitness that marks the operation of reason in science must be seen as the extreme of a desire that, in appropriate balance with others, belongs to all forms of reason.

While we cannot set reason any clear-cut boundary, it is preferable not to think of it as embracing all modes of apprehension. We cannot tolerate its restriction to scientific reason, for there are realms like history, philosophy, and everyday thought from which reason cannot be excluded without totally violating our sense of its nature. But it would be better not to speak of art as an activity of reason, even though reason is not excluded from it. In the end, however, our chief concern is not the role of reason. Rather, it is the whole sphere of understanding, expression, and communication—the various modes of apprehension—and this sphere embraces not only science, history, philosophy, and everyday thought, but art as well; it embraces reason *and* emotion, scientific language *and* poetic language, explicitness *and* evocation, bareness *and* mystery.

KNOWLEDGE AND APPREHENSION

Some people are intensely averse to the idea that art embodies knowledge. They may not even admit the view that art embodies knowledge *of* things, rather than *about* them.

Such people will perhaps want to confine knowledge to the domain of reason, assuming without question that they know what reason's scope and limits are. If, in so doing, they identify reason with scientific reason and, hence, knowledge with science, we must of course disagree. But perhaps they will grant knowledge to other areas—to history, philosophy, and everyday life—and deny it to the arts. To my mind this denial would violate my sense of what it is to know and my experience of the arts. Moreover, as we have seen, there are many fundamental resemblances between art and realms to which knowledge is granted, and these resemblances render futile any attempt to maintain that knowledge is not also present in art.

My aim, however, is not to insist on a certain meaning for a certain word. It is rather to gain an understanding of things, and if the conveyance of this understanding is hindered by use of the word knowledge, then let us use another. Moreover, sometimes *knowledge* does not seem the best word to use in connection with art. It does not stress the power of art to express and convey what we feel. Nor does it emphasize the immediacy of art, the fact that art involves direct and intimate experience and that it is a prime way of imaginatively reliving, and distilling the significance of, experiences of active life. Because of this insufficiency, I have often used other concepts to indicate aspects of art that seemed to be of principal importance in a given context—for example, interpretation, expression, evocation, and imaginative reliving. It is important to have one concept, however, that can embrace all of these as adequately as possible. *Apprehension* seems to me to be the concept best suited to art and also to what is shared by the various modes of which I have spoken.

To apprehend is to be aware, to perceive, to grasp with the understanding. It is to express in a pattern of words, colors, or sounds. It is to discern sense and recognize meaning through order, relationships, contrasts, and harmonies. Apprehension is a dimension of existence through which we are not merely alive in the world but are conscious of the world, conscious of being and of being who we are and conscious of what is other than ourselves. Apprehension is every movement of our self that brings us to awareness of reality. Apprehension is present in art and in science, in history and in philosophy, in our everyday confrontation with things and in many other areas. What is apprehended and the way it is apprehended vary greatly—and often there is conflict between different approaches.

Our life demands various modes of apprehension. Our outlook on things and our actions become distorted if one mode is allowed to dominate. We become imprisoned by it because we are unaware of other possibilities, and we impose it tyrannically because we do not know its limits and dangers.

What is crucial, however, is not merely that the ways of apprehending are many and varied, but that they span fundamentally diverse attitudes, approaches to the world, and kinds of embodiment. The characteristics of these modes range from the utmost impersonality to intimate personal engagement; from a minimum of emotion to great passion; from doubt and skepticism to response; from critical analysis to perception of wholes; from the literalism of technical terms to the power and richness of poetic language and of shape, color, and sound; from explicit articulation to suggestion and evocation; from sharply bounded illumination to intimation and glimpses into the inexhaustible; from abstraction to concreteness; from the general and regular to the individual and unique; from method as principle to method as means; from clear-cut boundaries and mechanical order to flexibility and organic interrelation. What matters most is that this span be acknowledged and maintained, that the tensions be faced, not dissolved, that contrary movements of spirit be profoundly understood, cultivated, and given a proper place within the wholeness of apprehension—in each activity, in the individual's life, and in the social structure.

271

Chapter 11   LANGUAGE AND THE
REALM OF SYMBOLS

The destruction of language and its connection with the diminution of understanding and reason was discussed in Chapter 2. Returning to understanding and reason, the discussion in Chapter 10 led to the consideration of apprehension, which extends beyond what we can properly call reason. Now, in returning to language, the discussion will similarly be extended to a larger domain, one that encompasses all the shapes and forms in which men embody meaning.

The most appropriate term for all these shapes and forms —used frequently in recent thought—seems to be *symbol*. The language of daily affairs and the language of intimate dialogue, the language of technology, the conceptual structure of science, the language of poetry, the patterns of paint or stone or sound that are painting or sculpture or music— all these are parts of the vast realm of symbols by which man apprehends the world, articulates his insight and understanding, expresses feelings and desires, projects ideals, embodies order and values, guides action, and communicates with his fellow man.

Many different things, however, have been spoken of as symbols, including some with which we are not, at least not directly, concerned in this book (religious ceremonies, for example, and dreams). It is not feasible to examine here the question of whether the kinships suggested by this common appellation are valid, or how far valid and in what ways. Within the scope of this exploration such questions remain open. I believe that the views reached here are valid for the symbolic forms I speak of, but to what extent they apply to others could be decided only by further inquiry, which will not be undertaken here. Conversely, it must not be taken for granted that ideas applicable to such other forms can be carried over to the ones I am discussing; this, too, would be a matter for further examination.

PROSAIC IMPAIRMENT OF SYMBOLS

The predicament of language, and of symbols altogether, springs from the prosaic mentality. To begin with, the literalism of the prosaic mind diminishes the scope of symbols to bare, explicit statements. The prosaic mentality is blind to, and denigrates, whatever cannot be pinned down in stark prose. It ignores the power of language and other symbolic forms to express meanings through suggestion, intimation, and evocation.

In our discussion of the destruction of language we considered the doctrine that language has two separate functions, the referential and the emotive. The literalism of the prosaic mentality is at the heart of this cleavage: the most literal language—that of science—is considered to constitute the model referential language, while all uses of language not cast on this model are said to be emotive. Meaning must then be embodied in referential language, which at its most perfect is stark and totally explicit. Its scope becomes the scope of what the human mind can grasp. Emotive language does not embody apprehension. It is connected with the emotions of the speaker (or writer) and affects the emotions of the hearer (or reader), but has no content, sense, or meaning. Especially important, it is incapable of reaching the world beyond the subjective emotions.

It is clear that this prosaic division of language impairs most sectors of the symbolic realm. It is linked with the fallacious belief that science and quasi science constitute the sole modes of apprehension. It propels art—all art, not only literature, since all artistic symbols are considered emotive—into a purely subjective sphere, devoid of the power to embody awareness, perception, or insight into anything beyond the exclusively private. Indeed it leads at once to that destructive view in which art is not only restricted to the exclusively subjective but is seen as mere ejaculation, or release of subjective states. Other symbolic areas, such as history, philosophy, and personal dialogue are made suspect or are maimed by the idea that their language is usually a mixture of referential and emotive and that the latter contaminates the so-called objective validity of the former.

Mutilation of the realm of symbols has another cause, which, like literalism and the referential-emotive cleavage, springs from the prosaic mentality. This is the notion that symbols are essentially arbitrary, a notion that is related, first of all, to the modern rejection of what has been called the primitive view of symbols. The primitive mind (which is often understood to be identical to, or at least closely related to, the mythical or prescientific mind) makes no separation between symbols and reality, between words and symbolic objects and acts, on the one hand, and that which is expressed or symbolized by them, on the other. For the primitive, symbols are, or are a part of, the reality they symbolize. Or at least symbol and reality are conceived as standing in an integral relation, such as is implied in magic, for example, where words and ritual acts are supposed to have a direct effect on the course of events. The modern mind rejects such an integral relation and holds, on the contrary, that symbol and reality are entirely separate: the *word* water, for example, and the *reality* water are considered completely independent entities. The name of a thing, it is argued, is not intrinsic in the thing itself. The word refers to the real thing, but beyond this reference there is no tie: there is nothing in the reality and in the word-sound (or written equivalent) that constitutes a direct link between the two.

The fact that the symbol shows great variability also is held to be evidence of arbitrariness. It is pointed out that many different symbols correspond to the same reality. Thus, we have, not only *water*, but also *Wasser, eau, acqua*, and so on. A particular symbol therefore seems to be an arbitrary sound, shape, color, pattern, object, or movement corresponding to a certain meaning. The form of the symbol and its meaning appear to have no intrinsic connection.

Arguments concerning the difference between man and animals lend additional weight to the idea of the arbitrariness of symbols. There is a strong impetus (more or less obsessive ever since Darwin) to affirm that there is no fundamental difference between them. But though often stated as a dogma, doubt of which at once brands one as unenlightened, unscientific, and steeped in medieval beliefs, this affirmation meets with difficulties. A chief obstacle is presented by the realm of symbols and the belief that this realm is a unique possession of man.

Opponents of the belief that only man has symbols base their opposition on the notion of "conditioning"—the key concept of behavioral psychology. The famous dogs of Pavlov were trained—that is, "conditioned"—to exhibit at the sound of a bell behavior that they had originally exhibited only when presented with food. In this conditioned behavior, it is claimed, is the essence of the symbolic realm: the bell— the conditioned stimulus—functions as a symbol for food. Just as for man the word water symbolizes the liquid, so for the dog the bell supposedly symbolizes food. The bell, of course, is not the only such symbol: behavioral psychologists have been busy for half a century studying what they call "response" to innumerable conditioned stimuli. Nor is recognition of animals' capacity to become conditioned to such symbols confined to animal psychology: it is old knowledge that dogs and horses can be trained, that a dog will come to you when you call him and that a horse will stop at the shout "Whoa!"

Those who are bent on denying all significant difference between man and animal, and who believe in conditioning as the master key to the understanding of both, deem this view of the symbolic realm entirely satisfactory. Language, they say, differs only in complexity from whoas and Pavlovian bells. There are others, however, who consider this view fallacious in that it ignores a fundamental disparity between the animal's stimulus and the human's symbol. The argument usually advanced to demonstrate this disparity is that for the animal, the entity that serves as a stimulus (in these discussions often called a sign or signal) has a fixed connection to the reality it signals, whereas for a human, the entity that serves as a symbol has no such connection; that is, the symbol is arbitrary.[1] Thus, for the trained dog, food is signaled by a sound that the dog cannot change any more than a horse can replace "whoa" by some other signal for stopping. But for man, the reality symbolized is not bound to any particular symbol: the same meaning can be expressed in different ways, as is done by *water, Wasser, eau,* and *acqua.* Moreover, man can and does originate relations between symbols and what they symbolize: he can assign a new meaning to an old symbol, and he can use a variety of different symbols to symbolize a given object, idea, or event. Hence arbitrariness is seen as the property that sets apart the purely human realm of symbols from that of conditioned stimuli.

These three arguments for arbitrariness are important. By themselves, however, they do not disclose the full weight of what the symbol's arbitrariness is felt to be, nor the fallacy and destructiveness of this notion. To see this, one must consider still another of the notion's manifestations. It has its intellectual source in science, but can now be found in all areas of life, since scientific symbolism is currently taken, either unconsciously or deliberately, as the model symbolic realm. This is done unconsciously in that the mental life of even those who do not understand science is subject to the pervasive effect of science. It is done deliberately by those who feel that science is the only valid—or at least the highest and ideal—symbolic form. This feeling is widespread. Ernst Cassirer thought it essential to recognize that the "symbolic universe" has a scope far greater than science, far greater even than reason, a scope encompassing myth, religion, language, art, and history; but even he wrote that "science is the last step in man's mental development and it may be regarded as the highest and most characteristic attainment of human culture." [2]

A cornerstone of science is its use of technical terms, that is, concepts (and their written equivalents) whose meanings are pinned down by explicit definitions. It is here that we find the arbitrariness that supposedly characterizes all symbols. When the scientist defines a concept, he can use whatever verbal sound or visual shape he wishes and assign to it the meaning he desires. This does not mean, of course, that he capriciously changes symbols other scientists have used, or that he invents new ones indiscriminately; that would only foolishly complicate the mind's work and bring confusion instead of clarity. But it does mean that when he finds it expedient to do so, he can replace one symbol by another and he can assign whatever meanings he requires to whatever symbols he chooses or invents.

The notion of arbitrariness manifested here is much more sweeping than those in the arguments discussed earlier. Moreover, the earlier ideas are exemplified in the scientific symbol in especially obvious and complete form. First, the divorce between symbol and reality is total: the technical term has no intrinsic connection whatever with what it symbolizes; no matter what its properties, no matter where it is taken from (usually nonscientific language), or whether it is invented, its scientific meaning is in no way inherent in it but is assigned. Second, the scientific assignment of meaning satisfies to perfection the idea of symbolic variability: we choose a symbol and pin a meaning to it, but innumerable other symbols could be chosen in its place. We need not call an entity A; we can just as well call it B or C, provided only that we make completely clear which symbols mean what and that we abide with these symbols and meanings until new definitions are made—if and when they are thought desirable. Third, the process of defining scientific terms is precisely the process of deliberate selection or invention of symbols and imposition upon them of any desired meanings that is supposed to constitute the basic disparity between symbol and animal stimulus.

In view of the perfection of these three manifestations of arbitrariness in the scientific symbol, it is easy to understand that interpretations of arbitrariness are often informed, even if not overtly, by the scientific symbol and by the arbitrariness of its definition. But when this interpretation of arbitrariness is carried over from science and its relative, technology, to other symbolic areas, it cripples them. It imposes the prosaic mentality upon them.

The destructive impact of this interpretation makes itself felt in two ways. First, scientific arbitrariness implies the utmost literalism, for the purpose of scientific definition is to establish terms with clear-cut, explicit meanings. These terms are intended to be closed, rigid, unambiguous, devoid of shadings, connotations, and reverberations. They are incapable of carrying meaning by suggestion, intimation, and evocation, being specifically designed *not* to work in any of these ways: they are stripped of all flexibility and openness, of the power to function poetically and to express meanings that cannot be pinned down and spelled out—stripped, in short, of all the far-reaching resources of symbols with the sole exception of the utterly literal meanings that are explicitly assigned to them.

Second, scientific arbitrariness invites the referential-emotive mutilation. In fact, it drives this mutilation to an extreme by actually ejecting the emotive sphere altogether from the realm of symbols. Referential language becomes identical with language whose meanings can be arbitrarily assigned: words are conceived to have referents that are deliberately and explicitly imposed on them—the ideal model of this imposition being furnished by scientific terms. Emotive language and other emotive forms are ruled out as symbols because they lack this arbitrariness. They supposedly have no meaning, embody no apprehension, articulate nothing. They neither express nor convey understanding or insight. Sometimes they are explained as expressions of subjective states, these expressions, however, being viewed not as mental apprehensions, like artistic creations, but—as we saw in the chapter on art—as ejaculations, ventings, or automatic releases of feelings and impulses. There is an easy and favorite linkage here with animal cries (another avenue for denying human distinctiveness): emotive expressions are said to be essentially the same as the noises emitted by animals—when they are hungry, for example, or sexually excited, or afraid. Emotive language is thus not only relegated to the completely subjective realm, but is even robbed of its power to constitute utterance of this subjectivity. It is no longer utterance, speech, or articulation at all, but a form of noise, like squeals and grunts (another way of dehumanizing man). Another explanation of emotive language focuses on its effect on an organism instead of on its emission—and is based on the behavior of Pavlov's dogs. Referential language is regarded as truly symbolic because it conveys arbitrarily assigned meanings; emotive language, however, is identified with the conditioned stimulus, which simply elicits from the animal or human organism conditioned behavior.

While imposition of the arbitrariness of scientific symbols thus violates most nonscientific symbols, there is evidently considerable basis for the ideas of arbitrariness mentioned earlier. (It would, however, be better to avoid use of the word arbitrary in connection with symbols in general, as it may lead us to mistake the characteristics of all symbols for the arbitrariness of scientific ones.) It is perfectly true that symbol and conditioned stimulus are not the same and that the relationship between a man's existence and the symbol is different from the fixed connection between an animal's conditioned behavior and the conditioned stimulus. To prove this, it might be argued that men can and do assign meanings to arbitrarily chosen symbols, whereas animals, apparently, cannot. The argument easily becomes misleading, however, in that it is taken to apply to all symbols. The process of imposing definite meanings on arbitrary sounds or shapes applies to the technical symbols of science, not to all symbols. The symbols that do not have this scientific arbitrariness are not therefore conditioned stimuli. The human freedom and creativity manifested in the arbitrary definition of terms are not the only forms of freedom and creativity that can be found in the realm of symbols but not in that of conditioned stimuli.

However, to explore the disparity between symbol and conditioned stimulus any further would be to stray from what really matters to us. To take the conditioned stimulus, or rather the rejection of it, as the point of departure in interpreting the symbolic realm is bound to give rise to distortions. One's ideas become chiefly reactions against something fallacious and are thus governed by it. That symbols are fundamentally different from conditioned stimuli is indubitable, but the contrast does not go very far in helping us to see what they are. A solid grasp of the nature of language is necessary before anything can be gained by comparing it with signals for dogs and horses (whatever the proper interpretation of these signals may be). In our time, especially, when the penchant for reducing everything to primitive forms or biological ancestry or atomic constituents is so overwhelming, we must beware not only of this distortion itself, but just as much of allowing our thought to be ruled by opposition to it. Emphasizing the arbitrariness of symbols in order to show their distinctiveness, and thereby man's distinction from the animals, too easily and too often leads to the absurd notion that this distinction resides solely in scientific or technological symbols, or in others having the same arbitrariness, and that poetry, music, human dialogue, and religion, lacking such arbitrariness, are less distinctly human, or at least are lower manifestations of man's mental life. A theory that would make Shakespeare, Bach, Buber, and Kierkegaard relatively close to dogs, white rats, and monkeys, but would suppose a tenth-rate mind defining arbitrary mathematical symbols or contriving technological lingo to manifest the quintessence of humanity is, to put it mildly, ludicrous.

The variability of symbols is also an important characteristic: *Wasser, eau,* or *acqua* can indeed substitute for *water.* But here again the example easily misleads, especially because the notion of scientific arbitrariness always hovers about us. We are led to suppose that everything can be expressed equally well in different ways, that the particularity, the individuality, of a symbol is of no real import, because any number of other symbols can do its job. But this is a false assumption. The example of the word for water in different languages does not give a true picture of language as a whole. Different languages can say the same things only to a limited extent, only if we restrict ourselves to a relatively small, however important, portion of their scope. Different languages, as we have seen, provide more or less different views of reality. When we learn—really learn—a second language, we not only acquire the ability to say in a different way what we could already say before (for example, that we want sugar in our coffee), but we are enabled to think and feel and perceive and express things to which our original language does not provide equally good access. The limitations within which one language can substitute for another stand out especially in poetry, where the resources of each language are most fully employed. Read Shakespeare translated into French or Rilke into English and see how far the idea of variability of symbol takes you. This variability in fact becomes increasingly inapplicable as we move away from the realms of literalness. When we want to do no more than convey to the waiter in the restaurant what we want to drink, then *water* or *eau* can serve equally well, depending on the language of the waiter. But when *water* appears in a line of poetry, *eau* is likely to be a poor substitute. And this lack of variability exists not only among different languages but also within each individual language. Meanings cannot be transferred from one embodiment to a variety of others. Shakespeare cannot be paraphrased; nor can the import of a painting be put into another painting or into words: some words will be more appropriate than others, but none will be a substitute. Variability of symbols is not an illusion, but it does not properly characterize the whole symbolic universe. It applies best in the realms that have prosaic interests. In the technical terms of science it is at its height, because these terms have their meanings assigned by definitions and can therefore be replaced in these definitions by innumerable other terms.

There is also merit in pointing to the aspects of arbitrariness brought out in the rejection of a virtual identity between word and thing. Symbol and reality are neither one and the same nor so directly linked as to lead to magic. But once more, it is crucial not to be trapped by mere opposition, for this opposition leads to scientific arbitrariness, where the divorce between symbol and what is symbolized is complete. Virtual identity, on the one hand, and scientific arbitrariness, on the other, are not the sole alternatives. Rejection of the primitive view does not demand the complete wrenching apart of symbol and reality that is found in science. The primitive view is adequately refuted by the recognition that all relationships between symbol and reality involve not only these two entities but a third entity, man. Man's apprehension, expression, and communication are fundamentally involved in whatever exists between symbol and what is symbolized. Men grasp things mentally through symbols, embody meanings in them, listen to them and become aware through them, and communicate through them. The essential presence of man rules out the primitive view, in which man comes, as it were, upon a scene in which virtual identity of symbol and reality, or integral correspondence, exists without him. But the presence of man does not necessarily imply scientific arbitrariness, or necessarily mean a total divorce between symbol and reality, or make all symbols arbitrary objects to which meanings are given by explicit assignment, as with technical terms. On the contrary, many areas of the symbolic realm have a property opposite to scientific arbitrariness: unity of form and meaning.

UNITY OF FORM AND MEANING

We have seen that what is expressed by a work of art cannot be separated from the way it is expressed. There is no substitute for a particular artistic form or any part of that form. Each form is a unique embodiment of meanings. In science, the definition of technical terms often requires language that does not itself need definition, that does not itself consist solely of technical terms. The very process of definition thus presupposes that the meaning assigned to any technical symbol can be articulated in nontechnical language, that is, in a medium other than that belonging purely to science. But in art there are no extra-artistic resources to draw on. The poet, for example, cannot turn to extrapoetic symbols to assign meanings to words, metaphors, and sound patterns prior to using them in a poem. His task is to make the poem *as poem* express whatever is to be expressed. Its parts and elements carry their full poetic burden only within the poem itself. In a scientific inquiry such parts—the scientific terms—function as indicators, as convenient tokens for what can also be indicated in other ways (though some tokens are more convenient, helpful, or elegant than others). The meaning is simply pinned to some word or shape that then carries it through the inquiry. The word or shape has no potential for ripening to new meanings in new contexts—or rather, any such potential is disregarded as irrelevant and inadmissable. In art, on the contrary, it is just this potential that matters. The words, shapes, and sounds do not carry fixed, assigned meanings but have been made capable of carrying the desired meaning within the artistic form into which they have been forged. Significance is not put on from the outside: it rises from within, emerges from all facets of the form that the artist has put to work, and lives in this form. To vary the form is to vary the thing that does the symbolic work, the thing that possesses expressive power. There is not shape, on the one hand, and content, on the other—with the latter explicitly attached to the former—but rather, in the phrase of the painter Ben Shahn, "shape of content." [3] The symbolic shape in all its particularity is the means to meaning.

The notion of arbitrariness, therefore, cannot be brought to art. Symbol, the reality symbolized, and man stand in far more complex, substantial, and intimate mutual relationship in art than in science. Art interpenetrates the whole of man's being in the world; it is interwoven with the human self and reverberates with the world in which the self lives.

In contrasting unity of form and meaning with scientific

arbitrariness, I have referred to art because, of the three areas I have discussed at length, art manifests this unity to the greatest degree. But this unity is important also in history. The form into which a history is cast is by no means arbitrary. The content of a historical work cannot be extracted from it and put into a different shape. History is and must be embodied in literary language, not in technical terms. Unity of form and meaning is characteristic also of philosophy. And in the speech the individual holds with himself concerning his individual life—a speech akin at times to history, at times to philosophy, and at times to art—symbolic arbitrariness has little place. The same is true for the individual's meeting with others. The symbolic form in which he embodies his struggling insight into what intimately concerns him, in which he articulates his awareness and makes known his innerness, is the form that must carry his meanings. On each occasion we must mold a form as best we can to do its particular work. Each self-confrontation, each genuine dialogue with another person, is interpenetrated by processes of giving shape to unique symbolic forms that make tangible what we think and feel and desire. It is vital, therefore, to recognize that the arbitrariness that characterizes scientific symbols is not a property of all symbols, and to acknowledge symbols that have more intimate relationships to man and to the reality symbolized.

To appreciate uniqueness—hence the uniqueness of symbols —one must be responsive; one must be able to listen. Here is the crux of the mutilation of symbols by the prosaic mind. It uses, manipulates, and controls, but fails to listen; and it does this to symbols just as to the world with which symbols deal. Hence, the notion that symbols are essentially arbitrary is doubly prosaic: first, in that arbitrary symbols are those that characterize the pursuits that occupy the prosaic mind; second, in that symbols are treated solely as tools to use and replace without attention to their uniqueness, their concrete particularity. The symbol, for the prosaic mind, is "merely" a symbol. In itself it does not matter. Its own shape, form, quality, and integrity are of no account.

But in fact the nonarbitrary symbol must arrest us and make an impact; it must invite, help, and even compel us to listen. In contrast to the arbitrary symbol, whose meaning is assigned and is therefore readily and exhaustively conveyed, the nonarbitrary symbol is integrally bound with its meaning in its context and speaks only to those who can meet it receptively. It is not explicit, but evocative, and the quality and power of this evocation depend on all its properties and on our capacity to perceive them. It does not, like the arbitrary symbol, embody a clear-cut idea or abstracted property of things, but is charged with a dense, rich substance of meanings. We want and need its wealth of associations, echoes, shadings, ambiguities, radiations, and sensuous qualities, and we must attend to them. Each element potentially enriches—and in a bad symbolic form, interferes with—the total significance.

The realm of symbols is crucial to our existence. We must combat any unwarranted curtailment of it, fight the imposition of tidy doctrines that would mutilate it, and vehemently oppose every miscarriage, abuse, and distortion of it. We must cultivate our use of symbols, and vitalize them again and again to offset the inevitable enfeeblement from routine usage. New forms must be forged that are genuine embodiments of genuine meanings. We must do our utmost to embrace the full scope of the symbolic world, from literal to poetic modes, from arbitrary symbols to those in which form and meaning are inseparable, for the wholeness of man's life flourishes and decays with the wholeness of his symbolic realm.

Chapter 12 VALUES

THE PROSAIC MENTALITY AND THE WORLD

In Part One we noted that many of us are undermined by the belief, or at least the suspicion, that values have no grounding in the world—that everything is really value-neutral and that what we call values are in fact only projections of strictly subjective feelings and desires onto this neutral world. This belief is prosaic. Our dominant view of things stems from pursuits in which value is not discerned—science, quasi science, technology, and ordinary practical affairs—and we take it for granted that what is perceived in these realms constitutes the world (an assumption that becomes increasingly valid as the world we live in comes to conform more closely with the prosaic outlook). I am not saying that this conception of reality has been arrived at by deliberate reflection: the reverse would more nearly be true for most people, especially in our prosaic atmosphere, where big questions are always avoided in favor of what we call problems. With or without reflection, however, everyone lives with some notion of reality, and this notion—whether justified or not, consistent or not, or articulate or not—is what matters.

The prosaic notion that the world is identical with what we apprehend in our chief pursuits is completely fallacious. Science is one mode of human apprehension, not the only mode. It directs its attention to one or another isolated group of general properties and omits everything else. The same is true in technology and in our ordinary, practical lives: we have a specific, usually narrowly circumscribed goal and attend to nothing but a few elements that we think are involved in its achievement. We usually cannot attain success if we allow our attention to be diverted, any more than a man can cross a street through heavy traffic while admiring the sky.

But the source of our predicament, the reason for our emaciated view of the world, is that we are incapable of beholding anything besides traffic—we hardly ever get out of it, and even when we do, we retain our prosaic attitude. We approach the world in certain ways and remain ignorant of whatever these ways do not bring within our ken; and when someone tries to direct our attention to spheres that we have overlooked, we feel forced to deny their existence. We reduce inexhaustible reality to skeletal facts and then inflate these facts into what we think is reality. We harness ourselves to methods and techniques, and insist that what they don't deal with isn't there. Fixing our minds on a group of abstractions, we mistake them for the concrete reality from which they derive. We regard individual entities—people, objects, or events—as mere instances of a class and ignore the fact that their individuality infinitely transcends their class properties. We concentrate on whatever can be quantified and remain blind to what cannot. We curtail the meaning of the word experience to include only the kinds of experience that characterize empirical science and technology. Everything is treated as a means, and we consign to nonexistence whatever is not discerned in this approach. We take it for granted that using literal, explicit symbols is the only way to embody apprehension, and then we explain away what lies beyond their scope.

Moreover, not only are the views of the world afforded by our dominant pursuits partial, but by their very nature they preclude the discernment of values. Values arise in our meeting with individual, concrete entities: persons, objects, situations, or events. They are present when we read a particular book, contemplate this scene or bit of nature, are involved in an actual human relation, and are confronted by a specific action. This is not at all to say that we cannot reflect on the universal aspects of scenes of nature and books and people and actions. It is to say that such reflection must always be in touch with concrete entities and, equally, that value judgment must strive to do justice to concrete entities in their fullness and particularity.

Science, technology, and ordinary practicality all neglect individuality from the outset. They at once focus on a group of abstracted, generic, and, especially, quantified properties (the "facts") and disregard everything else that makes the individual entity what it is. The person's attention to the entity does not extend beyond the elements that enable him, rightly or wrongly, to treat it as one among many (a member of a class, a case, or a specimen) and as repeatable or replaceable. The individual entity is dealt with and explained without attention to its unique qualities. It is made subservient to a method, system, or specific aim, and is not allowed to disclose itself in the concreteness that is itself and to which values are tied. When an illness is viewed solely as a manifestation of certain biological principles or as an insurance case, there is no question of good or bad. When we confront illness as the suffering of a particular individual in a specific life situation and bound to relatives, friends, and responsibilities—then we have an experience replete with moral values.

OBJECTIVITY AND RESPECT IN APPREHENSION

The belief that values are purely subjective was shown in Part One to be coupled with the notion that there is only one approach that affords valid knowledge of things, the objective approach, which cannot discern values. Despite this insistence on objectivity, characteristic of the prosaic mentality, there are approaches to valid apprehension that are not objective. Common to all approaches to valid apprehension, however, is *respect* for whatever aspects and attributes of things, events, or persons are relevant to this apprehension. This means that we give these aspects and attributes the utmost attention and exercise the utmost care not to distort them.

Since there are various modes of apprehension, there are various modes of respect. Objectivity is one of them. If we insist that it is the only one and adopt it in all realms of life, then we are guilty of a gross lack of respect; we reduce and distort what confronts us by a dogmatic method. The impersonality that characterizes objectivity is appropriate only in science and practical or technical activities. Another way to achieve respect is through *responsiveness*. When we are responsive, we give complete attention to what is before us; we contain the self so as not to obtrude; we become still, and listen.

We may wonder whether the real drawback of the insistence on objectivity is, not the belief that only objectivity can reach true apprehension, but the restrictive notion of an objectivity that is appropriate chiefly to science. It would seem that by the word objectivity we should denote the most general characteristic of all ways by which a knower, or subject, approaches objects of knowledge in any field. In that case the more special objectivity of the scientific pursuit could be referred to as impersonal objectivity, since impersonality is one of its chief characteristics. But this view is not satisfactory, because the subject-object conception of knowledge itself contains fallacies. One of these is that the subject, the knower, is conceived of, not as a concrete and whole person, but as only a part or abstraction of a person, like pure consciousness, reason, or mind. A complementary fallacy is that this reason, or mind, is supposed to act impersonally, scrutinizing the object with detachment; this implies that the general objectivity of subject-object knowledge inevitably turns into impersonal objectivity. A further aspect of this fallacy is that the object, even if it should be a person, cannot be recognized as a person but is "objectified" into a thing. The concept of respect overcomes all these difficulties.

There can be no objective discernment of values, because values involve the concrete and individual, while the objective approach is intent on abstracted facts and on cases and specimens. Responsiveness, on the other hand, is a bringing of oneself to the concrete and hence permits the discernment of values.

Objectivity is a very special and limited mode of respect: it consists in respecting entities in the way and to the extent that is necessary to gain intellectual or physical possession of them, to exercise control over them; aspects of entities that are not involved in gaining control are disregarded; the entities themselves, in their own right, are of no concern to us. Just such concern, however, is necessary in the realm of values; it constitutes a more profound respect than that of objectivity for the otherness of what meets us. It is the respect that involves response.

The doctrine that values are entirely subjective is perfectly correct when it states that values have to do with emotions and desires—with a man's personal being. But it is not correct when it takes it for granted that this personal being has no place in apprehension but only distorts it and that values therefore cannot be apprehended. The idea that emotions are blind, or that they produce heat rather than light and that heat always obscures, is rooted in a failure to differentiate between *reaction* and *response*. In reaction we have no respect for the world that confronts us: the emotions aroused stem chiefly from our own being, which is wrapped up in itself, the confrontation with the world being only the spark that ignites them; our perception of the other is ruled by our own needs or desires or habits, and the emotions that spring from this distorted perception usually give rise to further distortion. In response, on the contrary, we are attentive and open to the world, we are fully present to what meets us, and our emotions are a vital part of this presence. While objectivity, or impersonal respect, is easier to achieve than respect that involves response, it is not adequate for all modes of apprehension. Responsive respect is the *sine qua non* of the discernment of values. Without the exercise of such respect we cannot hope to overcome the twofold evil of our time—the prosaic reduction of the world to what can be known in science and the complementary splitting of human existence into two separate realms, one devoted to control of the reduced world, and the other to hermetic subjectivity.

VALUES AND RULES

The question of values is usually considered to be identical with the question of rules for values. Most men, for example, generally live by rules according to which progress, profit, efficiency, and education are good, and idleness, poverty, pain, and theft are bad, taking it for granted that the meaning of each entity is clear-cut. Anthropologists who study the values of a society usually look for rules and codes that govern the conduct of its members. Moral philosophers have mostly taken it for granted that consideration of moral values means consideration of ethical rules, or a system of value propositions derived by logical deduction from a principle concerning the ultimate good.

There is much truth on the side of the anthropologist, sociologist, historian, or philosopher who claims that there can be no question of superiority among the rules and codes of different societies or historical periods. The subjectivist who rejects the so-called objectivist system of value propositions of traditional ethics because there is no way of reaching agreement on its principle of the ultimate good also has much justification. These relativist and subjectivist claims are very important, for they help us to emancipate ourselves from the parochialism and dogmatism by which a set of rules current in a particular time and place, or enunciated by a school of thought or belief, is raised into a universal norm of human conduct. This is not to say that it is meaningless to speak of human good, but rather that such good is not identical with rules—social, philosophical, or any other kind. The laws of a nation, for example, prescribe conduct, but an action that is legal is not therefore moral. If legality and morality were the same, then many Nazi atrocities would have been moral. If a set of rules were the norm of artistic value, then academicism would be the last word in art.

The notion that values can mean only rules is a part of the prosaic mentality. This mentality knows only rules, clear-cut criteria, and literal propositions. But values are concerned with individual occasions and have their being in concrete human existence.

VALUE JUDGMENT

We cannot judge the right and wrong of an action by remaining detached and fitting it into a ready-made, abstract system. There are no established and clear-cut boundaries defining an action as a case of a class of such actions. To judge it as a case would be to judge without truly knowing what is being judged. A genuine value judgment is a decision that demands a person's intimate engagement. This does not mean that he is being merely subjective, however. His engagement is that of response. A person is called on to attend to the particular action with the utmost respect, to apprehend it in its uniqueness, and to judge it out of all his understanding of human existence.

Since judgment is a personal act, it cannot be passed on to an impersonal authority. It involves risk. Judgment requires that the judging individual be responsive to some part of the world and hence that he risk his self in the impact this part of the world may have upon him. He risks his self also in that there is no absolute assurance of the rightness of his judgment and in that it may place him in opposition to his society and have consequences that expose him and others to pain, difficulty, and danger.

These risks are among the chief reasons for the popularity of both the belief that values are fixed in rules and explicit standards, and the belief that values are entirely subjective. Both beliefs give comfort and security. For a holder of the first belief, fixed rules serve as an external authority that relieves him of the difficulties encountered in being truly present to the world. He imposes the rules on every occasion, thereby both avoiding the possibility of finding that he is in the wrong and escaping responsibility for the consequences of a personal decision. The subjectivist also fails to respond to a situation that demands his response, and he avoids the risk and responsibility of judgment by taking refuge in the subjectivity of feelings or the right to private opinions. He as well as the adherent to rules seeks security through abdication of a human burden.

A man can have no absolute assurance of the rightness of his judgments, because man is fallible and finite. His utmost effort at respect may not fully succeed, and his understanding may be faulty; he can never be aware of everything; he often has to sacrifice one thing to another even when both seem equally worthy, or to inflict injustice in one situation for the sake of more encompassing justice in another. Hence judgment must be made with genuine humility. This is utterly different from the humility of one who refuses judgment on the grounds that the individual never has the right to judge; such an attitude is pseudo humility, for it is an excuse for hiding from a basic demand of human existence. Genuine humility requires acknowledgment of man's potentials and the shouldering of his burdens without self-righteousness and with ever-renewed awareness of man's finitude.

The personal nature of value judgment by no means implies

that in arriving at judgments the person is entirely on his own. It is true, of course, that our sense of values must very largely grow out of our own life experience and our reflection upon this experience. We come to know good and evil through our meetings with people, through the sustenance or injury we give each other. Our own joy and sorrow, and those of others furnish constant schooling. But our sense of values needs to be guided and nurtured in many other ways as well. We see others' actions, speak with others, and profit from their understanding or, perhaps, learn from their lack of it. We recognize genuineness or falseness in the various modes of life with which we come into contact. We meet a person whose existence strikes us forcefully as being right and helps us to find our own direction. In addition to such encounters with men, we turn to the things men have made that embody values, especially in the areas of culture. Here we can learn most from the areas that are directly concerned with man and are concerned with him in ways that seek to discriminate and express values—though not by giving rules. History, philosophy, the arts, and criticism of the arts, for example, can help us by selecting and highlighting what is important and worthy, intensifying our awareness, liberating us from parochialism, and causing us to reflect on likenesses and differences between things, as well as on harmonies and discords, antecedents and consequences, meaning and lack of it, and on many other matters that have to do with values. Art and many activities of reason manifest values continuously, through selection, emphasis, and interpretation, and not only when judgment appears in an especially obvious form, as when a historian praises or condemns an action in so many words or a philosopher asserts that something is just or unjust. Values permeate the very language of historical, philosophical, and critical thought and, even more, the symbolic media of the arts, which engage us in immediate experience of concrete individuality and thereby inevitably communicate values. The arts help us to form our sense of values by leading us to wider and deeper experience and to better and more mature reflection.

Other disciplines that are concerned with man—such as anthropology, sociology, and psychoanalysis—can contribute to the maturity of our judgment by providing a wider perspective on the conditions of human life and the interrelations of its elements, and an understanding of some of men's inner tensions, difficulties, and potentials. They also contribute directly to our sense of values in so far as they do not insist on being value-neutral sciences. And even a discipline that does not concern itself with man and is scientific, hence value-neutral in the view of the world it offers, can contribute in a limited yet important way to our sense of values in so far as we participate in it as a human activity. From such a discipline we learn respect for scientific fact and the importance of unprejudiced thought, explicit language, and public agreement. Indeed, we learn these values so thoroughly that we may easily be led to the inconsistent subjectivization of values of the prosaic person, who is so under the spell of the values of science that he imposes them on all of life. He fallaciously converts the values of which he has immediate experience into a dogmatic set of abstract rules, and forces all other realms to conform to them.

Finally, fundamental value principles—by which I mean something radically different from prosaic rules and codes—are vitally important. Religious laws and commandments, philosophical principles, and the sayings of sages provide us with indispensable counsel. They are articulations of insights concerning man and the world to which we must listen and bring a personal response if we would grasp their meaning. Some are bound to particular times and places, while others have universal import; learning to discriminate among them is itself a part of the growth of personal judgment. We must grasp their inner life as it is embodied in their particular historical form. The more literal the symbols in which they are embodied, the less likely they are to be adequate to the vast variety of human existence. Only flexible and evocative symbols that call for personal response are capable of expressing the kind of wisdom that is crucial to all men at all times. Respect for commandments and principles is part of the humility that judgment requires. When we do not heed the past, we are in danger of being imprisoned by the predilections, illusions, and obsessions of the present. On the other hand, though we have the utmost respect for the past, our judgment must still be our own if we are not to be prisoners of literalized codes from the past. Judgment indeed cannot help but be ours, because the commandments and laws that are the most universal—for example, "Thou shalt love thy neighbor as thyself"—are not literal and explicit prescriptions for specific and clear-cut actions, but calls to us whose significance we grasp only when we can truly listen and recognize that they command the whole of our being.

Chapter 13 MAN AND THE WORLD

In Part One I discussed the prevalent divorce between learning and man's life. This situation is linked to the prosaic mentality. If we are obsessed with facts, we neglect to ask which
facts are worth knowing. If we look always for schemes of
abstractions and for tidy systems, even a potentially vital
subject is emptied of meaning. The rule of technical jargon
and literal language leads to spiritual sterility. The aims of
learning are forgotten if our stress is chiefly on methods.
Minutiae and a fetish of precision are the barren offspring of
too much technique. Where only such questions are asked as
lead to explicit answers, matters of intimate human concern
must be largely ignored. If learning consists of the study of
problems with clear-cut solutions, then no room is left for
matters of life.

The currently strong conviction that learning must be removed from life in order to have validity is a manifestation of
prosaic obsession with objectivity. Detachment and impersonality are said to be the roads leading to truth in all spheres.
The conflict between the desire for truth and other desires is
settled by making learning extraneous to life, so that the truth
it discovers becomes irrelevant to life's desires. The impulse,

298

therefore, behind the devitalization of learning is rarely, if ever, a passionate devotion to truth. More often it is merely a habit, an outcome of the prosaic attitude, which deals with everything at arm's length and is devoid of passion. There is no great clash here between truth and its foes; no penetrating and painful awareness in the depths of one's being that man is no simple entity and that needs, desires, and responsibilities often conflict; there is no struggle to achieve harmony in the face of tensions and conflicts. There is rather—often in the name of modesty and intellectual duty—a complacent and sometimes arrogant dismissal of human life and its demands. For learning to be valid it is not necessary to divorce it from life, and in fact such divorce often impairs learning's validity. All significant histories are linked to concerns of the present, and almost any philosophical issue—if really acknowledged, not toyed with like a crossword puzzle—has direct and fundamental significance for our life.

Specialism—that is, unlimited specialization—which is a chief cause of the isolation of learning from life, is also prosaic, for its very essence is fixed and standardized boundaries, with each area isolated from every other, thought channeled through a groove of abstractions, and activity defined and canalized by method. The specialist looks away from men and the world, ignores their demands and avoids their impact, and applies himself to solving problems. To solve problem after problem is the prosaic goal of specialism. What matters is that there be obvious activity that yields clear-cut results. The meaning and value of the activity are ignored.

Specialism means institutionalized activity and therefore impersonality. Here again it shows its prosaic character. Personal elements in ways of thought and modes of presentation are permitted only to a minimal extent. The individual's imagination and judgment are suppressed, and the connection between his life and the knowledge he seeks disappears. Specialism everywhere promotes this exclusion of the person. Specialism breeds prosaic minds, and prosaic minds further specialism.

We desperately need a reorientation of learning. We must integrate apprehension in all its scope with the whole of life. Too many minds now dissipate their powers in activities that contribute little to human life but increase our mental chaos and our consequent feeling of impotence. This feeling dissolves the self and often drives us into a total rejection of learning and into a cult of sheer irrationalism. The prosaic intellectual has become enslaved to schemes, systems, programs, projects, standards, rules, compartments, and institutions. He has abandoned the practice of judgment, which is the responsibility of every individual. He does not attempt to see what kind of knowledge is important for us as concrete men engaged in life and then to gain that knowledge as best he can. He makes himself a prisoner of some system by inserting himself into that system and seeking the smoothest possible adjustment to it. And he shuns awareness of this self-betrayal by never lifting his eyes and never interrupting his busyness.

Specialism is not necessitated by human finiteness. The alternative is not between specialism and the futile effort to attain infinite knowledge or, what is said to come to the same thing, between "solid" knowledge and superficiality. The alternative is between treating the mind as an irrelevant addendum to human life and accepting it as essential to man's being; between being ruled by methods, institutions, and standardized systems, and making personal, responsible judgments; between seeking the security of boundaries and compartments, and taking the risk of going where it is important to go; between ignoring man in the search for knowledge and accepting one's responsibility to foster him to the greatest possible extent of one's powers.

Learning must be guided by values. Genuine judgments have to be made as to what is worth knowing and how best to achieve it. In this process many factors must be weighed, for what merits attention at one time, may not merit it at another, and what is desirable in one situation, may be undesirable in another. Specialism ignores values. It sets up the tidy rule that knowledge is valuable for its own sake. This allows the specialist to escape from the burden and the risk of making a judgment on each concrete occasion by a safe and complacent appeal to a hackneyed and sacrosanct phrase. Thereby the whole of life and all values become subordinated to a fragment of themselves.

Values bear not only on the initial decision as to what learning to seek but also on choices being continually made while seeking it, and they are increasingly important as the pursuit is farther from science. To allow learning to be ruled by fixed boundaries set by specialism for content, method, or mode of expression is to lack respect for what is to be understood and to invite distortion. It is to violate ends by using improper means. Hence the relation to life of the knowledge being sought does not hinge solely on the initial decision; it rests also on the repeated valuations and choices involved in the study. The more closely a field is tied to human life and the deeper the personal engagement it requires, the more its merit and relevance are reduced if the person remains in the grooves that specialism fosters, and the more essential it is for him to be free to bring values to bear on his learning.

If the prosaic mentality must be overcome in the area of learning, this is even more true in art. To be prosaic is to be blind to art. This is the basic reason for the peripheral place and usually spurious esteem given to the arts in contemporary life. Art requires glad acceptance of the feelings. It is a realm of the individual and the personal. The uniform, the standard, and the clear-cut are incompatible with it. The prosaic mentality, to which everything is impersonal, is ruinous, for in art the self must be engaged. It must bring sensitive awareness and freely answering affections. This is a personal engagement very different from the engagement that is possible for the prosaic man, who is capable of reaction but not of response.

Clearly prosaic is the habit of regarding a work of art as an intellectual problem—of "going to work on it" as if it challenged one to account for it and explain it (in terms of psychology or sociology, or history or biography, or as an instance of form and technique), of dissecting it with the aim of making explicit what it is and what it means and how it achieves its meanings. In some of these approaches the work is actually not the focus of attention: attention is directed away from it to something else—for example, to psychological theories or biographical incidents in the artist's life. In other approaches attention is focused on the work, but attention of an inappropriate kind: the work is treated as if it were a phenomenon to be explained by general principles rather than a unique object of contemplation. In such prosaic approaches there is no response. Instead, an effort is made to subdue the work by assigning it to categories, to treat it as a soluble problem, or to reduce it to the kind of thing already known. Instead of a personal encounter with an individual thing as it is there is a detached examination of an alien object, a preoccupation with method, and the posture of impersonal objectivity.

This is not to say that it is impossible to enhance appreciation of art through conceptual thought and language: they are powerful instruments of human apprehension and communication, and we must use them. But when analysis is applied to art, it must be carried on with the greatest tact, the fullest respect for the work itself, thorough understanding of the inseparability of artistic content and form, and profound awareness of what cannot, and must not, be attempted in a critical, analytical approach. Otherwise, appreciation of the work is not enhanced but destroyed. The critical approach can lead to fuller response; but more often, because the disparity and inevitable tension between different approaches is not grasped by the critic, it obstructs response. It puts a wall between us and art, preventing direct encounter; it subdues the concrete individual entity by breaking it into fragments and so keeps it from making an impact upon us.

A chief reason for the predicament of art is clearly the literalism of the prosaic mind, which destroys or distorts the meaning of the artistic symbol. Literal interpretation of a work as a depiction of the world we live in too often leads us to react to the work of art as we react in everyday life to what is depicted. Such literalization especially threatens the verbal and visual arts, as we have seen, for language and visual representation are the most open to literal interpretation. This helps to explain why many scientifically inclined men genuinely understand music (which is not representational and therefore offers no possibility for literal interpretation) but do not understand representational painting and, especially, poetry.

But the prosaic mentality is a threat to the creator as well as to the beholder of art. The modern artist recognizes the danger of literalization. However, living in a prosaic world and not immune to its influences, he himself often regards art prosaically, especially those of its forms that are most exposed to prosaic literalism. He himself often does not respond to these forms as one must to art. This failure has led him to turn from the necessary and extremely difficult task of discouraging literalization and to attempt to solve the problem by the merely negative and easy reaction of insisting that artistic symbols must bear little or no resemblance to prosaic symbols. Thus, in literature, language is distorted and its meaning obscured. Word combinations, linguistic contrivances, visual patterns in print, and other devices are invented to produce novel effects; sound is separated from sense (in a misguided imitation of music) and treated as if nothing else were required. Analogous efforts to combat prosaic perception are made in the visual arts. If representation of the external world is not banished completely, the representational image is subjected to extreme distortion or fragmentation, and the aspects of the world to which images relate are deprived of their living interconnections or are juxtaposed in ways that are deliberately intended to be anything but similar to the ways in which they are connected in actual life. (I do not mean to imply that nonrepresentational art has no merit; my purpose is to reach a sound view of the relationship between art and the world, and to understand the current unsound attitude toward it.) It is ironical that many of the works created in reaction against the prosaic mind succumb to it after all: they invite intellectual analysis rather than response, because the symbolic form does not speak directly, through evocation. Such works are like puzzles, secret codes, or problems—to be solved and disposed of.

In speaking of these prosaic infections of art, I have already implied that certain other failures also spring from the prosaic mentality. Many a modern artist seems to be unaware of the intimate relation between symbol, reality, and man. Living in a prosaic climate, he has learned to treat the symbol as arbitrary, divorced from nature, independent of history, and devoid of organic links to man—something he can deform or invent and use at will. A work made in this way is not the unique embodiment of the artist's awareness or insight; it does not reveal to us the form in which something first sensed without form, at the center of his self, was born and given palpable being. It seems forced and contrived.

In the prosaic outlook, as we have seen, the world is fatally impoverished. The exponents of pure form and self-expression have succumbed to this prosaic outlook (though their sphere, art, is basically nonprosaic), and seeing nothing that could enrich their art in the outer world, they turn away from it. And while self-expression as it focuses on inwardness and emotions is opposed to the prosaic mentality, in a deeper way self-expression and the prosaic mentality are complementary. Thus, paradoxical as it seems at first, today's stress on the self in the realm of art parallels the prosaic mind's subjectivization of values. The cult of self-expression and the prosaic outlook are two sides of the same coin, for while the prosaic mind is focused on a skeletal external world and ignores innerness, self-expression focuses on innerness and ignores the world. The prosaic mentality conceives of the world as precluding response; self-expression accepts this view and withdraws into isolated subjectivity. Art must avoid both these distortions.

Today we extol creation, the new and the original, but all too often creation and the freedom it requires are thought to stem from utter subjectivity. In this view man frees himself from everything around him and creation is an expression and assertion of his self. But this is pseudo freedom. It is a delusion, because man cannot place himself outside the world, apart from nature, other men, and culture. "Pure" creation in the sense of an act that is totally unrelated and autonomous is impossible, a pathetic conceit. Such freedom is also destitution, because it means being divorced from and deprived of the world. Subjectivism is free as a blind man is free from shape and color. Man has no choice whether or not he will belong to the world; his only choices concern his ways of belonging. The subjectivist freedom is incapacity to respond; it is imprisonment in the prosaic mentality. The freedom of much modern self-expression is, in fact, lack of freedom of the self to engage with and be in the world. At its very best and rarest, art that stems from such lack of freedom (not really subjectivism then) is the desperate and chilling expression of the emptiness and terror of estrangement, the anguished cry that can only be given shape at the very edge of art with the utmost risk by the greatest of artists, a cry that comes from the very depth and center of lived suffering, from the knowledge of loss and aloneness, and the yearning for relation with an other.

305

The function of human creation is not simply to assert the self by being original. Nor is it to make an utterly new world, free from the world that is man's. The earth, sky, plants, animals, men, and things men created in the past are the very condition of life—life's wellspring and the elements of its predicament; and creation is the shaping of something significant from this spring and this predicament. To create is to enhance man's being in the world.

Artistic creation, especially, is fulfilled as it "weds man and nature," [1] unites man and man, and helps to transcend the distance and the isolation that always threaten. Art is fundamentally an affirmation, a yea-saying to the world and to man's life in the world—despite all that says "No." It reveals beauty and joy, evokes wonder, transforms and combats evil and ugliness, embodies values and shows meaning, and strives to transmute and harmonize. Art's very essence is to help us see and hear and know and feel; to make us come alive and respond.

Culture that is genuine belongs to life. It is not an irrelevant and superfluous addendum or the result of idle curiosity or an escape from boredom. Neither is it a sphere whose exaltation removes it from life, a sphere in which "we are shut off from human interests; . . . lifted above the stream of life." [2] To separate culture from life in this way would be to purify culture by making it sterile and to cede man's life in the world to the prosaic scheme; it would be to ignore—either facilely or desperately—human existence, and to abandon life to estrangement and vacuity. The function of genuine culture is to illuminate and enhance and help to make whole the life of man in the world.

MAN AND MAN

Response and Relation

Relation between man and man is the basic and the highest of man's relations with the world. The loss of man by man, the central calamity of our time, is the loss of true relation. At the root of this calamity we find again the prosaic mentality: relation is unknown to it.

Interhuman relation is response of one person to another. Such response differs from response in art and other realms of culture because it involves two or more beings capable of response, and at least the possibility of reciprocity. Also, in interhuman relation a person actively addresses another in word or deed (or in silence) and demands response—a response that in turn involves not only a receptive, but also an active, component.

Responding to a person is the contrary of approaching him with the prosaic interest of gaining mastery or control over him, either by explaining him or by using him. Despite the radical contrast, it is easy to deceive oneself about the two approaches. In the sexual sphere, for example, it seems that in being intently concerned with the partner one is responding to him. But the attention given is often the attention required to control and manipulate the other. The partner is nothing but the instrument for satisfying one's desire. Indeed the prevalent prosaic conceptions of man often see using and being used as constituting the basic character of sexual love and of all human interaction. Freud, for example, speaks of the sexual act as an act of aggression in which the partner is a love-object used to satisfy sexual needs. Because these conceptions ignore response, their effect is to undermine the possibility of its realization. Using a partner may satisfy the sex drive—as many prosaic thinkers interpret the desire for love between man and woman—but it negates true relation, for the user remains isolated and the other is not met as a self but is reduced to a means.

Even in activities whose ostensible purpose is to help other persons, the helper frequently manipulates and uses them. There are people who are constantly intent on "helping" others yet have never acknowledged another as the individual being he is and allowed him to make an impact upon them. If their help is rebuffed, they may even refuse to withdraw. At bottom, it is really their own needs they want to satisfy, and the other is the means for doing this.

Often we attend to the other person in so impersonal and specialized a fashion that we do not even recognize him as a concrete man, as a man who is alive and feels and hopes and suffers at the instant we confront him. We neglect to acknowledge that he too has longings and fears that are analogous to our own. We forget to think of him as one who, like ourselves, is surrounded by pressures and difficulties. We ignore the fact that he, too, is immersed in the human condition, endowed with potentials and burdened by troubles. We prosaically regard him as an entity in which we have a certain functional interest—an entity that has to be talked to, avoided, sold something, impressed, explained, or opposed.

If we seldom try to be aware of the other person as a man, even less do we try to be aware of him as the particular man he is, as this individual at this place and this time in his existence. Yet response requires that we turn toward the particular individual, that we engage ourself in a meeting of person with person. This involves listening. Many conversations are not dialogues but double monologues in which one person hardly hears what the other says, and the two trains of speech run beside or bounce off of each other, but never intertwine and unite. Some conversations are like debates or duels, in which the speaker's sole purpose is to assert himself over the other. He does not meet the other but is out to subdue him. Moreover, the aim is to subdue the other, not as a true opponent —who in his opposition is acknowledged to be a person, a concrete being—but merely as a means or a hindrance that is to be manipulated or swept away.

Sometimes a person seeks to make the other serve his interest not by engaging in a duel, but by "selling himself." He plays a role that he thinks will please the other or acts the part he thinks the other expects in the situation. He does not turn toward the other, but manipulates him, though not directly; he does it by manipulating himself, by maintaining a "surface of agreement," a "show of affection," by maneuvering, performing, and posing in ways that will make the other person act in accordance with his plans and satisfy his needs.[3] The seller of himself says to the other, as Erich Fromm puts it, "I am as you desire me." [4] There is no real listening, only the attention necessary to play the role. But in relation there is genuine dialogue. One person listens to the other, allowing him to be who he is, and addresses the other from his true self. The true self is *present* to the other; the words he speaks are not planned for effect, but are the disclosure of the speaker's being. In playing a role, the true self hides, or where playing has become the rule, is displaced by an amorphous, amoeboid entity that adjusts to each occasion.

In responding to a man we try to see him as he is, to know him in his concreteness and individuality. This requires self-extension similar to the self-extension necessary to understand history. But now another person is actually with us, and his existence demands that we turn toward him. We must try to put ourself in his place, to think his thoughts, to see with his eyes, and to feel the world as he does. This is not self-forgetting, denial or loss of our own being, or playing a role, but being truly present to the other.

Genuine relation has immediacy and directness, and is the opposite of prosaic impersonality and detachment. We allow the other to draw near, make ourself accessible, and ourself draw near to the other. We allow the other to touch our feelings and to affect our beliefs, desires, and passions. We go out to meet the other with our whole being.

Relation therefore involves openness, which means not shutting out the other and not shutting in the self. Openness is readiness for the nonsystematized and unfamiliar, the singular and unpredictable—the nonprosaic. The person we meet is beyond any system; he cannot be exhausted by categories, he cannot be reduced to what is already known. A closed self comes to encounter with plan and calculation. But genuine relation cannot be planned. It needs spontaneous presentness and openness—openness in listening and speaking, openness to the other's impact, and openness of self-disclosure.

Distrust and skepticism in human encounter, the enemies of openness, are often a means of avoiding the singular and are due to fear of what cannot be fitted into methods and systems. The prosaic person is insecure and anxiously guards his precarious stability. He is walled by protective devices and keeps aloof lest the other person affect him and threaten the props that sustain him; he subjugates the other person to impersonal schemes and figures him out like a problem, thereby trying to guard his own inflexible and brittle position. The distrustful person strives to assure himself that the other can be dealt with by familiar procedures and will not prove him inadequate; he admits only what can make no impact, by filtering otherness through the standardized system of criteria, tests, definitions, and credentials. However, the very foundation of human relation is the ability and courage to trust. The prosaic man's distrust of others is closely allied with his aggressiveness toward them. Aggressiveness is the striving, obvious or hidden, to satisfy, bolster, or reassure the self by using or silencing the other. The aggressive person tries to subdue another by words or acts so that the other's potential impact may be avoided. Unable to face and acknowledge his individuality, the prosaic man negates it by attack.

In response, on the contrary, we entrust ourself to the other. This entails risk, and the courage to risk. Relation is unforseeable and its consequences unforseeable. It may sustain or delight us; or it may shake our beliefs and habits and our very being. For in relation the self leaves all confines, emerges from singleness, and comes forth to respond to a real address; it forgoes the safety—which is empty and illusory

—of self-enclosure, of systems, standards, and weapons that use and subdue the world but separate the self from the world and give it the safety of imprisonment. The self comes forth in freedom to respond to another out of the depth and center of the self's being. The skeptic and the aggressor lack the courage to do this. They are ostensibly strong and sure of themselves, but in truth, afraid. Their courage is in their armor. Only the person who uses no walls or weapons to avert the unfortellable and thus protect a spurious selfhood can risk himself in relation.

Responsibility

Response to man involves responsibility, for a man is not a fixed entity, he is always susceptible of being either helped or harmed. His very existence as a man, and that means as the particular man he is, is not given and settled; it has to be realized anew in his every encounter with the world. A man is neither complete unto himself nor ever definitively a certain self. The question "Who are you?" addressed to him by word or deed can be a question that welcomes him and affirms his being, or it can be a question that rejects and denies. Because a man's self is not static, because possibility is perpetually interwoven with actuality, response to him always involves attention not only to who he is at that instant but also to who he may be in the next. What we do or fail to do with respect to a man, affects him, and we are therefore inevitably responsible for him. The only choice is whether we accept or ignore the responsibility. To ignore it is to fail to respond. For if we respond, then the predicament of his being, the pain he suffers, the hopes he has, and the potentials that are his to atrophy or blossom engage our responsibility. Responsibility is not subservience to a system of rules and duties. It means bonds, but not bondage. To be responsible is to shoulder others' burdens with courage and humility and to acknowledge that who they are and become is affected by ourself.

There is a notion common in our society that it is wrong to influence others, that such influence violates their individual rights. But this notion is based on a false understanding of human life and on a prosaic conception of influence. The notion is false because it fails to recognize that influence is inevitable, that individuality does not live in a vacuum. Everything has an influence on man; every part of his environment has an effect—climate, dwelling, furniture, street, car, food, job, people, words, noise, silence. It is impossible to be near a person and to have no influence upon him. The question is whether we acknowledge our influence and, if we do, what we make of it: whether we subdue, control, and make use of the other or accept responsibility for the integrity of his existence. The doctrine that we must leave another individual alone accepts the prosaic notion that influence means control, so that every influence violates him, but this doctrine is, in fact, a retreat from accepting responsibility for him.

We foster another, above all, by turning toward him in true relation. By being open ourselves we sometimes enable another to be open (although his opening may be a painful, shaking, and radical experience); by entrusting ourselves to him we may give him the courage to trust; by acknowledging him, we may help him attain harmony within his self and achieve the freedom to be in the world. "When a man is singing and cannot lift his voice, and another comes and sings with him, another who can lift his voice, then the first will be able to lift his voice too. That is the secret of the bond between spirit and spirit." [5]

Individualism and Collectivism

The usual conceptions of the individual and the group are radically inadequate, even though they are all too true to what in fact commonly exists. Such conceptions see either an atomic individual or else a group in which the individual is lost as a member. In the first view, individualism, the self is given so much importance that the world is obscured. In the second, group view, or collectivism, the system, organization, or collectivity is all-important, and the individual is an anonymous, faceless cipher and specialized function. But neither view knows anything of human relation. In neither does individual respond to individual, nor does man assume responsibility for man. The man who exemplifies the individualist overtly ignores others, the man who corresponds to the collectivist view is always in the midst of others, but acknowledges no one. The individualist makes others into means; the collectivist man treats others as the means to which they are reduced by the system. The individualist tries to escape from his emptiness by self-inflation; the collectivist, by pursuing the smoothest possible adjustment to the system. The individualist ignores responsibility in supposing that individual freedom means every man for himself; the collectivist ignores it in abdicating his and the other's freedom and blaming the system.

As the collectivist way of life advances, the individualist way becomes increasingly spurious. Sometimes it consists of little more than doing as one pleases and asserting one's "rights" over those of others; often it depends on means the collectivist system itself provides, such as "personalized" bank checks, "customized" mass-produced automobiles, and an endless stream of "original" novelties and gadgets. This spurious individualism deluges every part of existence and is found in the realm of learning as well as in industry. And art whose creativity consists of a blatantly contrived attempt to be different and whose subjectivity is empty promptly receives the attention and applause it seeks from the collectivity that "believes in individualism."

Neither individualism nor collectivism sees a man as a being who responds to others. Each divorces him from others and encloses him in empty subjectivity; each denies a man's responsibility to his fellow men. Both views correspond to prosaic conceptions of individual man and of the relationship between man and man. The individual man is not seen as a true individual: he is reduced, as is every individual entity by the prosaic mind, to a cluster of properties. His relationship with others is viewed as a system of interactions that can be spelled out or grasped in a diagram like that of an electric circuit or of the systematized interconnections of organizational roles. Hence relationship is thought to consist in controlling and being controlled, in using and being used, in discharging and receiving functional service. When control is concentrated, we have individualism; when it is dispersed, collectivism. The concrete uniqueness of individuals and the inexhaustible substance, the dense fabric, of their response and responsibility to each other are absent.

To grasp the fullness of individual man and of relation, we must transcend the prosaic outlook. The fullness of individuality and the fullness of relation go together. In responding to another, in opening the self to a personal encounter, in assuming responsibility for another being, a man is genuinely an individual self. His own being and his being in relation with another are one reality.[6]

MAN AND NATURE

Man must stand in a relation of response to nature. Today he takes two contrasting positions vis-à-vis nature, both under the sway of the prosaic mentality. In one position he perceives and treats nature as utterly alien; subduing it in mind and in action, he regards it as infinitely distant from himself, its master and exploiter. In the second position he attempts to join himself to nature by viewing himself in exactly the same way as he does nature, asserting, for example, that man is nothing but a physicochemical mechanism or that he is no more than an animal among animals. (His conception of an animal is, of course, prosaic.)

Relation requires that both man and nature be recognized in their concrete uniqueness. Both are infinitely more than is apparent to prosaic interests. Respect for what is other has a scope that includes, but is much greater than, the scope of objectivity. Many modes of apprehension are required to do justice to nature and to man.

The relationship between man and nature must not be reduced to their having common properties that are the focus of attention of various scientific studies. These properties must be acknowledged, but they exhaust neither man nor nature. The relation that is foreign to the prosaic mind is found in man's turning toward nature in a movement kindred to that of turning toward man. He refrains from obtruding with systems and tools that use and control, and instead opens himself in response. He meets nature in its concreteness and does not reduce it to abstractable properties. He makes himself accessible to its impact instead of going to work upon it and keeping it away from himself. He cherishes the shape, color, and scent of the fruits of the earth. He welcomes the sky, the air, and changes of weather instead of imprisoning himself in sterile, often windowless buildings that totally isolate him from nature. He seeks to become aware of nature's splendor and power. He perceives its bounty and its destruction, and he rejoices in the one and suffers from the other. He goes out to feel the earth and smell its ineffable fragrances. He is glad to witness the morning's awakening—the dew on the meadows, the first bird call and then the rising chorus, and the enlivening air. He learns to know intimately the summer sunlight on the ripening grain, the odor of fallen leaves in the autumn, and the crunch of snow in the cold stillness under the stars. He knows birth, maturing, and death.

Response to nature, analogous to the response to man, involves responsibility, although responsibility of a lower order. Nature is not in question as is man; it is not open to being affirmed or denied as he is, nor is human response essential to its being. But nature also can be hurt and healed, abused and protected. The man who responds to nature cares for it, not like one who merely wants to maximize its usefulness,

but like one who is concerned for its being, respects its otherness, and assumes responsibility for what it will become. He
is, as Saint-Exupéry says, a "gardener." [7] In response and
responsibility there is unity between man as man and nature
as nature.

MAN, WORLD, AND SYMBOL

The relation between man and the world requires all the
resources of the symbolic realm. If the symbol loses its power
for us, relation and the world retreat, and the reality expressed in the symbol disappears from our life; conversely,
when our relation to the world is impoverished, the symbolic
expression of what we have lost becomes meaningless to us.
The two losses are reciprocal. As the words *love* and *wonder*,
for example, are emptied of meaning, the realities they express
become more and more inaccessible; conversely, as the experience of love and wonder is diminished, the words are emptied
of meaning. And this is true not only for words but for all
symbols. Thus, man's response to the marvels of nature or
the human body diminishes together with the ability and the
desire to grasp these marvels in painting and sculpture. Literal
symbols and arbitrary symbols do not suffice, because they
get only at skeletal properties of things. The substance and
density of individual concreteness require symbols with evocative power, symbols whose shape is intimately linked with their
meaning.

The soundness of symbols is vital for the relation of man
with man. Literalness is good for answering scientific questions
or giving information about the operation of a machine, but
it is hopelessly inadequate when a man turns to you to engage
in a human relation. (And just as bad, or worse, are the
sentimental phrases and clever distortions of language to which
the prosaic mind—deprived of potent and genuine language—
has recourse.) The speech of human relation cannot be prosaic,
because the substance of relation cannot be exhausted in neatly

defined terms. A concrete encounter, a meeting of self with self, is beyond all systems and rules. To answer a man who speaks to you from the depth of his soul by asking him for explicit statements is to refuse to meet him, to refuse to listen. It is to demand instead that he reduce himself to an instance, or a case, that can be subsumed in a standard scheme. It is to compound disrespect for the word with disrespect for the man who speaks it. The speech of relation, just as the relation itself, must take shape in the lived occasion. What is said is inseparable from the way it is said. It cannot be carried by arbitrary symbols. All the resources of the symbolic sphere, all its potentials for grasping meanings in individual contexts are required, for every true relation is unique and therefore needs unique expression. The symbols that serve relation must partake of the qualities of art, and works of art themselves can become potent instruments of dialogue. Also, in an enduring relation other symbolic expressions arise that live only within this relation and become so charged with evocative power that things otherwise ineffable can be conveyed in the compressed intensity of an instant. A word, a gesture, a glance, an almost imperceptible smile, or a motion of the hand can convey a world.[8]

The centrality of the symbolic realm in man's life heightens the potential and danger of miscarriage in this realm. We easily become prisoners of symbols, so that instead of enhancing life, they distort it. As we have seen again and again, inappropriate symbols lead us to false and inadequate views and attitudes toward things. These symbols are imposed on the world, and the world is obscured and maimed. Instead of fostering our relation, they interfere with it.

Symbols, moreover, readily displace direct encounter. Men's attention and activity become confined to a sphere of symbols, leading them to complete estrangement from the world. Thus, in the modern world, where work is all but totally restricted to paper and type, symbols and their manipulation have become a wall between man and the world. An analogous situation exists in the realm of culture, where learning and art all too frequently become activities that keep men from direct meeting with nature and other men; these activities become a blinding routine, a shelter from the impact of active encounter and the responsibility it brings, an escape from meaningless surroundings, or an obsession. The very power of symbols that makes them so indispensable to man can also be his undoing. Symbols must never become his masters, but they must be tended and respected and given the vital place they deserve.

RESPONSE, CHALLENGE, AND PROBLEM

Response to the world, as we have seen, means turning toward the other, openness, and readiness to be touched. Further understanding of this way of being and of its absence from many lives is afforded by the fundamental contrast between response and the prosaic approach to things as a challenge and a problem.

The prosaic self lacks the shape and strength that are nurtured by genuine response. Its security depends on isolation and walls, and it is forever in need of reassurance. Therefore it treats every occasion as a means to gain reassurance—and an occasion that can be seen as a challenge is the perfect means. The prosaic man seeks reassurance through asserting his mastery over things or people and proving to himself that he is able to subdue them. The newer whatever confronts him looks and the more it seems to differ from what he has previously conquered, the more reassuring the conquering of it will be. At the same time, since he cannot respond to what confronts him as something that may deeply and unpredictably affect him, it must allow him to remain walled and protected, and to subdue it by the explanations, rules, and methods on which he has always depended. A situation that can be regarded as a challenge satisfies both requirements: it enables the prosaic man to consider it as new, different, and unique; yet, in its newness and uniqueness it is only another instance of what he can deal with in his usual ways, so he can remain fundamentally untouched and shun risk.

Just as the challenge precludes relation, so does the problem. A problem can be solved and put aside; and even if it cannot actually be solved, it is at least caught in a system. The self feels in control, and nothing is admitted that eludes its control or that cannot be completely grasped. A problem is something one keeps at a distance and need not meet face to face. To treat human beings as problems—whether in one's job or one's home—is to fail to acknowledge them as persons. To look always for standard ways for dealing with them—for example, in medicine, education, or charity—is to look away and to avoid response.

Chapter 14 WHOLENESS AND
THE PERSON

By *whole* I mean both unreduced and undivided. The man
who is whole acknowledges and unifies all elements of his
human self.[1] He does not try to escape from the complexity
and difficulty of human existence by suppressing parts of himself, thus transferring authority from a whole to a partial
being; nor does he attempt to resolve this complexity and
difficulty by splitting himself into compartments. He is neither
a mere part of a social system nor an isolated individualist.
The pressures on him and the demands from the world are
brought together in a center as rays in a focus, and his
approaches to the world issue from this center. He is always
himself.

The whole person, being capable of approaching the world
in diverse ways, accepts elements stressed by the prosaic
orientation, but is not chained to them; his approaches encompass the stance that distinguishes science as well as the stance
of art; he understands the treatment of things by standard abstractable properties as well as respect for uniqueness; he
appreciates the importance of explicit articulation but also the
importance of suggestion and evocation; he knows the attitude
of impersonality and also that of response; he embraces both

the approach whose aim is use and control, and that which accepts responsibility for the world.

But for us to be whole it is not enough to be capable of diverse approaches to the world and to be able to draw on diverse resources of the self in diverse encounters. For neither the self nor the self's interaction with the world can be systematized into separate compartments. The domination of mental and practical activities by such systematization is itself a chief factor in the prosaic mutilation of life. Wholeness means that the diverse resources of the self and diverse attitudes toward the world are not merely present side by side, but are unified.[2] It means that every activity is shaped by the whole self. If, for example, we express doubt with respect to another's beliefs, it is not because skepticism has destroyed our ability to trust or because trust has been permanently relegated to a separate realm, but because here and now, on this particular occasion, the whole self judges that doubt is in order. Doubt and trust subtend each other; they cohere in the unity that is the whole man. There are times to doubt and times to trust; there are realms where doubt is in the foreground (as in science) and realms where trust must be prominent (as in friendship); but only if both are acknowledged and kept in dynamic balance is a man whole and able to stand in appropriate relationship to the world. Similarly, when we speak with another, the occasion may call for explicit prose or it may call for poetic resources. A whole person recognizes different symbolic powers and the tensions between them, and tries to shape his speech to make it appropriate to each individual occasion.

Only if we become capable of taking different approaches to the world and of maintaining constant communion and a living balance among them can we hope to do justice to each moment of life. This is most difficult, for the ways in which we face the world easily become rigid, and to alter these ways is to transform our innermost being. Nothing requires more courage. Nothing is more desperately urgent for modern man.

If each part of the person is in communion with every other part, then no activity can be segregated from the rest of life. Each activity, while it stresses certain interests, values, and faculties, remains in touch with all other activities, capable of influencing them and being influenced by them. Only thus can an activity remain open to new aspects of the world and human life, and thereby keep its own soundness, instead of degenerating into dogmatic method, enshrined procedure, or domineering system.

CONCEPTIONS OF MAN

It is clear that the dissolution of man—his reduction and fragmentation—is rooted in the prosaic mentality. All its elements contribute to this dissolution, and so do the effects of these elements on apprehension, symbols, values, and man's relation to the world. Man cannot be whole if the conceptions he has of himself reduce and divide him, for what he thinks of himself has a pervasive effect on all he does and becomes. To do justice to man, one must not diminish understanding or raise a method above the reality to be apprehended. One must remember that what a person perceives depends on his attitude and that the attitude usually called objectivity is but a special and limited kind of respect; one must respect man fully and see him as the being he is, not reduce him to whatever likenesses he has (no matter how important) to things that are nonhuman. One must overcome the perverse and aggressive desire to degrade man and must not absurdly and stubbornly reverse the ancient error of anthropomorphizing the nonhuman world by dehumanizing man. One must look to various modes of apprehension in order to become aware of man's many aspects and his inexhaustible substance; one must be attentive to and cultivate all the resources of symbols; one must see man in the fullness of his being in the world, especially in the relation of man with man.

To be capable of seeing man thus is itself a manifestation of wholeness. Our striving to transcend the prosaic conception is a part of our striving toward wholeness. What a man believes is an inseparable part of who he is. This multiplies the difficulties of wholeness. But it also gives cause for hope, for whether growth toward wholeness takes place in the way one lives or in the views one holds, growth in the one may enhance the other.

FREEDOM

It is not necessary here to give a detailed refutation of the denials of the reality of freedom that are a part of modern conceptions of man. It is sufficient to note that these denials invariably proceed from a prosaic outlook. Man is reduced to what is seen of him by science and quasi science; he is made into an instance of general principles and is supposed to be exhaustively explained, or at least explainable, in explicit symbols. All this, we have seen, is radically mistaken, for what science does not perceive is not therefore nonexistent. Nor do purpose, self-government, and freedom require the negation or suspension of scientific laws. To suppose that they do is to take it for granted that science exhausts the world, to accept a prosaic outlook. To recognize freedom, one must look to other modes of apprehension than science. Freedom belongs to the person and can be known only by an approach that respects the person. We can know freedom in ourself, and we can know it in another through response that acknowledges the other as a person. Freedom resides first of all in the "inside" of human action, and to know it one must therefore be attentive to the inner experience of man.

Freedom is not chaos, chance, or license. Nor is it the individual's separation from the world. On the contrary, it is his capacity to respect the world, to apprehend it, to respond to and be responsible for it, and to judge and decide and engage in action.

One realm of man's being in the world in which freedom can be known is scientific apprehension—the realm from which denial of freedom chiefly issues. Like all apprehension, scientific apprehension involves the "inside" of human action and cannot be subsumed in scientific generalizations. If the individual is to recognize it for what it is, he cannot take the position of an alien observer of scientific activity, but must live the experience itself while thinking a scientist's thoughts. In doing so, he can discover what it means to be free or not free to think and can discover, as well, that only by himself, in freedom, can he make judgments of truth or error, imaginatively create a structure of thought, or decide what to observe, how to observe, and when an observation is valid. Without freedom there could be no science, no doctrine denying freedom, nor indeed, any doctrine at all.

Freedom as a capacity, as the power of the self to be in the world, is inseparably linked with wholeness. Any part of the person that is not acknowledged and integrated into a whole, like an outlaw attacks the parts ostensibly in control. In this is to be found the fatal error of those who make a cleavage between the rational and the emotional. Such persons do not acknowledge the emotions and take them into a unified self, but repress them or cast them out and suppose that in their detachment they are free from emotion and therefore rational. Instead, the emotions—prevented from constituting a vital element of the whole—impinge upon thought and curtail its freedom in unrecognized, underground ways. The very doctrine, for example, that in the search for knowledge one must expel emotion, that understanding can only be gained in detachment, is shaped under pressure of unrecognized emotions—not the least of which is fear of emotion and the consequent need to cling to the security of a sterile scheme. Only if the emotions are accepted as fully belonging to the self is it possible to prevent their turning into covert masters.

A person is not free to be in the world unless every part of him is potentially present at every moment of life. If, when faced with a predicament, for example, he cannot use reason to illuminate his position, he does not acquire the freedom to choose. If, when engaged in dialogue with another, he cannot draw upon whatever mode of expression is called for—explicit or suggestive, literal or evocative—he is not free to apprehend and convey what matters at the moment. If, in encountering nature or a work of man or a person, the individual's feelings are not ready to be affected, if the prosaic mentality stifles his soul so that he confronts the world only for mental mastery and practical use, then he is not free to respond, to open himself, to be in relation.

Only if all elements of the self can be called upon in every occasion is self-government possible. If one interest or one special activity of the person is isolated from everything that might demand its reassessment and change, this special interest or activity becomes an autonomous entity that is no longer answerable to the rest of life. In specialism—the institutionalization of isolated activities practiced by partial and divided selves—the activities are enshrined, and their practitioners are fettered. The whole self, on the other hand, is free to assess each special activity and, though the activity be valuable, to curtail and even sacrifice it (a heresy in our time) if other and greater values so demand.

Wholeness makes the difference between commitment and enslavement. Only in freedom can one commit oneself. Any end or activity that is not made answerable to the whole person becomes a prison, for the partial person, who is tied to the end, is incapable of seeing beyond it. The partial person does not choose a given end from among other ends and in view of a total situation but abandons choice and decision, not committing himself but giving himself up. Hence the bonds of commitment are replaced by the bondage of servitude; dedication changes to automatism; devotion becomes compulsion.

VALUES

Choice and commitment imply valuation, and valuation, like freedom, is linked with wholeness, for when any part of life is segregated from the rest, assessment of that part becomes impossible. Only if one part is balanced with other parts—only if it is seen in concrete context, and if all parts of the world and all parts of the self involved in a particular occasion are acknowledged and reconciled—can there be true valuation. Otherwise values become pseudo values—interests, methods, or goals isolated from all else, set up as values, and blindly affirmed.

The person who is conscious of wholeness judges again and again as the concrete occasion requires. He knows that no fixed system, set of rules, or clear-cut division can do justice to life. To judge an individual entity is not to determine its place in a ready-made public scheme. Neither is it to express a private whim or the spurious rights of individualism. Judgment is maimed when the person is not whole and therefore not free to respect what he judges. Genuine judgment is an act of giving the utmost respect to the world and striving for the utmost wholeness of self.

THE WHOLE PERSON AND THE WORLD

Wholeness does not reside in the individual as an isolated being but in the person who is in relationship with the world. This relationship is manifold: it must comprise control (of nature and other elements of the person's surroundings) as well as response; use as well as responsibility. In the whole self, moreover, interest in use and control is balanced by response and responsibility, and is thereby transmuted. This balance ensures that use does not degenerate into abuse—that nature, for instance, is husbanded, not despoiled—and that alteration is prevented from turning into tampering. Physical and mental mastery enter as essential elements into the totality of man's confrontation of the environment instead of being heedless obsessions. Practical action is informed by values pertinent to all of life, not by a monomaniac impulse. Mental apprehension is an act of the whole person and is not enslaved by dogmatic method, driven to deny what it cannot encompass, or used to dispose of the world and avoid its impact or to inflate the self.

Wholeness is crucial in man's relationship with man. No interaction with a human being should be, or needs to be, devoid of response. No matter what the occasion, what the purpose, or how restricted the contact, people must be acknowledged as human selves. Friendship and love can blossom and ripen only rarely in each man's life, but in every confrontation—even in the most narrowly functional exchange, a routine purchase, for example—it is essential to make that minimal response by which the other is recognized as a man; even here he must not be reduced to the embodiment of a function. Even when the other is as anonymous as a passenger in the subway or a passer-by on a city street, the person who is whole will meet the other as an individual being the moment the other enters, for whatever reason, the compass of the person's life. A glance, a smile, a nod, or a word can suffice to acknowledge the other in his unique and inexhaustible concreteness.

A man must never be disposed of by being categorized. Conceptual classification is important—the illumination shed by the discernment of regularities, scientific or other, is essential—but classifications and regularities must never be allowed to displace the concrete individual. A whole man, no matter how fruitful he finds the recognition of regularities for a specific purpose, never treats a human being as a mere instance or case. The physician, for example, who regards his patient as a case of pneumonia violates the patient as a man.

The patient is not a case of pneumonia but a man who suffers from pneumonia; and between these two entities and the ways of confronting them there is a measureless difference.

The response I speak of must not be confused with the devices often promoted by various branches of applied psychology to make people feel that they are being acknowledged as persons, when in fact they are not. The spurious and insulting posture of intimacy, the feigned interest, the backslap, the "friendly" smile, the patronizing use of first names, and the insidious manipulations by personnel management and public relations—doubly insidious because often the perpetrators have fooled even themselves into believing that they are in relation with others—are diabolical perversions of response.

Only a whole self is capable of genuine response, especially to a human being. The partial or divided person is afraid of encounter, afraid to expose his rigid and brittle stability. He cannot summon the courage to listen, to respect the unique, to open himself to the unreducible and unforseeable. He cannot risk himself, because his very existence is tied to division and suppression instead of to a unity in which all elements of the self and its confrontation with the world come together and cohere. Therefore the nonunified person will avoid the other. Distrusting him and being on guard, he will neutralize the potential impact of the other by reducing him to something he can deal with—the embodiment of a function, a commodity, a case, a problem, or a challenge whose conquest will yield reassurance. The divided person will seek to ignore the other entirely, or to ward him off by aggression; he will try to avoid the impact of the other's being by playing a role or by selling himself. A nonunified person cannot acknowledge another because he does not acknowledge himself; he is fearful of being brought up against his own self-betrayal. A whole person has the courage to be open, to risk himself, to be himself, because his being is an embracing unity. The courage to be oneself and the courage to respond to another are inseparable.

For the whole man no activity, goal, method, or interest remains uninformed by true relation to other beings. He assesses and shapes every pursuit with respect and concern for men as men. He allows no transformation of the physical, social, or cultural environment to take place without consideration for persons. Nor does he make business, government, law, medicine, learning, or art into a compartmentalized self-justifying pursuit in which response and responsibility are ignored. But today we avoid response and disavow responsibility, either by appealing to the duties of a job or profession, by disclaiming competence outside our specialty, or by calling on the name of progress. These and other protestations are but ways of hiding in publicly approved shelters, of escaping from the complexity of human life into simple and comforting solutions and keeping the self untouched by others; they are ways of avoiding the weight and risk of freedom and judgment, and hence the responsibility for ourself and others—in short, of evading the burden of being whole. To respond to others and be responsible for them is the very essence of being a man.

THE LIVED CONCRETENESS OF BEING WHOLE

The wholeness of the person is not simple. Man's interests, values, needs, faculties, and approaches to the world are varied and cannot be harmonized easily. The unified self must encompass tensions, frictions, and contrarieties.

Current formulas for living, in their effort to provide escape from these tensions, destroy wholeness by either reducing man to a partial man who is blind to most of the world or by splitting man and the world into corresponding isolated compartments. The whole person, in contrast, acknowledges the complexity of life with its various and disparate claims, and maintains a balance that embraces them.

This balance cannot be spelled out in a set of rules. No clear-cut system can do justice to the wholeness of human life.[3] All rules, criteria, and methods are themselves elements of life that must be taken into a larger unity. To look for a tidy system of wholeness would be to make yet another attempt to divide the self and the world into compartments so as to escape the tensions inherent in man's existence; it would be to disavow freedom and replace judgment and decision with conformity to an external authority, to evade response to the unforseeable and unique, and to relieve oneself of the heavy and joyous burden of responsibility for the world. The balance required for wholeness is one that is lived in the here and now of concrete occasions, with their multifarious and often opposing claims, values, and demands on the self. It has its being in the way a person seeks to understand a certain issue before him, makes a certain decision to act, reads certain words in a book, looks at a certain tree, and responds to a certain man who steps up to him. Such a balance means that all parts of the self are present, or potentially present, at every moment of life, ready to be touched and to influence each other, to respond, and to act—to be in the world.

There is no final perfection to be reached. Man is more whole or less whole, but his wholeness is never a static condition to be achieved and thereafter maintained in fixed form. It must be sought again and again, often with difficulty and pain. Every moment of life, each new experience, each new encounter, has to be taken into the self, and each may call for a wholeness more encompassing and more profound than has yet been attained.

NOTES

NOTES

CHAPTER I. DIMINUTION OF MAN'S
UNDERSTANDING

1. Galileo Galilei, *Dialogues concerning Two New Sciences*, trans. Henry Crew and Alfonso de Salvio (New York, 1914), p. 160.
2. *Ibid.*, p. 166.
3. Hans Reichenbach, *The Rise of Scientific Philosophy* (Berkeley, Calif., 1951), p. 4.
4. A. d'Abro, *The Evolution of Scientific Thought* (2d ed.; New York, 1950), pp. 354–55.
5. *Ibid.*, p. 355.
6. Reichenbach, *Rise of Scientific Philosophy*, p. 316.
7. C. H. Waddington, *The Scientific Attitude* (2d ed.; Baltimore, 1948), p. 35.
8. The claim that history is scientific or quasi-scientific has been more prevalent in recent times among philosophers than among historians (though even among the former, efforts have been made with varying success to view history as a valid nonscientific realm). Historians have more often, deliberately or unconsciously, imitated science in less obvious ways, or, occasionally, they have let mere reaction against it define their paths. The nature of such imitations and reactions will be seen in Part Two and Part Three.
9. Carl G. Hempel, "The Function of General Laws in History," *The Journal of Philosophy*, XXXIX (1942), 35–48.
10. Ernst Nagel, "Some Issues in the Logic of Historical Analysis," *The Scientific Monthly*, LXXIV (1952), 163, reprinted in Hans Meyerhoff (ed.), *The Philosophy of History in Our Time* (New York, 1959), p. 205.
11. Reichenbach, *Rise of Scientific Philosophy*, p. 308.
12. Thomas C. Cochran, "The Social Sciences and the Problem of Historical Synthesis," in Fritz Stern (ed.), *The Varieties of History* (New York, 1957), pp. 348–59.
13. José Ortega y Gasset, *Toward a Philosophy of History*, trans. Helene Weyl (New York, 1941), p. 178: "... the science, the

reason, in which modern man placed his social faith is, speaking strictly, merely physico-mathematical science together with biological science, the latter based directly on the former ... in short, ... what is called natural science or reason."

CHAPTER 2. DESTRUCTION OF LANGUAGE

1. Thomas C. Cochran, "The Social Sciences and the Problem of Historical Synthesis," in Fritz Stern (ed.), *The Varieties of History* (New York, 1957), p. 350.
2. Jan-Albert Goris, Introduction to the Anchor Books edition of Henri Pirenne, *A History of Europe,* trans. Bernard Miall (New York, 1958), I, xvi.
3. *Ibid.,* p. xiv.
4. The cleavage of language appears even in such a thinker as Ernst Cassirer (see, for example, *An Essay on Man* [New Haven, 1944], p. 115, where it is between propositional and emotional language), who was intent on interpreting language in all its fullness. It is widely accepted in the behavioral sciences.

CHAPTER 3. NULLIFICATION OF VALUES

1. In this book, except in a very few places, I have not addressed myself to such questions as those concerning God, faith, or revealed law—that is, to specifically religious matters. This does not mean that such matters need not concern modern man. The understanding of man and world toward which the book reaches leaves open questions as to the existence of God and a relation between man and world, and God.

CHAPTER 4. LOSS OF THE WORLD

1. Miguel de Unamuno, *The Tragic Sense of Life,* trans. J. E. Crawford Flitch (New York, 1954), p. 1.
2. Erich Kahler, *The Tower and the Abyss* (New York, 1957), p. 42.
3. One of Western society's most inspiring goals has been the education of the masses of men, the expansion of their lives through the wealth of culture. Its realization required the surmounting of social, political, and economic obstacles: access to the products of the spirit was denied to the majority of men by a dominant social class anxious to safeguard its privileges, or by an exploiting government basing its powers on men's ignorance, or by the crushing burden of poverty. Gradually, with much struggle, men have been overcoming these obstacles. But even as they have done so, the goal has vanished—not alone for the masses of men, but for all. Education as concerned with the understanding and appreciation of thought and art, the illumination of the mind, the refinement of feeling, the cultivation of judgment, the capacity for effective and civilized action, the irra-

diation of every province of life, education in this sense, is all but extinct.

4. José Ortega y Gasset, *Toward a Philosophy of History*, trans. Helene Weyl (New York, 1941), p. 181.

5. The phrase "being in the world" is not intended to be the equivalent of Martin Heidegger's *In-der-Welt-sein*. There are certainly basic similarities in meaning, as my general outlook has fundamental points of agreement with Heidegger's (as seen in his book *Sein und Zeit* ["Being and Time"]) and with those of other thinkers who also may broadly be characterized as existentialist; but there are equally fundamental differences, whose nature, extent, and depth varies with the far-reaching variations among these thinkers.

CHAPTER 5. DISSOLUTION OF THE PERSON

1. Robert A. Millikan, *Science and the New Civilization* (New York, 1930), p. 18.

2. See Erich Kahler, *The Tower and the Abyss* (New York, 1957), chap. iii.

CHAPTER 6. THE PROSAIC MENTALITY

1. For an illuminating discussion of the dismissal of "meaningless questions," see Joseph Wood Krutch, *Human Nature and the Human Condition* (New York, 1959), chap. ix.

CHAPTER 7. SCIENCE

1. This discussion of scientific cognition and its public character has implied the existence of an external world—an "objective reality"—that becomes known to scientific thought and that pursues its course independently of our efforts to know it. This is an implication with which the modern mind is sometimes not at ease. Philosophical thought has often denied either this independent existence or man's ability to know it. And the rise of modern physics, with its emphasis on the role of the observer in the cognizing process, has been widely interpreted as rendering meaningless any notion of an independent external world. Whatever their merit, however, these ideas do not invalidate the assertion of the public character of science. Suppose we are not entitled to claim that science discovers order in nature, but can only say that it coordinates our sensations, so that the problem of a common world to be sensed is (apparently) not even raised. We will then have to make parallel changes in the language we use to speak about knowledge. This is an extremely difficult (perhaps impossible) undertaking, because our language everywhere implies an independently existing world. But in attempting to make the changes, the public character of science comes even more into the foreground, for instead of being able to ground each individual's observations in an underlying reality and judging the validity of his

beliefs by their correspondence to this reality, we must now restrict ourselves to demanding agreement among different observations and beliefs. The susceptibility to agreement has been an integral part of scientific thought since its inception, but modern physics and especially the theory of relativity have given it new and powerful emphasis. (Modern writers have been exceedingly impressed by the relativity of scientific observations, that is, by the banishment of the absolute, the assertion that what everyone sees is relative to his frame of reference. They have been much less impressed by the interconnections between different observations, by the requirement that different observations be capable of being brought into accord by means of a uniform and consistent system of conceptual relationships, and this has had unfortunate philosophical repercussions. At the heart of the theory of relativity is the scheme whereby different observers can test their agreement.) Whether or not we permit ourselves to envisage an independent world while speaking of the nature of science, we continue to assert that science always seeks an understanding to which all competent investigators can agree. Indeed, disagreement on the part of anyone generally thought to be competent instantly places an onus on others to seek to reconcile their views by various means: by showing the dissenter to have erred on this occasion, by modifying established views, by showing that the disagreement can be explained in ways that leave established views undisturbed, or by the establishment of new schemes that encompass and reconcile the discrepancy.

CHAPTER 8. HISTORY

1. Bertrand Russell, *A History of Western Philosophy* (New York, 1945), p. 834.
2. Ernst Nagel, "Some Issues in the Logic of Historical Analysis," *The Scientific Monthly*, LXXIV (1952), 162–69, reprinted in Hans Meyerhoff (ed.), *The Philosophy of History in Our Time* (New York, 1959), pp. 203–15.
3. Carl G. Hempel, "The Function of General Laws in History," *The Journal of Philosophy*, XXXIX (1942), 39.
4. See, for example, Ernst Cassirer's assertion that "art and history are the most powerful instruments of our inquiry into human nature," in *An Essay on Man* (New Haven, 1944), p. 206.
5. José Ortega y Gasset, *Toward a Philosophy of History*, trans. Helene Weyl (New York, 1941), p. 183.
6. Henri Pirenne, *A History of Europe*, trans. Bernard Miall (New York, 1958), II, 3.
7. *Ibid.*, p. 28.
8. R. G. Collingwood, *The Idea of History* (London, 1946), p. 213.
9. Pirenne, *History of Europe*, p. 29.
10. This quotation and the two that follow are from Cassirer, *Essay on Man*, pp. 175, 184, 177.
11. The quotations in this paragraph are from Collingwood, *Idea of History*, p. 213.

12. Pirenne, *History of Europe,* p. 29.
13. Theodor Mommsen, "Rectorial Address," in Fritz Stern (ed.), *The Varieties of History* (New York, 1957), p. 195.
14. Theodor Mommsen, *The History of Rome,* trans. W. P. Dickson (New York, 1900), V, 6.
15. The quotations in this paragraph are from Thomas C. Cochran, "The Social Sciences and the Problem of Historical Synthesis," in Stern, *Varieties of History,* pp. 350–58.
16. Henri Pirenne, "What Are Historians Trying To Do?" in Stuart A. Rice (ed.), *Methods of Social Science* (Chicago, 1931), reprinted in Meyerhoff, *Philosophy of History,* pp. 87–88.
17. Karl Popper, *The Open Society and Its Enemies* (3d ed.; London, 1957), II, 263.
18. *Ibid.;* also Morris R. Cohen, *The Meaning of Human History* (La Salle, Ill., 1947), p. 38.
19. Popper, *Open Society,* II, 264.
20. Hempel, "General Laws," p. 47.
21. Two objections will perhaps be made to my argument. The first questions the justification for saying that geological knowledge of an event concerns a group of abstracted properties which also characterize any number of other events. The second takes the opposite path and denies the justification of claiming for historical events a uniqueness other than that belonging to scientific events.

   As to the first objection, where are the other events, it asks, to which the group of abstractions supposedly applies? Are not the events of geology unique? They *are* unique in two ways: first, in the strict sense in which every event is unique, including those studied by theoretical science; second, in that our special interest in establishing geological happenings at definite places and dates is rarely found in theoretical science, where the specific occurrence is only attended to as a test for the universal laws it exemplifies. But geological events are *not* unique in that they are repeatable with respect to a group of abstracted properties. To clarify this, it is helpful to distinguish two kinds of events with which the geologist deals, those of specifically geological interest, and others treated primarily by sciences whose laws are made use of in geology. The first kind comprises such processes as volcanic action, flooding, sedimentation, erosion, and glaciation, particular occurrences of which are viewed as repeated instances of the appropriate class—in the same way as is done in the theoretical sciences. The second kind are events of the past that, one takes for granted, followed the same laws of physics and chemistry as do the events now studied by these sciences. Hence one uses these laws in geology, and the events they explain therefore constitute particular repeatable instances of them just as do the events of physics and chemistry.

   The second objection to my distinction between the individuality of geological and historical events grants what has just been said, but denies that the individuality of events in history is any different from that in geology and hence in all science. Thus it is asserted that "history can 'grasp the unique individuality' of its objects of study no more no less than can physics or chemistry." (Hempel,

"General Laws," p. 37.) This, evidently, is a denial of the argument advanced earlier in this chapter that the knowledge of individual occurrences sought by history is very different in nature from that sought by science. But when we examine the sort of grasping of unique individuality that is denied, we find that it is something called "complete description," a process that would "require a statement of all the properties exhibited by the spatial region or the individual object involved," as well as explanation of the object "in the sense of accounting for *all* its characteristics by means of universal hypotheses." *(Ibid.)* This, I agree, is rightly asserted to be impossible: the "task can never be accomplished." Moreover, whoever tries to approach this "complete" grasping merely succeeds in suffocating the mind in endless properties and labyrinthine complexity of explanations. But why should we suppose that those who claim that history looks toward the individual, concrete happening intend anything so foolish?

The objection is clearly based on a premise that is itself the very issue in question, namely, that all knowledge is patterned on science in that it views the individual object in terms of a group of abstractable properties correlated by universal laws. If that were so, then a fuller grasp of the individual indeed could only mean more such properties and more, as well as more complex, laws. This would make history a superscience and is clearly an untenable view, so the alternative conclusion is drawn, that history's grasp of individual objects is no more than that of physics. But neither is this conclusion in accord with what we have already said about history, nor are we compelled to it, since its premise is in question. We will do better to abide with the contention that history does indeed provide fuller knowledge of the concrete event—a contention that, I trust, has received some clarification and support already and that will be further elucidated in the sequel—and seek to understand in what way this is accomplished.

22. Donald W. McConnell, *Economic Behavior* (New York, 1939), pp. 894–95, quoted in Hempel, "General Laws," p. 40.
23. Cohen, *Meaning of Human History*, pp. 37–38.
24. Hempel, "General Laws," p. 42.
25. Cohen, *Meaning of Human History*, p. 52.
26. Hempel, "General Laws," p. 41.
27. Popper, *Open Society*, II, 268.
28. *Ibid.*, p. 264.
29. Johan Huizinga, "The Idea of History," in Stern, *Varieties of History*, p. 291.
30. *Ibid.*, p. 299.
31. G. G. Coulton, *Medieval Panorama* (Cambridge, 1938), p. 69.
32. Pirenne, *History of Europe*, p. 26.
33. Jacob Burckhardt, *The Civilization of the Renaissance in Italy*, trans. S. G. C. Middlemore (New York, 1954), p. 5.
34. The quotations in this paragraph are from Collingwood, *Idea of History*, pp. 219, 296, 303, 301.
35. *Ibid.*, p. 214.

36. *Ibid.*, p. 296.
37. *Ibid.*, p. 301.
38. Hempel, "General Laws," p. 44.
39. *Ibid.*, p. 40.
40. Cohen, *Meaning of Human History*, p. 38.
41. W. H. Walsh, *An Introduction to Philosophy of History* (London, 1951), p. 65.
42. This and the following quotations in this paragraph are from Popper, *Open Society*, II, 264, 265.
43. *Ibid.*, p. 265.
44. This and the following quotation are from Cohen, *Meaning of Human History*, p. 38.
45. McConnell, *Economic Behavior*, pp. 894–95.
46. Ortega y Gasset, *Toward a Philosophy of History*, p. 185; compare Walsh, *Philosophy of History*, pp. 66 ff.

CHAPTER 9. ART

1. The quotations in this paragraph are from Rudolf Carnap, *Philosophy and Logical Syntax* (London, 1935), reprinted in Morton White, *The Age of Analysis* (New York, 1955), pp. 218–19.
2. Robert Bridges, *John Keats: A Critical Essay* (London, 1895), p. 83.
3. Carnap in White, *Age of Analysis*, p. 219.
4. *Ibid.*
5. See, for example, Susanne K. Langer, *Problems of Art* (New York, 1957), pp. 95, 96, 106.
6. Rainer Maria Rilke, *The Notebooks of Malte Laurids Brigge*, trans. M. D. Herter Norton (New York, 1949), p. 26.
7. John Constable, quoted in Herbert Read, *The Philosophy of Modern Art* (New York, 1955), p. 17.
8. Giorgio Vasari, "Life of Leonardo da Vinci," in Ludwig Goldscheider, *Leonardo da Vinci* (London, 1959), p. 20.
9. *Ibid.*, p. 14.
10. The problem of the expression of meaning by a work of art is discussed by Wilbur Marshall Urban in *Language and Reality* (New York, 1961). Urban admits that nonverbal artistic forms can express things that language cannot express (at least not "directly"). But what is thus expressible, he claims, is very limited, for example, the specifications of light and color, and the peculiar feeling in a Cézanne landscape. If we want to go beyond this, Urban says, to "the artist's way of envisaging reality," that is, to "what the picture 'says,'" then we must make use of language—we must give an interpretation of the painting in linguistic terms (pp. 265–66). Moreover, the language of interpretation of either nonverbal or verbal art, that is, the language in which we can express what the painter or "the poet really says" (pp. 487, 488), is always literal (in the sense of "'according to the letter'" [p. 433], though no language is ever purely literal [p. 435]). This theory seems to me to be largely due to the common and understandable, but none the less unjustifiable bias of a philosophical thinker toward his own medium

of expression. I agree, of course, that art may be interpreted and that such interpretation takes place in relatively literal language. But while such interpretation may help us to a deeper understanding of a work of art and may go on to show us important relationships between the work and other artistic and nonartistic matters, it is still the work itself that is the most adequate expression of its meaning, and we must return to it if we wish to grasp this meaning.

11. *Goethe's Gespräche mit J. P. Eckermann* (Leipzig, 1908), I, 395, "Als ob ich das selber wüsste und aussprechen könnte! " (My translation.)

12. Cited in Archibald MacLeish, *Poetry and Experience* (Boston, 1961), p. 14.

13. Archibald MacLeish, "Ars Poetica," in *Collected Poems 1917-1952* (Boston, 1952).

14. Roger Fry, *Vision and Design* (New York, 1956), p. 15.

15. *Ibid.*

16. Clive Bell, *Art* (London, 1949), p. 28.

CHAPTER 10. UNDERSTANDING AND APPREHENSION

1. José Ortega y Gasset, *Toward a Philosophy of History*, trans. Helene Weyl (New York, 1941), p. 181.

2. For especially striking illustrations of this see the comparisons between Indo-European and American Indian languages by Benjamin Lee Whorf, "Science and Linguistics" and "Languages and Logic," in *Language, Thought, and Reality* (New York, 1956).

3. See *ibid.*, especially pp. 236-37.

4. Johan Huizinga, "The Idea of History," in Fritz Stern (ed.), *The Varieties of History* (New York, 1957), p. 297.

5. Aristotle, *Ethica Nicomachea*, trans. W. D. Ross (Oxford, 1925), 1094b.

6. Ernst Cassirer, *An Essay on Man* (New Haven, 1944), p. 143.

7. See, for example, *ibid.*, p. 186.

8. Rainer Maria Rilke, *Letters to a Young Poet*, trans. M. D. Herter Norton (New York, 1954), p. 29.

9. Hans Reichenbach, *The Rise of Scientific Philosophy* (Berkeley, Calif., 1951), p. 4.

10. Martin Buber, *Eclipse of God*, trans. Maurice S. Friedman (New York, 1957), p. 73.

11. This is the view, for example, of Susanne K. Langer in *Philosophy in a New Key* (Cambridge, Mass., 1942) where all mental activity is assimilated to reason. (See, for instance, pp. 91, 126.) A chief motivation for this assimilation is Mrs. Langer's opposition to the usual identification of reason with discursive thinking and relegation of all nondiscursive forms to irrationality, instinct, and blind feeling. I am entirely in accord, of course, with the opposition, but I cannot agree with this conception of reason.

CHAPTER II. LANGUAGE AND THE REALM OF
SYMBOLS

1. See, for example, Leslie A. White, *The Science of Culture* (New York, 1949), chap. ii.
2. Ernst Cassirer, *An Essay on Man* (New Haven, 1944), p. 207.
3. The title of one of his books, *Shape of Content* (Cambridge, Mass., 1957).

CHAPTER 13. MAN AND THE WORLD

1. John Dewey, *Art as Experience* (New York, 1934), p. 271.
2. Clive Bell, *Art* (London, 1949), p. 25.
3. See Erving Goffman, *The Presentation of Self in Everyday Life* (New York, 1959), where such conduct is viewed as being the very thing that constitutes human interaction.
4. Erich Fromm, *Man for Himself* (New York, 1947), p. 73.
5. Martin Buber, *Tales of the Hasidim*, trans. Olga Marx (New York, 1947), I, 126.
6. My view of individualism, collectivism, and relation has deep kinship with that of Martin Buber. See, for example, in *Between Man and Man* (New York, 1965), "What Is Man?"—especially pp. 199–205.
7. Antoine de Saint-Exupéry, *Wind, Sand, and Stars*, trans. Lewis Galantière (New York, 1939), pp. 60, 305.
8. My claim that many symbolic forms, including nonlinguistic ones, are important to express meanings and to communicate with our fellow men must by no means be supposed to constitute a "depreciation of the word." Wilbur M. Urban is perfectly justified in protesting against "one of the characteristic tendencies of our modern 'depreciation of the word' to hold that it is precisely the ideal of thought and its communication to break through the 'husk of language' to non-linguistic forms of expression." (*Language and Reality* [New York, 1961], p. 265.) In the last few years the depreciation of language has in fact been nearing disaster as a result of the infatuation with visual and "mixed" media of mass communication, on the part not only of the masses but of many intellectuals as well. However, I must disagree with Urban's claim that "all adequate expression ... must ... be linguistic, for only linguistic communication is ultimately intelligible." (*Ibid.*) It is as fallacious to depreciate nonlinguistic as linguistic communication. (See also above, chap. 9, n. 10.) If today we fail to accord to nonlinguistic forms their justified and vital place within the whole realm of symbols, we shall only fan the flames of the new obsession that is threatening the word.

CHAPTER 14. WHOLENESS AND THE PERSON

1. Relatively few modern writers are profoundly concerned with the

341

wholeness of man. Outstanding among those who are concerned, are Martin Buber, Erich Kahler, and Lewis Mumford.

2. Compare Lewis Mumford's conception of the "organic person" in *The Condition of Man* (New York, 1944), p. 419.

3. Compare Lewis Mumford on the fallacy of systems, in *The Conduct of Life* (New York, 1951), p. 175.

INDEX

INDEX

Absoluteness, 265–67, 294
Abstract and concrete, in apprehension, 239–46
Abstracted elements, in scientific knowledge, 103–4
Abstractions, interest in, 82
Aggressiveness, 92, 307, 310
Applied science, history as, 132–35
Apprehension: of the abstract and the concrete, 239–46; attitudes in, 246–55; and clear-cut boundaries, 227–34; and communication, 255–57; and desire for certainty, 265–67; embodiment of, 234–39; and knowledge, 222–25, 257–59, 269–71; and method, 225–27; and reason, 267–69; and respect, 289–92; and social and personal contexts, 259–65
Arbitrariness, of symbols, 274–83
Art: and clear-cut boundaries, 228, 232; communicability in, 255–57; creation, 305–6; and explicitness, 238–39; form and meaning, 186–87, 205–10, 283–84; and knowledge, 183–86; and inner experience, 192–96; isolation from life, 56–60; and outward world, 196–200; particular and universal in, 202–5, 242–45; personal element in, 247–48; and prosaic mentality, 301–5; and reason, 269; as representation, 180–83, 200–202; response to art, 210–17, 251–52; as self-expression, 179–80, 187–92
Articulation of knowledge, 104–6

Challenge, 92, 318–19

Clear-cut boundaries, 83, 85–86, 90–91, 227–34
Cognitive language. *See* Referential language
Collectivism, 312–14
Communication: and apprehension, 255–57; in science, 104–6
Comparison, and historical knowledge, 139–41
Concreteness: in apprehension, 239–46; in human relation, 308–9; and values, 289; and wholeness, 329–30
Conditioning, and symbols, 275–76, 280–81
Control: in human relation, 307; of nature, 326; of outward world, 91–92
Creation, human, 305–6

Detachment. *See* Objectivity
Distrust, 92–93, 310

Education: mass education, 50 (n. 3); and values, 37–38
Emotion: and art, 57–58; and reason, 267; suppression of, 44, 47, 55–56, 72–76, 186–87, 261–62. *See also* Objectivity
Emotive language, 22–23, 184–85, 273–74, 279
Environment, and person, 65–67
Everyday life: and communication, 257; and human relation, 44–46; and knowledge, 222–25; and prosaic interests, 84–87, 89–90
Everyday thought, explicitness, 235
Exhaustive articulation, 104–6, 239

345